HOLY VISIONS ~ SACRED STORIES

HOLY VISIONS
SACRED STORIES

*Realities from the Blessed
Anne Catherine Emmerich*

CHARLES S. TIDBALL

SteinerBooks

2012
SteinerBooks
An imprint of Anthroposophic Press, Inc.
610 Main Street, Great Barrington, MA 01230
www.steinerbooks.org

Cover image: The Space Window, National Cathedral,
Washington, D.C.; image used by permission under
the Creative Commons Attribution 3.0 License
Cover & book design: William Jens Jensen

Printed in the United States of America

Library of Congress Cataloging-in-Publication Data
Tidball, Charles S.
 Holy visions, sacred stories : realities from the blessed Anne Cath-
erine Emmerich / Charles S. Tidball.
     p. cm.
Includes bibliographical references.
ISBN 978-0-88010-645-0 — eBook ISBN: 978-0-88010-747-1
 1. Jesus Christ—Biography. 2. Bible stories, English.—N.T. Gos-
pels. I. Title.
BT301.3.T53 2011
232.9'01—dc22
[B]
                                                    2011010096

CONTENTS

	List of Maps	*vi*
	Introduction	*vii*
1.	Journey to the Childhood Home of John the Baptizer	1
2.	Travels with Eliud in Lower Galilee	6
3.	Journey to the Baptism in the Jordan River	12
4.	The Forty Days in the Wilderness	17
5.	The Wedding at Cana	25
6.	The First Festival of the Passover	32
7.	The Healings at Capernaum	39
8.	The Sermons on the Mount	46
9.	The Death of John the Baptizer	62
10.	Second Festival of the Passover	72
11.	The Transfiguration	77
12.	Journey to Cyprus	89
13.	Third Festival of the Passover	99
14.	The Raising of Lazarus	107
15.	Journey to the Tent City of the Kings	113
16.	Journey to the Birthplace of Abraham	125
17.	The Long Journey to Egypt	128
18.	Last Journey to Jerusalem	133
19.	Fourth Festival of the Passover	138
20.	The Passion of Jesus Christ	156
21.	Resurrection	188
22.	The Ascension	206
23.	Pentecost	210
	Appendix: The Bare Bones Story	214
	Bibliography	216
	About the Author	217

List of Maps

Figure 1.   Journey to the Childhood Home of John the Baptizer   2

Figure 2.   Travel with Eliud in Lower Galilee   7

Figure 3.   Journey to the Baptism in the Jordan River   13

Figure 4.   The Forty Days in the Wilderness   18

Figure 5.   The Wedding at Cana   26

Figure 6.   The First Passover   33

Figure 7.   The Healings at Capernaum   40

Figure 8.   The Sermons on the Mount   47

Figure 9.   Death of John the Baptizer   63

Figure 10.   Journey to the Second Passover   73

Figure 11.   The Transfiguration   78

Figure 12.   The Journey to Cyprus   90

Figure 13.   The Raising of Lazarus   108

Figure 14.   Journey to the Tent City of the Kings   114

Figure 15.   Journey to the Birthplace of Abraham   126

Figure 16.   The Long Journey to Egypt   129

Figure 17.   The Last Journey to Jerusalem   134

INTRODUCTION

Anne Catharine Emmerich's visions have been called into prominence principally by those who have found it possible to use her recollections to establish dates for many of the important events in the life of Jesus, and to make possible the construction of maps showing routes and places visited by Jesus during his earthly life. We do know, from appropriate records, that she was born in 1774 and died in 1824. We are also aware that during her later years she began having daily visions of the life and work of Jesus, and that word of her visions reached Clarence Brentano, who came to her side and recorded her visions regularly for some three years. His records have become the primary source of Anne Catharine's visions for those who have wished to use her amazing revelations, even as Brentano's notes, translated from German into English, form the basis for this book.

Anne Catharine's visions speak of many events that can be found in the canonical Gospels, making it clear that she knew her Bible. In addition, her passing references to writings of the Hebrew Scriptures and their relevance to Gospel stories remind us that she not only knew the Bible, but also appreciated connections between events of Hebrew writers and those of later Christian commentators. In this way, her visions expand *our* understanding of Jesus beyond the "abbreviated" texts of current Christian biblical writers. Indeed, they make us acutely aware of the tireless, generous and loving life of the One who came among us so that we may have life and have it more abundantly.

In the pages that follow, you will find Anne Catharine's versions of many familiar stories, for example: the Baptism, the Forty Days in the wilderness, the Sermon on the Mount, the Transfiguration, the Raising of Lazarus, the Passion, the Resurrection, and the Ascension. However, you will also find many descriptions of Jesus' healing, his teaching (especially of children), his compassion, and his relationships with friends, followers, and disciples. It is these stories that were perhaps too "ordinary" to take space from the "larger intent" of the Gospels. Nevertheless, they bring forward the person of Jesus, both fully human and fully divine, who provided compassion and caring to all who came into his presence. Thus, it is that this book of the lesser as well as the greater Signs and Wonders is brought to you. Not to provide better representations of events described in Holy Scripture; rather that you may find something here that enlightens your mind and enlivens your spirit, such that you may indeed have life and have it more abundantly.

I have already written a book that deals with the same material in a different manner.[1] It contains all the justifications and footnotes that document where the several mutually reinforcing parts come from. The presentation in that prior version provides the scholarship for those who are willing to believe that the improbable can actually have taken place. But that book has not reached many people. Now I am trying a different approach. If I can present these relatively unknown facets of the life of Jesus Christ as stories, perhaps they can achieve the broader recognition they deserve.

The Contribution of Scholarship

Much of current New Testament scholarship has been preoccupied with a search for the "historical Jesus." The inconclusive nature of that effort pits those who are reluctant to support the miraculous against the witness of the original oral tradition. This holds true even before documents were created to testify to the authenticity of unusual events that occurred some two thousand years ago. Ironically, the gospel accounts were created by those who would fit my broad definition of visionaries. Since that time, there have been more recent visionary sources that have tended at one extreme to be dismissed as heresy, or at the other extreme, to be ignored. One result of the confusion in the New Testament record is that contemporary fiction has emerged to fill the void. It has been overwhelmingly popular, so great is the hunger for a better understanding.

---

1   Tidball, *Jesus, Lazarus, and the Messiah: Unveiling Three Christian Mysteries.*

In addition, modern scholarship has made it clear that the twists and turns occurring after the first century brought about "an enforced orthodoxy" that was more politically inspired than were the visions of the saints. Yet there should be a *via media* that permits the use of witnesses over the centuries without insisting that first-century documents have either to be inviolate or to be dismantled, theme by theme, as the bias of the authors or their redactors.

Then, there is the matter of the timing. The early church sought confirmation of actual dates for important events in the life of Jesus Christ. However, wanting to put them all in the same liturgical year, along with extended periods for Advent, Lent, and the days leading up to Pentecost, has not helped to refine an actual calender. Today, following the careful analysis of Robert Powell (b. 1947) in both his *Christian Hermetic Astrology: The Star of the Magi and the Life of Christ* (1991) and his *Chronicle of the Living Christ: The Life and Ministry of Jesus Christ* (1996), we have a better basis for actual dates than ever before. These have been carefully corrected by Powell, and they have been used here with the confidence that they are as accurate as is possible at this time.

Similarly, a word is appropriate about the maps presented with many of the stories. They were created by Helmut Kaplan Fahsel in his monumental work *Der Wandel Jesu in der Welt*. Using the information in the visions of the Blessed Anne Catherine Emmerich (1774–1824), Fahsel went to the holy land and actually traced the steps of Jesus Christ to create his maps. The original map numbers are shown in the figures, since not all the relevant maps are used here in telling these stories. However, it should be noted that some of the maps cover journeys that are not present in the New Testament.

A Sampling of Visionaries

Chronology and travel detail may be less important when presenting stories, but it is worthwhile to identify some visionary sources and to acknowledge that they represent different sorts of individuals. I have used the word visionary in a broad sense. Chronologically, the first person on the list, Saint Francis of Assisi (1181–1226), is also the earliest visionary known to have received the stigmata. This designates individuals who bear on their body the wounds suffered by Jesus on the cross. It is considered by some to be the highest outward sign of a close union with the Christ. Sister Emmerich and Judith von Halle (b. 1973) also share this distinction.

By contrast, another visionary, Dr. Rudolf Steiner (1861–1925), was a mystic of a different kind. He had a conventional education that led to a Ph.D. degree, but over time it became obvious that he had access to extraordinary information. He spoke of his source as the "akashic record," which he characterized as "that mighty tableau where everything that ever happened in the evolution of the cosmos, the Earth, and humankind is written in an unchangeable script." The akashic record is not a new concept. The word *akasha* comes from the Sanskrit language, and the idea has been with us for milennia. Doctor Steiner left an impressive corpus of information, including a more sophisticated cosmology than that in the Old Testament. It places the descent of the Godhead (Jesus Christ) into a broad context that includes the concept that individuals from other traditions of faith were involved in the complex preparation for the incarnation of the Christ being. This element has not been recognized, either by the canonical gospels or by the orthodoxy that evolved during the several centuries after the actual events.

Others on the list of visionaries include the Blessed Jacobus de Voragine (1230–1298), Archbishop of Genoa, who compiled an extensive catalog of the lives of Christian saints. Also on the list of visionaries are followers of Doctor Steiner and modern authorities on early Christian history. Finally, the author wishes to affirm that this is *not* a work of fiction. Nevertheless, to maintain the narrative flow, the sources used for each event are not detailed. The fact that a minimal number of endnotes have been presented may cause some confusion over proper names. The latter have been used intentionally and are consistent with my previously mentioned volume. In the Hebrew tradition, a change in name was often used to recognize a significant event in the life of an individual. For example, after Jacob wrestled with an angel he was called Israel (Genesis 32:28). This happens frequently in this volume. To facilitate understanding these changes in proper names, Table 1 has been provided below which indicates the changes in name for key individuals. The changes in proper names are linked to important events such as the transfer of individualities, the baptism of Jesus of Nazareth by John the Baptizer, the Resurrection, and Pentecost. The second table summarizes the major events found in the appendix. Some of the latter have already taken place before the first pages of chapter 1.

The stories that follow are based primarily on two different translations of the visions of Sister Emmerich. In addition, the visions of Saint Birgitta of Sweden (1303–1373) and those of several contemporary visionaries supplement this information. The author is also indebted to the scholarship of The Jesus Seminar.[2]

Setting the Stage

As indicated, this narrative is based on more recent visionary information than was available in the early parts of the first millennium, when certain decisions determined which accounts would be accepted into the New Testament. Regrettably, the orthodoxies established by various elements of the emerging Christian church created views that were not as broad-minded as the visionary record. To put it simply, just as there is only one physical world perceived by our senses, there is only one spiritual world. The fact that each of the world religions claim diverse views of this spiritual world is less than ideal.

Further, before embarking on a new telling of the Good News, it is necessary to recognize that the four Gospels are biographical sketches, in contrast to the visionary record, which is more like a daily journal. Interestingly, even the canonical gospels contain information that has not been adequately processed by Christian scholars. The first such example is the idea that there were two holy families, each with a "Joseph," who was a direct descendant of King David; each with a Mary; and each with a baby, who was called Jesus. This was clear to some, because the nativity story as told in the Gospel according to Matthew differs from the nativity story as told in the Gospel according to Luke. The most striking difference is found in the two genealogies; in Matthew's gospel, the lineage

---

2   A group of about 150 critical scholars and laity, founded in 1985 by Robert Funk under the auspices of the Westar Institute.

PROPER NAMES

Blessed Virgin Mary: see Solomon Mary	Became Mary Sophia at Pentecost, May 24, 33 CE
Jesus Christ: see Jesus of Nazareth	Was transfigured, April 3, 31 CE Was crucified, April 3, 33 CE Became the Christ at the Resurrection, April 5, 33 CE
Jesus of Nazareth: see Solomon Jesus and Nathan Jesus	Became Jesus Christ at the baptism by John, September 23, 29 CE
Mary Sophia: see Blessed Virgin Mary	Taken to Ephesus by the Apostle John, circa 35 CE Died in Ephesus at age 65, August 15, 44 CE
Nathan Jesus: born December 6, 2 BCE	Received Zarathustra individuality from Solomon Jesus, April 3, 12 CE Became Jesus of Nazareth, April 3, 12 CE
Nathan Joseph: birth date not known	Died before the Passover, 29 CE
Nathan Mary: born July 17, 17 BCE	Gave birth to Nathan Jesus, December 6, 2 BCE Died, August 4, 12 CE
Solomon Jesus: born March 5, 6 BCE	Transfer of Zarathustra individuality to Nathan Jesus, April 3, 12 CE Died on June 4, 12 CE
Solomon Mary: born September 7, 21 BCE	Gave birth to Solomon Jesus, March 5, 6 BCE Fled to Egypt with Solomon Joseph and Solomon Jesus, February 29, 5 BCE Solomon Holy Family returned from Egypt to Nazareth, September 2 CE Merger of two Holy Families occurred after death of Nathan Mary, 12 CE Became Blessed Virgin Mary at baptism, September 23, 29 CE
Solomon Joseph: birth date not known	Fled to Egypt with Solomon Mary and Solomon Jesus, February 29, 5 BCE Solomon Holy Family returned from Egypt to Nazareth, September 2 CE Died before Passover, 12 CE
The Christ:	Ascended into Heaven, May 14, 33 CE

goes from David to Solomon, whereas in Luke's gospel the lineage goes from David to Nathan, an older brother of Solomon. We can distinguish between these two holy families by appending the name of the Davidic ancestor in front of the names *Joseph, Mary,* and *Jesus.*

There are other significant differences, too, which have been summarized by Alfred Heidenreich. Some include the hometown (Bethlehem for the Solomon holy family, and Nazareth for the Nathan holy family); the time of the birth (before the death of King Herod for the Solomon family, and after the death of King Herod for the Nathan family); the visitation by the Magi (only to the Solomon family; but when they return from Egypt, they go to Nazareth, where both the Solomon Jesus and the Nathan Jesus lived in the same town for some ten years).

A next logical question might well be: Why were there two holy families? Dr. Steiner makes a point of indicating that the spiritual world prepared for the incarnation of the Godhead in ways that have not been obvious to the orthodoxies that have emerged.

The Incarnation of the [Godhead] was a unique event. The spiritual world prepared for this occurrence by making sure that the human vehicle for the Incarnation was properly suited. The usual incarnation consists of a single individuality attaching itself to the same physical body for an entire lifetime in the material world. In this instance, at the onset, an individuality that was representative of the kingly tradition incarnated in the physical body of the Solomon Jesus. Then, several years later, a second individuality, a representative of the priestly tradition, incarnated in the physical body of the Nathan Jesus. After a suitable period of maturation, the individuality of the Nathan Jesus was joined by the individuality of the Solomon Jesus, which entered the prepared vehicle of the Nathan Jesus. After further maturation, this joint individuality departed to make way for the incarnation of the [Godhead]. Without this elaborate preparation, an ordinary human entity would not have been able to tolerate the presence of the [Godhead] as its individuality.

The preparation of the spiritual world for this event extended beyond any single faith tradition and included elements of ancient Indian, ancient Persian, and ancient Egypto-Chaldean religious faiths. The Hebrew people were selected as the vehicle for the Incarnation of the Godhead, because a number of the elements in their tradition were a reasonable approximation of spiritual reality.

CHAPTER I

JOURNEY TO THE CHILDHOOD HOME
OF JOHN THE BAPTIZER

MAY 29 TO JUNE 30, 29 CE

On the morning of Sunday, May 29, when Jesus of Nazareth was twenty-six years old, he set off on a month-long journey from Capernaum in Galilee to the region of Hebron in Judea and then back to Capernaum. For the first part of the journey, as far as Nazareth, he was accompanied by his stepmother, the Solomon Mary. Between Capernaum and Nazareth, they passed through Bethulia. There, Jesus of Nazareth saw Nathanael Chased among a group of men standing under a fig tree. Jesus of Nazareth came by at the moment Nathanael was glancing over at the women's game and struggling against a sensual temptation that had seized him. As Jesus of Nazareth passed, he cast upon Nathanael a warning look. Without knowing Jesus of Nazareth, Nathanael was deeply moved by his glance and thought, "That man has a sharp eye." Nathanael felt that Jesus of Nazareth was more than an ordinary man. He became conscious of his guilt, entered into himself, overcame the temptation, and from that time kept a stricter guard over his senses.

When Jesus of Nazareth and the Solomon Mary arrived at Nazareth, she decided to wait there for Jesus of Nazareth's return. She stayed with her niece, Mary Cleophas. Jesus of Nazareth continued on his way that same evening, accompanied by two young friends from Nazareth, Parmenus and Jonadab. Jesus of Nazareth and his two friends directed their steps toward Jerusalem. Without stopping, they traveled through Samaria the whole next day. They arrived at Lazarus' castle in Bethany on the

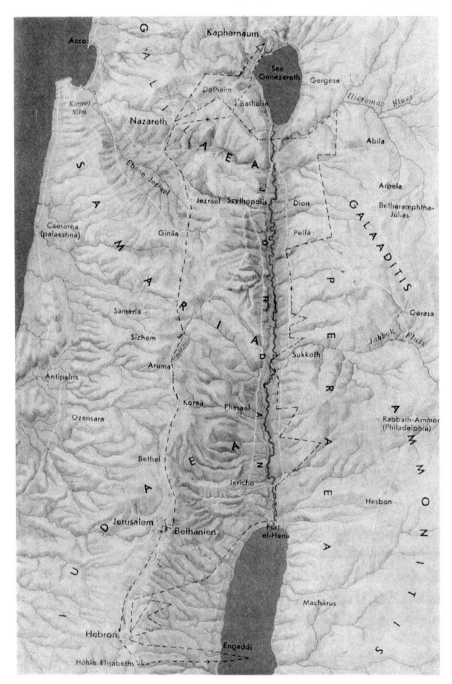

FIGURE 1: *Journey to the Childhood Home of John the Baptizer*
May 29–June 20, 29 CE *(all maps are from Powell, 1996)*

following day. After talking with Lazarus, Jesus of Nazareth and his two friends visited the Temple in Jerusalem. That evening they traveled further, journeying through the night to Hebron. The next day, Jesus of Nazareth parted company with Parmenus and Jonadab. He then went into the desert region south of Hebron and found his way to Elizabeth's Cave, where the young John the Baptizer had stayed, having been brought there by his mother Elizabeth. In the wilderness south of Hebron, Jesus of Nazareth remained alone in prayer, preparing for his mission.

Jesus of Nazareth then made his way to Hebron for the Sabbath. That evening, Friday, June 3, he visited the synagogue for the evening Sabbath celebration. The next day, after the morning service at the synagogue, Jesus of Nazareth visited the sick to console and help them, but he did not heal anyone. Wherever he went, he evoked amazement; he appeared to all as a wonderful and benevolent person. Even the possessed grew quiet in his presence. Some people thought at first that he was John the Baptizer, but then they realized that he was another prophet, as yet unknown. That evening, Jesus of Nazareth left Hebron and traveled by night to the Jordan River.

Early in the morning, Jesus of Nazareth arrived at the point where the Jordan River flows into the Dead Sea. Crossing the river by boat, he then proceeded northward, on the east side of the Jordan River, to the region north of Pella where he visited many sick people, consoling them, and exhorting them to prayer. At one place, some people knew of the prophecies of Simeon and Anna, and they questioned him as to whether he was the one to whom they referred. In response to that question, Jesus of Nazareth taught concerning the nearness of the Messiah and gave indications as to how one would be able to recognize him. It was a common thing for people to follow Jesus of Nazareth from one place to another out of the love he inspired.

For several days, Jesus of Nazareth remained on the east side of the Jordan River. Everywhere he went, he helped others. Then he crossed the Jordan River and went to the little town of Dothaim, west of the Sea of Galilee. At the time, Dothaim was a sparsely settled place, but its soil was good, and its meadows extended down to the sea. It contained a large building like a madhouse, in which lived many who were possessed. On Jesus of Nazareth's arrival, they became furious and dashed themselves almost to death. The keepers could not bind them. Jesus of Nazareth entered and spoke to them, and they became calm. He addressed to them a few more words, after which they quietly left the house and repaired to their several homes. The people were astonished.

On Friday, June 17, Jesus of Nazareth arrived at Nazareth, the town where he grew up. He received a cool reception when he visited various acquaintances of his parents. He wanted to attend the evening Sabbath service in the synagogue to teach there, but he was turned away. Instead, he addressed a crowd of people in the marketplace, including Pharisees and Sadducees. Jesus of Nazareth spoke of the Messiah, saying that he would be different than anyone imagined him to be. He also called John the Baptizer a voice in the wilderness.

John the Baptizer's fame had spread to Herod Antipas, who sent messengers to him from his castle at Callirhoe, east of the Dead Sea, where he was staying. Herod invited John to visit him, but John turned him down. About this time, Herod traveled in his coach, along with some of his soldiers, to a place about five hours south of Ainon, and invited John to visit him there. John the Baptizer came to a hut nearby, and Herod went alone to talk with him. Herod asked John why he chose to live in a miserable hut, saying that he would have a larger house built for him; but John replied that he did not need a house, that he had all he needed, and that his sole will was to serve God. He spoke solemnly and decisively, standing at some distance from Herod, and then returned to the place of baptism.

During those days, Jesus of Nazareth went from place to place, visiting especially those villages through which John the Baptizer had passed several weeks earlier on his journey through Palestine. Everywhere he went, Jesus of Nazareth taught in the synagogues and consoled the sick; but he did not perform any healing miracles. About this time, Jesus of Nazareth was teaching in a synagogue concerning the nearness of the Messiah, the baptism of John the Baptizer, and the need for repentance. The people started to voice their disapproval. They whispered, mockingly, "Three months ago his father, the carpenter, was still alive. [The death of the

Nathan Joseph is not well determined. It has been indicated to be before the Passover of the year 29 CE.] He worked with him. Now he has traveled and returns to impart his wisdom."

On June 30, Jesus of Nazareth was in Cana, where he visited his widowed cousin Mary, the daughter of Sobe, and the sister of Mary Salome. Mary Salome was married to Zebedee; their two sons, James and John, later became disciples, but, here in Cana, Jesus of Nazareth was not accompanied by any of those who were to become his close followers.

CHAPTER 2

TRAVELS WITH ELIUD IN SOUTHERN GALILEE

AUGUST 27 TO SEPTEMBER 29, 29 CE

On Saturday, August 27, in his Sabbath teaching at Jezrael, Jesus of Nazareth warned against setting oneself apart from others through pride. His attention was directed especially to those of the Nazarite sect, many of whom had set themselves apart from others living in the town who had married pagans. The next day, the Nazarites invited Jesus of Nazareth to eat with them. During the course of the meal, some Nazarites spoke about circumcision. Jesus of Nazareth declared that circumcision would soon be replaced by baptism through the Holy Spirit as the sign of the new covenant. The following Monday, Jesus of Nazareth visited a group of rich tax collectors living between Jezrael and Aphake. They had their own synagogue where Jesus of Nazareth taught. The next day, Jesus of Nazareth continued to teach the tax collectors, exhorting them to receive the baptism of John the Baptizer. The tax collectors offered Jesus of Nazareth presents; however, he declined them.

Toward evening, Jesus of Nazareth arrived at Kisloth, a city on Mount Tabor, inhabited mainly by Pharisees. They had heard of him. But they were displeased at seeing him followed by publicans—whom they looked on as malefactors, the possessed—who were known to be such.

The next day the Pharisees of Kisloth-Tabor invited Jesus of Nazareth to a meal, so that they could ensnare him in his own words. On arriving, the first thing that Jesus of Nazareth did was to ask where the poor were. To the displeasure of the Pharisees, Jesus of Nazareth then sent out his disciples to round up the poor of the town and bring them to the meal.

On Friday, September 2, Jesus of Nazareth passed through the Edron valley, accompanied by some followers. He came to the shepherd village

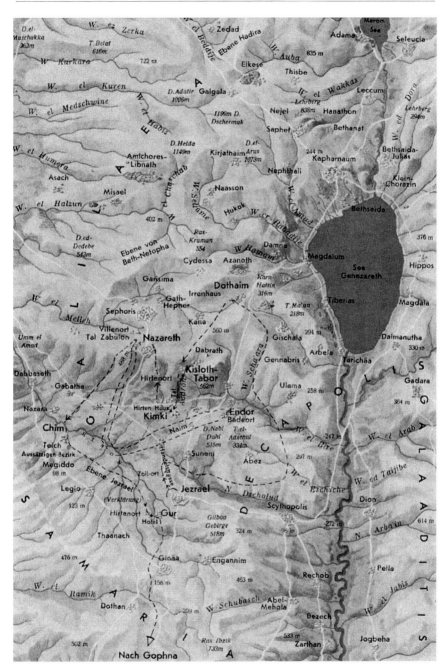

FIGURE 2: *Travel with Eliud in Lower Galilee*
August 27 to September 19, 29 CE

of Chimki. That evening, he taught in the synagogue there. The following day, Jesus of Nazareth again taught in the synagogue, expounding several parables that the Pharisees mocked as childish. That night, Jesus of Nazareth stayed with a poor family and healed the mistress of the house, who was suffering from dropsy. Sunday evening, in the synagogue at Chimki, the Pharisees were greatly angered at the teaching of Jesus of Nazareth that warned against taking life too lightly as had been done in the time of Noah. Jesus of Nazareth also spoke of the coming of the Messiah, saying, "You are expecting him to appear surrounded by worldly glory. But he is already come, and he makes his appearance as a poor man. He will teach truth. He will get more blame than praise, for he wills justice. But separate not from him, that you may not be lost. Do not be like those children of Noah who mocked him when he so laboriously built the ark that was to save them from the flood. All they that did not deride him went into the ark and were saved." The Pharisees accused Jesus of Nazareth of speaking as if he were the Messiah himself, and—amid the uproar—they put out the lights. That night, Jesus of Nazareth and his disciples left Chimki and went northward.

On Monday, September 5, Jesus of Nazareth and his traveling companions went to a shepherd village between the Edron valley and Nazareth. There they ate with some shepherds. The shepherd hosts led in Jesus of Nazareth and his followers, about twenty in number, equal to that of the shepherds themselves. All washed their feet, a separate basin being assigned to Jesus of Nazareth. He asked for more water and, after using it, requested it not be thrown out. When all were ready for table, Jesus of Nazareth questioned the shepherds, who seemed anxious about something, as to the cause of their trouble. He asked if there were not some of their number absent. In answer to his questions, they acknowledged that they were sad on account of two of their companions who were lying sick of leprosy. Fearing that it might be the unclean leprosy, and dreading that Jesus of Nazareth might not come to them on that account, they had taken care to conceal them. Then Jesus of Nazareth ordered them to be brought before him, and sent some of his disciples after them. At last, they appeared so closely enveloped from head to foot in sheets, that it was with great difficulty that they could walk, though each was supported on either side. Jesus of Nazareth commanded them to wash in the water he had used for his feet. They obeyed, and the crusts fell from them leaving the scars behind. Then Jesus of Nazareth and his five disciples went on to Nazareth and put up in a community of Essenes on the outskirts of the town. Jesus of Nazareth stayed with the venerable Eliud, an elderly Essene widower who was cared for by his daughter.

The following day, while the five disciples visited friends and relatives in Nazareth, Jesus of Nazareth talked with the aged Eliud, who had had many deep, mystical experiences. The Solomon Mary and Mary Cleophas also visited Jesus of Nazareth. In the course of conversation with the Solomon Mary, Jesus of Nazareth told her that he would go to Jerusalem *four* times for the Festival of the Passover, but that the last time would be one of great affliction for her. The editors of the German edition of Sister Emmerich's visions thought there were only *three* Festivals of the Passover between the baptism and the crucifixion of Jesus of Nazareth because they were not aware of a 313-day gap in the transmission of visions to Clemens Brentano.

On Wednesday, September 7, Jesus of Nazareth spent much of the day in deep conversation with Eliud. This pious and devout Essene told Jesus of Nazareth of his mystical experiences concerning the coming of the Messiah. Jesus of Nazareth was able to interpret these experiences for Eliud and to answer many of his questions regarding the things he had seen in visions That evening, Jesus of Nazareth and Eliud visited the place where the Nathan Joseph had worked as a carpenter.

On the next day, Jesus of Nazareth and Eliud set off on a journey southward from Nazareth, passing through the valley of Esdrelon, and then turning eastward in the direction of Endor. They arrived at a small village close to a well-known spring. At the synagogue, Jesus of Nazareth taught concerning the Messiah and the Kingdom of God, which he affirmed was not of this world. He also expounded many passages from the prophets. That night, Jesus of Nazareth and Eliud stayed at an inn near the synagogue.

Setting off early on the next day, Jesus of Nazareth and Eliud journeyed around Mount Hermon and came to Endor. There they visited a sanitarium—a bathing spot for invalids—where Jesus of Nazareth taught the sick and told two parables. There was no synagogue in Endor, so, for the Sabbath, they returned to the synagogue at the village where they had been the previous day. After the Sabbath morning service in the synagogue, Jesus of Nazareth and Eliud went back to Endor. The inhabitants of the town were Canaanites, some of whom secretly worshipped an idol of the goddess Astarte. Jesus of Nazareth reprehended them for this practice. Then, accompanied by Eliud, Jesus of Nazareth returned to the synagogue for the service at the close of the Sabbath. That evening, he and Eliud set off for Nazareth. They arrived at Eliud's home in the early hours of the morning. A number of the disciples of Jesus of Nazareth, Essenes, and some other people—including two Pharisees from Nazareth—gathered together to hear his discourses. The Pharisees invited Jesus of Nazareth to come to them and later conducted him to the synagogue. There he taught concerning Moses and the prophecies of the coming of the Messiah. That night, he stayed at an inn nearby, together with his five disciples.

On the night of September 14, Jesus of Nazareth set off with Eliud for the little town of Chim, southwest of Nazareth. At daybreak, they reached Chim. Not far from the town was an isolated leper settlement. Eliud tried to restrain Jesus from entering it, that he might not be defiled. For, as Eliud urged, if it were discovered that he had been there, he would not be allowed to go to the baptism. But Jesus of Nazareth replied that he knew his mission, that he would enter, for there was in it a good man sighing for his coming. They had to cross the Kishon River. The leper settlement lay near a brook formed by the waters of the Kishon that flowed into a little pond in which the lepers bathed. The water thus used did not return to the Kishon. The lepers dwelt in scattered huts. There were no others in the place except those that attended the infected. Eliud remained at a distance and waited for Jesus of Nazareth who entered one of the most remote huts in which lay stretched on the ground a miserable creature entirely enveloped in sheets. He was a good man. Jesus of Nazareth addressed him. He raised himself, and appeared to be deeply touched by Jesus of Nazareth's coming to visit him. Jesus of Nazareth then told him to rise and stretch himself in a trough of water that stood near the hut. He obeyed, while Jesus of Nazareth held his hands extended over the water. The rigid limbs of the leper relaxed, and he was made clean.

Jesus of Nazareth and Eliud then made their way south through the valley of Esdrelon. They continued walking in the dark, in deep conversation. Around midnight, Jesus of Nazareth said to Eliud that he would reveal himself, and, turning toward heaven, he prayed. A cloud of light enveloped both of them and Jesus of Nazareth became radiantly transfigured. Eliud stood still, utterly entranced. After a while, the light melted away, and Jesus of Nazareth resumed his steps, followed by Eliud, who was speechless at what he had experienced.

At dawn, they approached the huts of some shepherds. The shepherds already knew Jesus of Nazareth. Leading them to a shed, they washed the feet of the two guests and prepared a meal for them. Afterward, Jesus of Nazareth took leave of Eliud, first blessing him and then embracing him before going on his way. Jesus of Nazareth then traveled to the mountain village of Gur. He celebrated the beginning of the Sabbath there alone in his room at an inn, having requested a roll of the scriptures to be brought to him from the synagogue. The following day, September 19, the last Sabbath prior to his baptism, Jesus of Nazareth spent the entire day in his room, alone, and in prayer.

CHAPTER 3

JOURNEY TO THE BAPTISM IN THE JORDAN RIVER

SEPTEMBER 19 TO 26, 29 CE

In the mountain village of Gur, Jesus of Nazareth got up before day-break and proceeded further. Toward evening he arrived at Gophna on Mount Ephraim, north of Jerusalem. After eating a meal at an inn, he was escorted to a house where he stayed overnight. The next morning, Jesus of Nazareth went to the synagogue and asked for the scriptures of one of the prophets. He then interpreted the prophecies, saying that the time had arrived for the coming of the Messiah. After spending much of the day teaching in the synagogue, Jesus left Gophna. That evening, he arrived at the shepherd village of Bethel, where he met up with two groups of people on their way to be baptized by John.

On the following day, Jesus of Nazareth went to the synagogue and taught concerning baptism and the nearness of the Messiah. During the evening meal at the inn where he was staying, some of the guests denounced Herod's unlawful connection with his brother's wife. Jesus of Nazareth concurred but said that whoever judged others would also be judged.

The next morning Jesus of Nazareth left Bethel early and arrived that evening at a little village called Giah on Mount Amma, facing the Gibeon desert. There, he ate a meal and talked.

On the following morning, Jesus of Nazareth walked about in the courtyards and gardens of Lazarus' castle, teaching those who were pres-ent. Then Martha took Jesus of Nazareth to visit her sister Mary, known as Silent Mary, who lived by herself like a hermit in an isolated part of the castle. Jesus of Nazareth was left alone to talk with Silent Mary, who

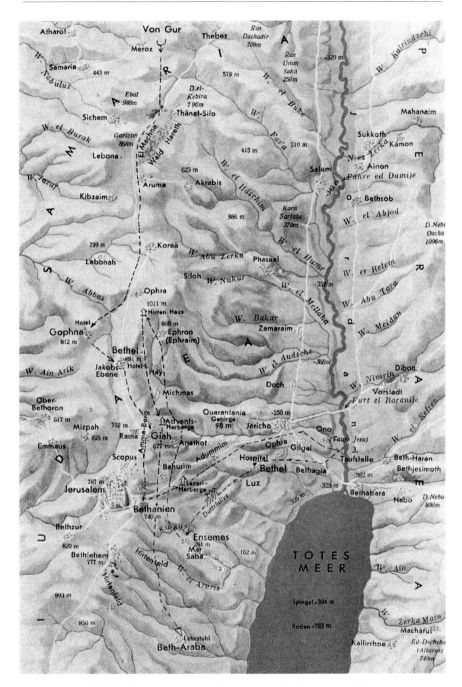

FIGURE 3: *Journey to the Baptism in the Jordan River*
September 18–26, 29 CE

lived in continuous vision of heavenly things. Normally silent in the presence of other people, Silent Mary began to speak of the mysteries of Jesus of Nazareth's incarnation, passion, and death. After saying some prayers, Jesus of Nazareth returned to talk with Martha who expressed her deep concern regarding her other sister, Mary Magdalene. Although the New Testament mentions both Mary and Martha as sisters of Lazarus, note that the visionary record includes a third sister, Silent Mary, and also clarifies that the Mary who is Martha's sister is, in fact, Mary Magdalene.

At about half-past one, the Solomon Mary arrived, accompanied by Mary Chuza, the widow Lea, Mary Salome, and Mary Cleophas. After a light meal, Jesus of Nazareth and the Solomon Mary, retired to talk with one another. Jesus of Nazareth told the Solomon Mary that he was now going to be baptized and that his real mission would begin with that event. He said that they would meet again briefly in Samaria after the baptism, but that he would then go into the desert for forty days. The Solomon Mary was much troubled when she heard this, but Jesus of Nazareth answered by saying that he must now fulfill his mission and that she should renounce all personal claim upon him.

Dr. Steiner provides some more details about this conversation. He suggests that it brought about a new spiritual alignment in the Solomon Mary. The strange effect of this conversation was that the soul of the Nathan Mary came down from the spiritual world and united with the soul of the Solomon Mary. Dr. Steiner put it this way: "Virginity was reborn, as it were." To acknowledge that change in this narrative, the Solomon Mary will be referred to as the Blessed Virgin Mary, until her next change in status calls for yet another name.

That evening, Lazarus gave a feast for all who were present. During the meal, Jesus of Nazareth again alluded to the persecutions that lay ahead of him, saying that those who allied themselves with him would suffer with him. The final step in the preparation for the incarnation of the Godhead also occurred at this time. According to Dr. Steiner, the Zarathustra individuality that had been transferred from the Solomon Jesus to the Nathan Jesus, at the time of the Festival of the Passover in the year 12 CE, returned to the spiritual world in order to make way for the descent of the Godhead.

That same night Jesus of Nazareth, accompanied by Lazarus, set off in the direction of Jericho to make his way to the place of baptism.

On Friday, September 23, Jesus of Nazareth went on ahead of Lazarus and arrived at the place of baptism some two hours before him. This place of baptism was located on the west side of the Jordan, just south of the village of Ono. A large crowd had already assembled there to hear John the Baptizer's preaching when Jesus of Nazareth arrived about daybreak. The Baptizer felt Jesus' presence among the crowd; he was fired with zeal and preached with great animation concerning the nearness of the Messiah. Then John began baptizing. By ten o'clock he had already baptized many people.

Jesus of Nazareth now came down to the baptizing pool where the Baptizer was being helped by Andrew, later to become one of the twelve, and by Saturnin, a young Greek of royal blood from the city of Patras, who also became one of Jesus of Nazareth's closest disciples. When Jesus of Nazareth came down among the aspirants to the pool of baptism, the Baptizer bowed low before him, saying, "I ought to be baptized by you, and yet you come to me?" Jesus of Nazareth answered, "Suffer it to be so now, for we will fulfill all justice for you to baptize me." Then the Baptizer suggested that Jesus of Nazareth follow him to the island.

In the water off the southern shore was a red triangular stone that sparkled in the sunlight. It was sunk close to the margin of the basin, the flat side toward the center of the well, the point toward the land. In the well, in front of the triangular stone, there stood a green tree that had a slender trunk. Saturnin received the garments of Jesus of Nazareth as he disrobed, and handed them to Lazarus, who was standing on the edge of the island. Now Jesus of Nazareth descended into the well, and stood in the water up to his breast. His left arm encircled the tree, his right hand was laid on his breast. On the southern side of the well stood the Baptizer, holding in his hand a shell with a perforated margin through which the water flowed in three streams. He stooped, filled the shell, then poured the water in three streams over Jesus of Nazareth, one on the back of the head, one in the middle, and the third over the forepart of the head and on the face. John's words, when baptizing Jesus of Nazareth, were "May God through the ministry of his cherubim and seraphim, pour out his blessing over you with wisdom, understanding, and strength!" After this, Jesus of Nazareth stepped on the red triangular stone that lay to the right of the descent into the well, while Andrew and Saturnin each laid one hand upon his shoulder, and the Baptizer rested his hand on the head of Jesus of Nazareth. This part of the ceremony over, they were just about to mount the steps when there came from Heaven a great, rushing wind like thunder. All trembled and looked up. A cloud of white light descended. Above Jesus of Nazareth a winged figure of light flowed over him like a stream. The heavens opened. There was an apparition of the Heavenly Father and, in a voice of thunder, God said, "You are my beloved Son, today I have begotten you." Jesus of Nazareth was perfectly transparent, entirely penetrated by light; one could scarcely look at him. There were angels around him. Satan and his minions were observing this event at a distance.

Meanwhile Nicodemus, Obed, John Mark, and Joseph of Arimathea, had also arrived to join Lazarus in witnessing the baptism of Jesus of Nazareth. John the Baptizer then told Andrew to announce the baptism of the Messiah throughout Galilee. On the assumption that the physical incarnation of the Godhead took place at the baptism, in this narrative Jesus of Nazareth, the prepared vehicle for the Incarnation of the Godhead, will henceforth be called Christ Jesus.

John himself continued baptizing and preaching, while Christ Jesus journeyed with his followers in the direction of Jerusalem, traveling until he reached a little place called Bethel, where there was a kind of hospital. In Bethel, Andrew and Saturnin baptized a number of people, following Christ Jesus' instructions. This baptism differed in several respects from John's baptizing. Christ Jesus and his disciples then celebrated the Sabbath in Bethel. After the close of the Sabbath, Andrew took leave of Christ Jesus and departed for Galilee to proclaim the baptism of the Messiah there.

CHAPTER 4

THE FORTY DAYS IN THE WILDERNESS

OCTOBER 11 TO NOVEMBER 30, 29 CE

After teaching in the synagogue at Dibon, Christ Jesus found that some sick people had been brought there into the open court. They cried out, "Lord, thou art a prophet! Thou hast been sent from God! You can help us! Help us, Lord!" He healed many of them. That evening he was received at a banquet in his honor. Afterward, Christ Jesus arranged with the disciples to meet him on the following morning at a place outside the town. Then Christ Jesus left the inn where they were staying and went to pray alone on the mountain. Early in the morning the disciples met up with Christ Jesus and journeyed with him northward from Dibon.

On Friday, October 14, Christ Jesus and his disciples passed by Gerasa and arrived at the town of Great Chorazin where they celebrated the Sabbath. The next day, Christ Jesus taught in the synagogue in Great Chorazin until the close of the Sabbath. Then Christ Jesus went to the inn where the Blessed Virgin Mary together with Peter's wife, Suzanna of Jerusalem, and several other holy women were awaiting his arrival. Christ Jesus talked with the Blessed Virgin Mary and again told her that after going to Bethany he would go alone into the wilderness.

On the evening of October 19, Christ Jesus and his disciples arrived at a hostel near Bethany that had been put at their disposal by Lazarus. Lazarus came to greet them. Talking with the disciples, Christ Jesus spoke of the dangers facing those who follow him. Christ Jesus said that each disciple should consider carefully—during the coming period of separation from him—whether that person really wanted to continue being a

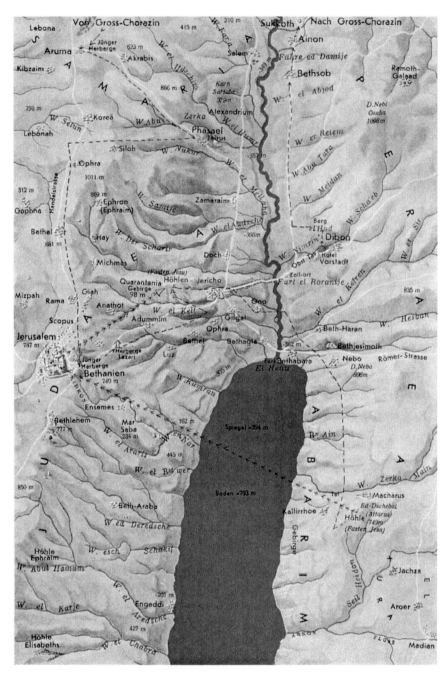

FIGURE 4: *The Forty Days in the Wilderness*
October 11 to November 30, 29 CE

disciple. Christ Jesus then took leave of the disciples and made his way to Lazarus' castle at Bethany, accompanied by Lazarus and the two nephews of Joseph of Arimathea, Aram and Themini. Here, many friends from Jerusalem were expecting him.

The following day, Christ Jesus had a conversation with Silent Mary. Her bearing toward Christ Jesus was somewhat different from that of the last interview, for she cast herself down before him and kissed his feet. Christ Jesus made no attempt to prevent her, and raised her up by the hand. With her eyes turned heavenward, she, as once before, uttered sublime and wonderful things. She spoke of God, of his Son, and of his Kingdom just as a peasant girl might talk of the father of the village lord and his inheritance. Her words were a prophecy, and the things of which she spoke she saw before her. Silent Mary considered herself a captive, for her body appeared to her a prison, and she longed to go home. Christ Jesus spoke to her lovingly, consoling her and saying, "After the Pasch, when I come here again, you shall indeed go home." Then as she knelt before him, Christ Jesus raised his hands over her and blessed her.

On the next day, Friday, October 21, Christ Jesus set off in the direction of Jericho. For the first part of the journey, he traveled with Lazarus. The latter accompanied Christ Jesus as far as a hostel, which he owned, close to the wilderness. Here they parted company, and Christ Jesus continued on his way, alone and barefoot. As the Sabbath began, Christ Jesus climbed a mountain, called Mount Quarantania, about one hour's distance from Jericho. Here he started his forty-day fast and spent the night at prayer in a cave. Christ Jesus knelt with outstretched arms and prayed to his heavenly Father for strength and courage in all the trials that awaited him. For the whole of the Sabbath and the following night, Christ Jesus remained in prayer on Mount Quarantania. A vast cloud of light descended upon him, and he received consolation from on high. Christ Jesus offered up to the Father the fruits of all his future labors and sufferings so that these fruits should benefit his followers in all ages to come. So intense was Christ Jesus' praying that his sweat became tinged with blood.

On Sunday, October 23, Christ Jesus descended from Mount Quarantania before sunrise. He walked toward the Jordan River, which he crossed on a beam of wood, and journeyed east of the town of Bethabara into the wilderness beyond the Dead Sea. Eventually, he reached a very wild mountain range east of Callirrhoe where he ascended the forbidding Mount Attarus. This savage and desolate mountain lay about nine hours distance from Jericho. Here Christ Jesus continued to pray and fast, spending the night in a narrow cave near the summit of the mountain.

From Monday, October 24 to Wednesday, November 30, Christ Jesus stayed at the mountain cave on Mount Attarus, praying and fasting. Throughout the whole period, Christ Jesus was daily submitted to temptation. Early in this period, Satan appeared at the entrance to the cave. He had adopted the form of the son of one of the three widows, a youth especially loved by Christ Jesus. Satan made a noise to attract attention, thinking that Christ Jesus would be displeased at his disciple's following him against his prohibition. Christ Jesus did not look toward him even once.

Foiled in this first ruse, on the subsequent day Satan tried another. He sent seven, eight, or nine apparitions of the disciples into the cave. In they came one after another, saying to Christ Jesus that Eustachius had informed them that he was there, and that they had sought him with much anxiety. But Christ Jesus' only reply was, "Withdraw, Satan! It is not yet time," and all the phantoms disappeared.

The next day Satan drew near under the form of a feeble old man, a venerable Essene, toiling painfully up the steep mountain. Approaching the cave, with a loud groan he fell fainting from exhaustion at its entrance. But Christ Jesus took no notice of him, not even by a glance. After the apparition had made an appeal to help him, Christ Jesus uttered a few words only, such as, "Retire Satan! It is not yet time." Only then was it obvious that it was Satan, for as he turned away and vanished, he became dark and horrible to behold.

When Satan next came to tempt Christ Jesus, he assumed the appearance of old Eliud. Satan must have known that his passion and cross had been shown to Jesus by the angels, for Satan said that he had a revelation of the heavy trials in store for him, and that he felt he would not be able to resist them. For a forty day's fast, he continued, Christ Jesus was not in a prepared state; therefore, urged by love for him, he had come to see him once more, to beg to be allowed to share his wild abode and to assume part of his vow. Christ Jesus noticed not the tempter, but raising his hands to Heaven, he said, "Father, take this temptation away from me!" Satan was then transformed into a horrible figure that vanished.

On another day as Christ Jesus knelt in the cave praying, Satan arrived in a glittering robe borne, as it were, through the air up the steepest and highest side of the rock. This precipitous, inaccessible side faced to the east; in it were some apertures opening into the cave. Christ Jesus did not glance toward Satan, who was now intent on passing himself off for an angel. Hovering at the entrance of the cave, Satan spoke, "I have been sent by your Father to console you." Christ Jesus still did not turn toward him. Then Satan flew around to the steep, inaccessible side of the rock and called to Christ Jesus to witness a proof of his angelic nature since he could hover there without support. But Christ Jesus did not notice him. Seeing himself foiled in this attempt, Satan again became quite horrible, and made as if he would seize Christ Jesus in his claws. His figure grew still more frightful and then he disappeared. Christ Jesus did not pay attention to his departure.

Satan came next in the appearance of an aged solitary from Mount Sinai. He was quite wild, almost savage looking, with his long beard and scanty covering, a rough skin being his only garment. But there was something false and cunning in his countenance as he climbed painfully up the mountain. Entering the cave, he addressed Christ Jesus, saying that an Essene from Mount Carmel had visited him and told him of the baptism, also of the wisdom, the miracles, and the present rigorous fasting of Christ Jesus. Hearing which, notwithstanding his great age, he had come all the way to see him, to converse with him, for he had long experience in the practice of mortification. He told Christ Jesus that he should now desist from further fasting, that he would free him from what remained, and went on with much more such talk. Christ Jesus, looking aside, said, "Depart from me, Satan!" At these words, the evil one grew dark and, like a huge, black ball, rolled with a crash down the mountain.

When Christ Jesus began to hunger, and especially to thirst, Satan appeared in the form of a pious hermit and exclaimed, "I am so hungry! I pray give me of the fruit growing here on the mountain outside your cave. Then let us sit together and talk of good things." Christ Jesus answered the false hermit, "Depart from me! From the very beginning, you are *the* liar. Do not harm the fruit!" Then Satan as a little somber figure hurried off, a black vapor exhaling from him.

Satan next appeared to Christ Jesus in the cave as a magician and philosopher. Satan told him that he had come to him as to a wise man, and that he would show him that he, too, could exhibit marvels. Then he produced an apparatus like a globe hanging on his hand. A look into Satan's globe disclosed the most magnificent scenes from nature, lovely pleasure gardens full of shady groves, cool fountains, and richly laden fruit trees. All seemed to be within one's reach, and all was constantly dissolving into ever more beautiful, more enticing scenes. Christ Jesus would not look at the tempter, much less into the globe as Satan desired, but turning his back on Satan, Christ Jesus left the cave. As soon as he turned his back on him, Satan vanished.

Christ Jesus was now suffering from hunger and thirst; he appeared several times at the entrance of the cave. Toward evening on November 27, Satan ascended the mountain in the form of a large, powerful man. He had furnished himself with two stones as long as little rolls, but square at the ends, which as he had mounted he molded into the perfect appearance of bread. There was something more horrible than usual about him when he stepped into the cave and confronted Christ Jesus. In each hand he held one of the stones, and his words were to this effect, "You are right not to eat of the fruit, for it only excites an appetite. But, if you are the beloved Son of God over whom the Holy Spirit came at baptism, behold I have fashioned these stones so that they look like bread. Do now change them into bread." Christ Jesus did not glance toward Satan, but he did say, "Man does not live by bread alone!" Then Satan became perfectly horrible. He stretched out his talons as if to seize Christ Jesus, at which action the stones still resting on his arms became visible, and then Satan fled.

Toward evening of the following day, Satan appeared in the form of a majestic angel sweeping down toward Christ Jesus with a noise like the rushing wind. He addressed boasting words to Christ Jesus, along this line, "I will show you who I am, and what I can do, and how the angels bear me up in their hands. Look yonder, there is Jerusalem! Behold the Temple! I will place you on its highest pinnacle. Then cast your self down, and we will see if the angels carry you down." While Satan thus spoke, and pointed out Jerusalem and the Temple, it seemed that both of them were quite near, just in front of the mountain. Christ Jesus made no reply, and Satan seized him by the shoulders and bore him through the air. Satan flew low toward Jerusalem, and placed Christ Jesus upon the highest point of one of the four towers that rose from the four corners of the Temple. Christ Jesus uttered not a word. Then Satan flew to the ground and cried up to Christ Jesus, "If you are the Son of God, show your power and come down also, for it is written, 'He has given his angels charge over you, and in their hands they shall bear you up, so that you do not dash your foot against a stone.'" Christ Jesus replied, "It is written, 'You shall not tempt the Lord, your God.'" Satan, in a fury, returned to Christ Jesus, who said, "Make use of the power that has been given you!" Then Satan seized him fiercely by the shoulders and flew with him over the desert towards Jericho. This second flight appeared longer than the first. Satan was filled with rage and fury. He flew with Christ Jesus now high, now low, reeling like one who would vent his rage if he could. He bore him to Mount Quarantania, the same mountain one hour from Jericho upon which Christ Jesus had started his fast. Satan flew with him to the highest peak on the mountain, and set him upon an inaccessible, overhanging crag much higher than the cave.

It was night, but while Satan pointed around, it grew bright, revealing the more wonderful regions in all parts of the world. The devil addressed Christ Jesus in the following vein, "I know that you are a great teacher, that you are now about to gather disciples around you and promulgate your doctrines. Behold, all these magnificent countries, these mighty nations! Compare with them poor little Judea lying yonder! Go rather to these." As Satan pointed around, one saw first vast countries and seas, with their different cities into which kings in regal pomp and magnificence and followed by myriads of warriors were triumphantly entering. As one gazed, these scenes became more and more distinct until, at last, they seemed to be in the immediate vicinity. Satan pointed out in each the features of special attraction. This was a most wonderful vision, so extended, so clear, so grand, and magnificent! The only words uttered by Christ Jesus were, "You shall adore the Lord your God and him only shall you serve! Depart from me, Satan!" Then Satan in an inexpressibly horrible form rose from the rock, cast himself into the abyss, and vanished as if the earth had swallowed him up.

At the same moment, a myriad of angels drew near to Christ Jesus, bent low before him, took him up as if in their hands, floated him down gently to the lower rock outcropping and into the cave in which the forty day fast had begun. When Christ Jesus had overcome the last temptation, the twelve angels of the twelve apostles served him heavenly food. These twelve angels were accompanied by the seventy-two angels of the seventy-two disciples. An incredible blessing and consolation emanated from this heavenly celebration of Christ Jesus' triumphant victory over temptation. That evening, Christ Jesus descended from the mountain; he then traveled through the night until he reached the Jordan River.

During Christ Jesus' fast, the Blessed Virgin Mary in the house near Capernaum had to listen to all kinds of speeches about her divine son. They said that he went wandering about, no one knew where; that he neglected her; that after the death of the Nathan Joseph it was his duty to undertake some business for his stepmother's support. Throughout the whole country, the talk about Christ Jesus was rife at this time, for the wonders attendant on his baptism, the testimony rendered by the Baptizer, and the accounts of his scattered disciples had been everywhere noised abroad. The Blessed Virgin Mary was grave and composed, for she was never without an internal vision of Christ Jesus, whose actions she contemplated, and whose sufferings she shared.

CHAPTER 5

THE WEDDING AT CANA

DECEMBER 20 TO 31, 29 CE

Today, Tuesday, December 20, Christ Jesus and his traveling companions, which included Andrew, stayed at an inn just outside the town of Tarichea. Christ Jesus was visited there by Lazarus, Saturnin, Obed, the son of Simeon, and the bridegroom Nathanael who was soon to be married at Cana. Nathanael invited Christ Jesus and everyone else to attend his wedding. That evening, they remained at the inn and celebrated the Feast of the Dedication of the Temple. On the following day, Christ Jesus and some of his disciples gathered at the inn and prayed together, lighting the candles for the Feast of the Dedication. Andrew busied himself writing letters with a reed upon strips of parchment. These were to be sent by messengers to Philip, Peter, and his stepbrother Jonathan, notifying them that Christ Jesus would be in Capernaum for the Sabbath.

On the next day, Christ Jesus went to Capernaum accompanied by Andrew, Saturnin, Obed, and several disciples. On the way, Andrew parted company with Christ Jesus and went to meet his stepbrother Jonathan, who was with Philip. He told them that Christ Jesus was truly the Messiah.

In Capernaum, Christ Jesus and his traveling companions stayed at a house belonging to Nathanael, the bridegroom. Here there was a messenger from Cades who had been waiting two whole days to see Christ Jesus. Now he approached him, cast himself at his feet, and informed him that he was the servant of a man from Cades. His master, he said, entreated Christ Jesus to return with him and cure his young son who was afflicted with leprosy and a dumb devil. This man was a most faithful servant;

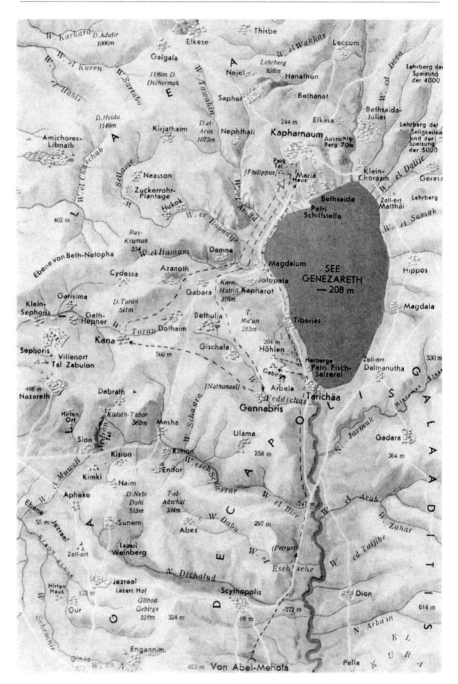

FIGURE 5: The Wedding at Cana
December 20, 29 CE – January 2, 30 CE

he placed his master's trouble before Christ Jesus in very pathetic words. Christ Jesus replied that he could not return with him, but still the child should receive assistance, for he was an innocent boy. Then he directed the servant to tell his master to stretch himself with extended arms over his son, to recite certain prayers, and the leprosy would disappear. After which, he, the servant himself, should lie upon the boy and breath into his mouth. A blue vapor would then escape from the boy and he would be freed from dumbness. Later, the master and the servant did cure the boy, as Christ Jesus had directed. There was a reason for the command that the master and the servant should stretch themselves alternately on the boy. The servant himself was the true father of the child, of which fact, however, the master was ignorant. But Christ Jesus knew it. Both had therefore to be instrumental in freeing the child from the penalty of sin.

On the evening of Friday, December 23, at the start of the Sabbath, Christ Jesus taught in the synagogue at Capernaum. Many friends and relatives were in attendance, including the Blessed Virgin Mary. In connection with the lighting of candles at the Feast of Dedication, Christ Jesus spoke of the light that should not be hidden under a bushel.

Christ Jesus taught again, morning and afternoon, in the synagogue. At the close of the Sabbath, he and his disciples went for a walk in the little vale nearby. Philip, who was modest and humble, hung back. Christ Jesus turned and said to him, "Follow me," whereupon Philip, filled with joy, joined the other disciples.

The following day, the Blessed Virgin Mary and her companions set off along the road leading to Cana. Christ Jesus and his disciples went by a more circuitous route. They traveled through Gennabris, where Christ Jesus taught in the synagogue. While he did so, Philip sought out Nathanael Chased, who worked in Gennabris as a clerk. Philip found Nathanael and said to him, "We have found him of whom Moses in the law and also the prophets wrote, Jesus of Nazareth, the son of Joseph." Nathanael replied, "Can anything good come from Nazareth?" Philip then said to him, "Come and see." Philip and Nathanael then set off along the road to Cana and soon caught up with Christ Jesus. Philip called out, "Master! I bring you here one who has asked, 'Can anything good come from Nazareth?'"

Christ Jesus, turning to the disciples, said, as Nathanael came up to them, "Behold, a true Israelite in whom there is no guile!" Christ Jesus uttered the words in a kind, affectionate manner. Nathanael responded, "How do you know me?" Meaning to say, "How do you know that I am true and without guile, since we have never spoken to each other?" Christ Jesus answered, "Before Philip called you, I saw you when you were standing under the fig tree." These words Christ Jesus accompanied by a significant look at Nathanael intended to recall something to him.

This glance of Christ Jesus instantly awoke in Nathanael the recollection of a certain passerby whose warning look had endued him with wonderful strength at the moment in which he was struggling with temptation (see May 29, 29 CE). He had indeed been standing at the time under a fig tree on the pleasure grounds around the warm baths, gazing upon some beautiful women who, on the other side of the meadow, were playing for fruit. The powerful impression produced by that glance, and the victory that Christ Jesus had then enabled him to gain, were fixed in his memory. Now that Christ Jesus reminded him of it and repeated the significant glance, Nathanael became greatly agitated and impressed. He felt that Christ Jesus in passing had read his thoughts, and had been to him a guardian angel. He recognized, therefore, in Christ Jesus his savior and deliverer. Humbling himself before him as he uttered these significant words, Nathanael exclaimed, "Rabbi! You are the Son of God!"

Everyone then went on to Cana where Christ Jesus was received by the bridegroom, Nathanael, (not the same as Nathanael Chased above) and by the bride's father, Israel, by the bride's mother, and by the Blessed Virgin Mary. That night, Christ Jesus stayed at a house belonging to one of the Blessed Virgin Mary's cousins. On the next day, about a hundred guests had gathered in Cana to attend the wedding. That evening, Christ Jesus taught in the synagogue concerning the significance of marriage, husbands and wives, continence, chastity, and spiritual union.

On the third day after Christ Jesus' arrival in Cana, the marriage ceremony took place at about nine o'clock in the morning. The nuptial ceremony was performed by the priest in front of the synagogue. The rings exchanged by the young pair had been presented to the bridegroom by the Blessed Virgin Mary after Christ Jesus had blessed them for her. After the ceremony many other articles, such as scarves and other pieces of clothing, were bestowed upon the poor gathered around. Before the wedding banquet all the guests assembled in the garden. The women and maidens sat on a carpet in an arbor and played for fruit. But for the amusement of the men, a game was contrived by Christ Jesus himself in the summerhouse.

In the center of the house stood a round table with as many portions of flowers, leaves, and fruits placed around the edge as there were players. Christ Jesus had, beforehand and alone, arranged these portions, each with reference to some mysterious signification, for the prize that fell to the players severally was significant of his own individual inclinations, faults, and virtues. This Christ Jesus explained to each man as the prize that was won was assigned. What Christ Jesus said about each prize was quite unintelligible to all that it did not concern. It was received by the bystanders as only a pleasant remark. But each felt that Christ Jesus had cast a deeply penetrating glance into his own interior. Nathanael, the bridegroom, won a remarkable piece of fruit. After the bridegroom had eaten the fruit he had won, he became very much agitated. He grew pale, and a dark vapor escaped from him, after which he looked much brighter and purer, yes, even transparent when compared with what he had been before. The bride, too, who at a distance was sitting among the women, became after eating her piece of fruit quite faint. A dark shadow appeared to go out from her.

The game in the garden was followed by the nuptial banquet. Christ Jesus had taken the responsibility for arranging the banquet. When the food was brought in, a roasted lamb, the feet bound crosswise, was set before Christ Jesus. As he carved the lamb, wonderful words fell from his lips. He said that the lamb had been separated from its companions and cut into pieces, so that it might become in them a nourishment of mutual union. So, too, must one who would follow the Lamb renounce one's own field of pasture, put one's passions to death, and separate from the members of one's family. Then would one become, as it were, a nourishment to unite, by means of the Lamb, one's fellows to the Heavenly Father.

At a later time, when the Blessed Virgin Mary saw that there was no wine, she said to Christ Jesus, "They have no wine." Christ Jesus had promised the Blessed Virgin Mary that he would provide the wine. But the wine he was about to provide was more than ordinary wine; it was symbolic of the mystery by which he would one day change wine into his own blood. His reply, "My hour has not yet come," contained three meanings: first, the hour for supplying the promised wine, second, the hour for changing water into wine; and third, the hour for changing wine into his blood. The Blessed Virgin Mary said confidently to the servants, "Do all that he tells you to do."

After a while, Christ Jesus directed the servants to bring him the jugs that were used in the Jewish rite of water purification. He told them to turn them upside down to prove that they were empty. Then Christ Jesus ordered each to be filled with water. The servants took the six jugs to the well and filled them. Then they were placed on a side table and Christ Jesus went to them and blessed them. As he retook his place at the table, Christ Jesus called to a servant, "Draw off now and bring some to the steward." When this latter had tasted the wine, he approached the bridegroom and said, "Every man at first sets forth good wine and when all have well drunk, then that which is worse. But you have kept the good wine until now." He did not know that the wine had been provided by Christ Jesus. Then the bridegroom and the bride's father drank of the wine, and great was their astonishment. The servants protested that they had drawn only water. And now the whole company drank the water that had been changed into wine.

This miracle gave interior strength to all who drank the wine. They became convinced of Christ Jesus's power and of the lofty nature of his mission. Faith entered their hearts, and they were inwardly united as a community. Here, for the first time, Christ Jesus was in the midst of his community. He wrought this miracle on their behalf.

After the banquet, Nathanael the bridegroom had a private conversation with Christ Jesus in which he expressed his desire to lead a life of continence. His bride came to Christ Jesus with the same wish. Kneeling before Christ Jesus, they took a vow to live as brother and sister for a period of three years. Christ Jesus bestowed his blessing upon them.

On the following day, Christ Jesus taught in the house where the wedding banquet had taken place. Several guests, including Lazarus and Martha, departed from Cana. That evening, in a festive procession, the bride and bridegroom were conducted to their house.

On Friday, December 30, most of the remaining guests, including the Blessed Virgin Mary and the other holy women, left Cana. In the evening, with the beginning of the Sabbath, Christ Jesus taught in the synagogue concerning the marriage ceremony and the devout sentiments of the bridal pair.

The next day, Christ Jesus taught in the synagogue morning and afternoon. When he came out of the synagogue, in the presence of the priests, he healed six people and raised from the dead a man who had died as a consequence of falling from a tower. After the close of the Sabbath, Christ Jesus and his remaining disciples set off for Capernaum.

CHAPTER 6

THE FIRST FESTIVAL OF THE PASSOVER

MARCH 16 TO MAY 26, 30 CE

Today, Thursday, March 16, Christ Jesus celebrated the Feast of the Dedication of the Temple of Zorobabel in the synagogue at Ginnim. That evening, he and the disciples continued on their way to Jerusalem for the Festival of the Passover, walking through the night.

The following day, after walking through Samaria, Christ Jesus and his disciples arrived at a shepherd's inn. As it was Friday, Christ Jesus led them in a celebration of the Sabbath at the inn. After the close of the Sabbath, Christ Jesus and his disciples continued on their way to Bethany. That night Christ Jesus stayed at Lazarus' castle.

On the next day, Christ Jesus and Lazarus went to Jerusalem. By midday, the holy women and friends of Christ Jesus from Jerusalem were gathered at the house of Mary Mark. They ate a meal together with Christ Jesus, who spoke of the nearness of the kingdom of heaven. That evening, Christ Jesus and Lazarus returned to Bethany where Saturnin and some of John's disciples came to him.

The following morning, Christ Jesus went to Jerusalem again. He visited the son of Obed, the son of Simeon, and ate a meal there. After eating, Christ Jesus walked the streets of Jerusalem. Nicodemus also came from Jerusalem to hear Jesus.

On the next day, Christ Jesus went to Simon the Pharisee's inn in Bethany. Many disciples and holy women gathered there and ate together with Christ Jesus. During the meal, he made numerous allusions to the prophets and the fulfilling of their prophecies. He spoke of the wonders attending

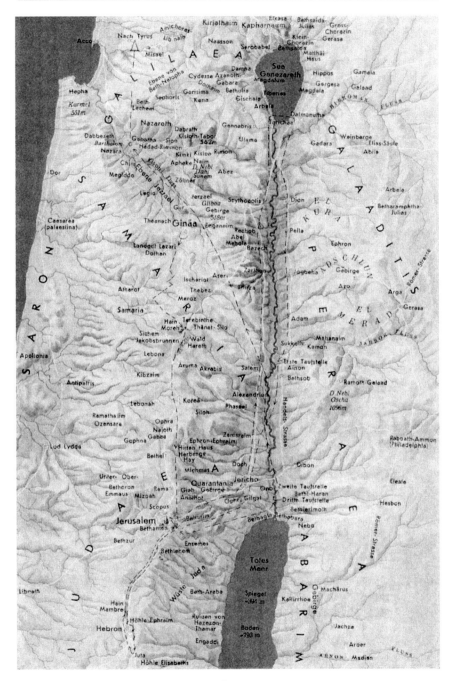

FIGURE 6: The First Passover
March 16 to May 26, 30 CE

the conception of John the Baptizer, and of his now being engaged in preparing the way. He drew their attention to man's indifference respecting the completion of the time marked by the prophets. "It was fulfilled thirty years ago, and yet who thinks of it excepting a few devout, simple-minded people? Who now recalls the fact that three kings, like an army from the east, followed a star with childlike faith seeking a newborn King of the Jews, whom they found in a poor child of poor parents? They spent three days with these poor people! Had they been coming to the child of a distinguished prince, it would not have been so easily forgotten!" Christ Jesus, however, did not at that time say that he himself was that child.

On the following day, accompanied by Lazarus and Saturnin, Christ Jesus visited the homes of the sick in Bethany and healed a number of people.

That evening, with the start of the first day of the Hebrew month of Nisan, the New Moon festival was celebrated in the synagogue at Bethany. On the next day, together with Lazarus, Saturnin, Obed and several other disciples, Christ Jesus was present at the service in the Temple at Jerusalem. Christ Jesus' presence evoked mixed emotions in the people there, ranging from deep sympathy to hatred.

On the next day in the great hall of Lazarus' castle in Bethany, Christ Jesus taught his disciples. He spoke about his youth. Among other things, he said: "It is now exactly eighteen years since a *bachir* (youth) in the Temple argued eloquently with the doctors of the law, who were filled with wrath against him." Christ Jesus then related what the *bachir* had taught. That evening, Friday, March 24, 30, he celebrated the Sabbath in the synagogue at Bethany.

This morning Christ Jesus with Obed, who served in the Temple, and the other disciples of Jerusalem, went again to the Temple at Jerusalem for the celebration of the Sabbath. They stood two by two among the young Israelites. Christ Jesus wore a white, woven robe with a girdle, and a white mantle like those used by the Essenes, but there was something very distinguished about him. His clothing looked remarkably fresh and elegant. He chanted and prayed from the parchment rolls in turn with the others. There were some prayer leaders present. The people were again struck with the sight of Christ Jesus. They were astonished; they wondered at him, though without having said a word to him. Even among themselves they did not speak openly of him, but it was obvious the wonderful impression he made on many. Around two o'clock in the afternoon, he and his disciples ate a meal together at a place adjoining the Temple. Christ Jesus remained at the Temple for the rest of the day, returning to Bethany at about nine o'clock in the evening.

On the morning of the following day, Christ Jesus was in the Temple again, accompanied by about twenty disciples. Afterward, he taught in the house of John Mark. Then he returned to Bethany where he and Lazarus shared a meal with Simon the Pharisee.

Later that week, Christ Jesus proceeded to the Temple. The Pharisees were angered to see him again. Afterward, he returned to the home of Joseph of Arimathea. Everywhere, preparation was underway for the Feast of the Passover.

On Saturday, April 1, Christ Jesus went to the Temple for the Sabbath. Together with Obed, he entered the inner court, where the priests and Levites were holding a discourse concerning the Festival of the Passover. The whole assembly was thrown into consternation by the appearance of Christ Jesus at the sacrifice of the Paschal lamb—meaning the Lamb of God would soon be fulfilled, so that the Temple and its services would then come to an end. The Pharisees were angry and astounded at his whole bearing. They did not undertake anything against him. Although it was forbidden for ordinary people to come into this part of the Temple, Christ Jesus had entered it in his capacity as a prophet.

That evening, after the close of the Sabbath, Christ Jesus returned to Bethany and conversed at length with Lazarus' sister, Silent Mary. Part of the time she sat up on her couch, and part of the time she walked around her chamber. She now had perfect use of her senses. She distinguished between the present and the future. She recognized in Christ Jesus both the Savior and the Paschal Lamb, and she knew that he was to suffer frightfully. All this made her inexpressibly sorrowful. The world appeared to her gloomy and an insupportable weight. But most of all she was grieved at human ingratitude, which she foresaw. Christ Jesus spoke long with her of the approach of the Kingdom of God and his own Passion, after which he gave her his blessing and left her. She was soon to die.

The following day, Christ Jesus healed publicly in Bethany. Among those who came to be healed were some who were blind and some who were lame. In the afternoon, he taught again in the Temple. That evening, a group of Christ Jesus' friends and supporters from Galilee came to celebrate the Passover in Jerusalem. The Blessed Virgin Mary and the holy women also arrived and stayed at the home of Mary Mark.

On Monday, April 3, Christ Jesus and his disciples went to the Temple. There Christ Jesus found vendors ranged around the inner court selling their wares. He admonished them in a friendly manner and suggested they retire to the court of the Gentiles. He and the disciples helped them move their tables. Today, for the first time Christ Jesus healed the sick in Jerusalem.

On the next day, a multitude of people were gathered in Jerusalem. Arriving at the Temple, Christ Jesus and his disciples again found the vendors there. Christ Jesus admonished them more severely this time, and set about forcibly removing their tables to the outer court. Some pious Jews approved of his action and called out, "The prophet of Nazareth!" The Pharisees, put to shame by Christ Jesus' action, were angered by the crowd's response. Later, as Christ Jesus left the Temple, he healed a cripple. All was quiet on the streets of Jerusalem that evening, for people were busy in their homes cleansing out the leaven and preparing the unleavened bread.

The following day was the day of preparation for the Passover, and Saturnin slaughtered the three lambs that Christ Jesus and the disciples were to eat. The Passover meal took place in the great hall at Lazarus' castle. Christ Jesus taught, and they sang and prayed together until late in the night.

At daybreak Christ Jesus and his disciples went to the Temple. Christ Jesus taught in the forecourt. Vendors had again erected tables to sell their wares, and Christ Jesus demanded that they withdraw. When they refused, Christ Jesus drew a cord of twisted reeds from the folds of his robe. With this in hand, he overturned their tables and drove the vendors back, assisted by the disciples. Christ Jesus said, "Take these things away; you shall not make my Father's house a house of trade." That afternoon, Christ Jesus healed about ten people—some crippled, some dumb—in the forecourt of the Temple. This gave rise to much excitement and jubilation. Summoned to answer for his action, Christ Jesus rebuked his interrogators. He then returned to Bethany, where he celebrated the Sabbath.

On the following day, Christ Jesus remained for the whole day at Lazarus' castle. At the close of the Sabbath, some Pharisees, wishing to take Jesus into custody, went to the home of Mary Mark, thinking to find him there. However, only the Blessed Virgin Mary and the holy women were there. After addressing the women sharply and telling them to leave the city, the Pharisees went away. The women then hurried to Bethany, where they found Martha together with Silent Mary. The latter died just a few hours later, in the presence of the Blessed Virgin Mary.

That night, in spite of the open persecution directed at Christ Jesus, Nicodemus came to Bethany and visited Christ Jesus at the invitation of Lazarus. They spoke privately throughout the night as recorded in John 3:1–12.

Before daybreak, Christ Jesus and Nicodemus went to Jerusalem to Lazarus' castle on Mount Zion. Joseph of Arimathea joined them there. Later, a whole group of about thirty disciples came. Christ Jesus gave instructions about what the disciples should do during the coming period.

Several weeks after that, Christ Jesus was at Ono where he himself had been baptized. While he was teaching before the multitude, a stranger approached mounted on a camel. He was followed by six attendants, who rode on mules. It was a delegation from King Abgarus of Edessa. The king was sick; he had sent presents to Christ Jesus, and he implored him to come to Edessa and cure him. The young man who was commissioned to bear the king's letter to Christ, Jesus was vainly trying to reach him. Christ Jesus told one of the disciples to make room for the man. Christ Jesus continued his discourse a while longer, but then sent the disciple to tell the envoy that he might approach and deliver his message.

Casting himself on his knees before Christ Jesus, the messenger bowed low, as did also his attendants, and said, "Your slave is the servant of King

Abgarus of Edessa. He is sick. He sends you this letter in which he indicates that he believes you are the Son of God, and prays you to accept these gifts from him." Then the slaves approached with the presents: woven stuffs, thin plates of gold, and very beautiful lambs. Christ Jesus replied to the envoy that the good intentions of his master were pleasing to him, and he commanded the disciples to take the gifts and distribute them among the poorest of the assembled crowd. The envoy was also an artist, and he had been told, if Christ Jesus could not come, that he should bring back a portrait of him. When Christ Jesus had read the letter, he called for some water, bathed his face, pressed the soft stuff in which the letter had been folded to his countenance, and returned it to the envoy. The latter applied it to the picture he had vainly been trying to perfect, when behold! The likeness instantly became a facsimile of the original. The artist was filled with delight. He turned the picture, which was hanging by a strap, toward the spectators, cast himself at Christ Jesus' feet and left immediately. It became known later that the sight of this image effected a deep transformation in the king's life.

Later that month, several of John the Baptizer's disciples traveled down the Jordan to join Christ Jesus, and a controversy arose between the disciples of John and one who had been baptized by one of Christ Jesus' disciples—a controversy concerning the difference between the baptism and purification. Furthermore, as Christ Jesus now had so many disciples, John's remaining disciples complained to him that everyone was going over to Christ Jesus. John replied that he had come to bear witness as the forerunner of the Messiah; and that he was satisfied.

Around this time, Christ Jesus left the place of baptism, and his disciples returned to their homes in different parts of the country. It was now that Herod Antipas imprisoned John the Baptizer in his castle at Callirrhoe. Christ Jesus crossed the Jordan and made his way through Samaria toward Tyre.

CHAPTER 7

THE HEALINGS AT CAPERNAUM

AUGUST 8 TO 26, 30 CE

On Tuesday, August 8, Christ Jesus made his way toward Lower Sephoris. He was accompanied by his cousins Tharzissus and Aristobolus.
The following day, Christ Jesus taught in the synagogue at Lower Sephoris
before a large number of people assembled from the country around. He
also went with his cousins out of the city, and gave instructions here and
there to little crowds of people that followed him or were waiting for him.
On his return, Christ Jesus cured many sick persons outside the synagogue,
then entering, he taught of marriage and divorce.

He reproached the doctors with having made additions to the Law.
He pointed to a certain place in a roll of parchment, accused one of the
oldest among them of having inserted it, convicted him of fraud, and commanded him to erase the passage. The old man humbled himself before
Christ Jesus, prostrating himself at his feet in the presence of all the others.
He even acknowledged his fault, and thanked Christ Jesus for the lesson
just received. That night Christ Jesus spent the entire night in prayer.

On the morning of Friday, August 11, Pharisees from Upper and
Lower Sephoris drew Christ Jesus into a great dispute concerning the
strict teaching on marriage and divorce that he had recently expounded
in Lower Sephoris. In this region divorces were obtained on insignificant
pretexts, and there was even an asylum for the reception of repudiated
wives. Christ Jesus demonstrated to them the falsity of their justifications
and rebuked them for the ease with which the marital bond was dissolved
in their region.

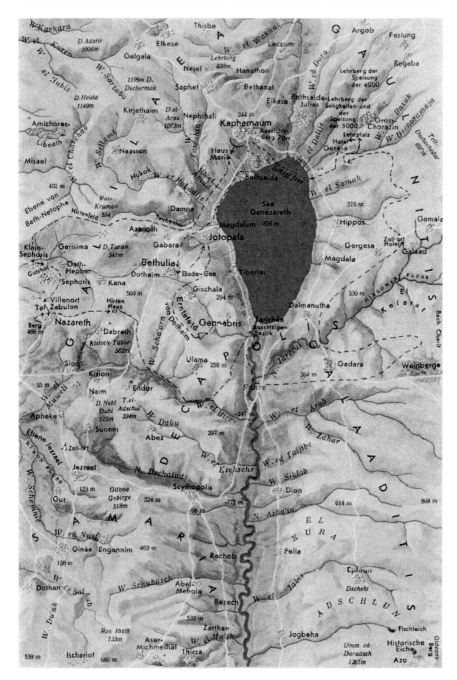

FIGURE 7: *The Healings at Capernaum*
August 8 TO 26, 30 CE

That afternoon, when Christ Jesus went to Nazareth where he was brought up, he went to the synagogue at the start of the Sabbath, as was his custom. He stood up to do the reading, and was handed the scroll of the prophet Isaiah. He unrolled the scroll and found the place where it was written: "The spirit of the Lord is upon me, because he has anointed me to bring good news to the poor. He has sent me to announce pardon for prisoners and recovery of sight to the blind; to set free the oppressed, to proclaim the year of the Lord's amnesty."

The manner in which Christ Jesus read this text gave his hearers to understand that the prophecy referred to him. That the spirit of God had descended upon him. That he, himself, had come to announce salvation to poor, suffering humanity. That all wrong should be made right, widows should be consoled, the sick cured, and sinners forgiven. His words were so beautiful and so loving that, wondering and full of joy, they said to one another, "He speaks as if he himself were the Messiah!" They were so carried away with admiration for him that they became quite vain of the fact that he belonged to their own city.

The next day, Christ Jesus taught again at the synagogue at Nazareth and sharply reproached the Pharisees for their misinterpretation of the law. At midday, he dined with an Essene family. He then returned to teach at the synagogue some more. He spoke of the fullness of time, of his own mission, of the last chance of grace, of the depravity of the Pharisees, and of the punishment in store for them if they did not reform. They became more and more displeased especially when he said, "You say to me, 'Physician, cure yourself! In Capernaum and elsewhere you have wrought miracles. Do the same here in your native city.'" But Christ Jesus said, "No prophet is welcome in his own village; no physician cures those who know him."

Then comparing the present to a time of famine and the different cities to poor widows, he said, "There was a great famine in Israel at the time of Elijah, and there were many widows in those days, but the prophet was sent to none but the widow of Sarepta. And there were many lepers in the time of Elijah, but he cleansed none but Naaman the Syrian." Thus Christ

Jesus compared Nazareth to a leper who was not healed. Those in the synagogue became enraged at being likened to lepers, and rising up from their seats, they stormed against him and made as if they were about to seize him. But he said to them, "Observe your own laws and break not the Sabbath! When it is over do what you propose to do." They allowed him to proceed with his discourse, though they kept up the murmuring among themselves and addressed scornful words to him. Soon after, they left their places and went down to the door. Christ Jesus, however, continued to teach and explain his last words, after which he, too, left the synagogue.

Outside the door, Christ Jesus found himself surrounded by about twenty angry Pharisees who laid hands on him, saying, "Come up with us to a height from which you can advance more of your doctrines! Then we can answer you as such teaching ought to be answered." Christ Jesus told them to take their hands off him, that he would go with them. They surrounded him like a guard, the crowd following. The moment the Sabbath ended, jeers and insults arose on all sides. They raged and hooted, each trying to outdo his neighbor in the number and quality of his scoffing attacks on Christ Jesus. "We will answer you!" they cried, and thus shouting and raging, they led Christ Jesus up the mountain. Ascending, they reached a lofty spur that, on the northern side, overlooked a marshy pool, and on the south formed a rocky projection over a steep precipice. Here they intended once more to call Christ Jesus to account and then to hurl him down. They were not far from the scene of action when Christ Jesus, who had been led as a prisoner among them, stood still, while they continued their way mocking and jeering. At that instant, two tall figures of light came near Christ Jesus, who took a few steps back through the hotly pursuing crowd, reached the city wall on the mountain ridge of Nazareth, and followed it till he came to the gate by which he had entered the evening before.

On August 13 Christ Jesus met with four disciples—Saturnin, Parmenus, and the Greek brothers Tharzissus and Aristobolus—on their way from Nazareth to Tarichea. They walked together, arriving around four o'clock that afternoon. Here in Tarichea Christ Jesus healed five lepers. He and the four disciples proceeded on to the Jordan River, which they crossed that night. On the following day, Christ Jesus and the four disciples made their way to Galaad, where they stayed at an inn on the outskirts of town. The next day they went northward to the town of Gerasa, where they arrived that evening. Here Christ Jesus received a message sent by the Blessed Virgin Mary on behalf of a widow of Nain who was possessed. This widow was an acquaintance of Maroni, the widow of Nain whom Christ Jesus had visited there on August 2. Receiving the message, Christ Jesus healed the possessed woman from a distance.

After healing many in Bethsaida, Christ Jesus made his way to the synagogue in Capernaum. It was the start of the Sabbath, and also the beginning of the month of Elul. In Capernaum, many Pharisees, including the fifteen newcomers who were there to investigate him, listened to Christ Jesus' teaching. The number of people in Capernaum on that day was great. The possessed had been released from their places of confinement and ran crying out along the streets to meet Christ Jesus. He commanded them to be silent and delivered them; whereupon, to the astonishment of the multitude, they followed him quietly to the synagogue and listened to his instruction. They gave him the Scriptures, and he taught from *Isaiah* that God had not forgotten his people: "Sing for joy, O heavens, and exalt, O earth; break forth, O mountains, into singing! For the Lord has comforted his people, and will have compassion on his suffering ones. But Zion said, 'The Lord has forsaken me, my Lord has forgotten me.' Can a woman forget her nursing child, or show no compassion for the child of her womb? Even these may forget, yet I will not forget you."

He then explained from the preceding verses that the impiety of men could not restrain God, could not hinder him from realizing his thoughts of mercy. They were astounded by his interpretation of the prophet Isaiah, whispering to one another: "Never before has a prophet taught like this!" But they had no reply to Christ Jesus' sermon.

The scene took place there, in which Christ Jesus healed a man who was possessed. At this moment, right in their synagogue, a person possessed by an unclean spirit shouted, "Jesus! What do you want with us, you Nazarene? Have you come to get rid of us? I know who you are: God's holy man!" But Christ Jesus said to the spirit, "Be quiet and get out of him!" Then the unclean spirit threw the man into convulsions. Letting out a shriek the spirit came out of him. The people were all amazed. They asked themselves, "What is this? A new kind of teaching backed with authority! He gives orders even to unclean spirits, and they obey him." Thus, his fame spread rapidly everywhere throughout Galilee and even beyond. Later, after teaching again in the synagogue, Christ Jesus withdrew to a lonely place where he spent the night in prayer.

It was afternoon on Tuesday, August 22, when Christ Jesus arrived at Jotopata. He washed his feet and ate a meal at an inn outside the city. The disciples went before him into Jotopata to the chief of the synagogue, and requested the key for their leader, who wished to teach. The people hurriedly gathered in crowds. The Doctors of the Law and the Herodians, a secret sect of the Jews who opposed the rule of Rome, were all expecting to snare him in his doctrine. When Christ Jesus had taken his place in the synagogue, they put to him questions upon the approach of the Kingdom, the computation of time, the fulfilling of the weeks of Daniel, and the coming of the Messiah. Christ Jesus answered in a long discourse, showing that the prophecies were now fulfilled. He spoke, too, of John the Baptizer and his prophecies, whereupon they took occasion to warn him, hypocritically, to be careful of what he said in his instructions, not to set aside the Jewish customs, and to take a lesson from John's imprisonment! What he said of the fulfillment of the weeks of Daniel, of the near coming of the Messiah, and of the King of the Jews, was excellent and quite in accordance with their own ideas. He told them, *they* might seek where they would, but they would not find the Messiah. Christ Jesus had, though rather vaguely, applied the prophecies to himself. They understood him well enough, but they pretended that such things could not happen to anyone, and that they had failed to catch his meaning. In reality they wanted to force him to speak out more clearly, so they might acquire language they could use against him.

Christ Jesus said to them, "How you play the hypocrite! What turns you away from me? Why do you despise me?" Then he cast into their face Herod's shameful deeds, his murders, his dread of the newborn King of the Jews, his cruel Massacre of the Innocents, and his frightful death, the

crimes of his successors, the adultery of Herod Antipas, and the imprisonment of John the Baptizer. He spoke of the hypocritical sect of the Herodians who were in league with the Sadducees, and showed them what kind
of a Messiah and what sort of a Kingdom of God they were awaiting. The
Herodians, seeing themselves discovered, blanched with rage when Christ
Jesus referred to Herod's misdeeds and laid open the secrets of the sect
before the people. They were silent and, one by one, left the synagogue.

A few days later, Christ Jesus and a number of his disciples arrived at
Gennabris at the start of the Sabbath. Christ Jesus taught in the synagogue,
which was very full. Afterward he was invited to a meal by a Pharisee. The
following morning, Christ Jesus taught again in the synagogue. Herod
Antipas had sent some spies to Galilee to hear what Christ Jesus was
preaching. Christ Jesus referred to them in these words, "When they come,
you may tell the spies to take word back to Herod not to trouble himself
about me. He may continue his wicked course and fulfill his designs with
regard to John the Baptizer. For the rest, I shall not be constrained by him.
I shall continue to teach wherever I am sent in every region, and even in
Jerusalem itself when the time comes. I shall fulfill my mission and account
for it to my Father in heaven."

That evening, after the close of the Sabbath, Christ Jesus was invited
to a banquet to celebrate the completion of the harvest. He spoke from the
scriptures: "Is it not to share your bread with the hungry, and to bring the
homeless poor into your house; when you see the naked, to cover them,
and not to hide yourself from your own kin?"

He asked whether it was not customary to invite the poor to such feasts
of thanksgiving. Christ Jesus expressed this by saying, "Where are the
poor?" Then he sent his disciples out to bring in the poor from the streets.

CHAPTER 8

THE SERMONS ON THE MOUNT

NOVEMBER 16 TO DECEMBER 10, 30 CE

On November 16, Christ Jesus and some disciples who were traveling with him, left Megiddo in the direction of Mount Tabor. Christ Jesus taught as they walked along. Toward evening they arrived at a small shepherds' place at the foot of the northwest side of the mountain. Here Christ Jesus taught and they all spent the night. The next morning, Christ Jesus and his disciples walked in the direction of Capernaum, arriving there shortly after the beginning of the Sabbath. They went to the synagogue where Christ Jesus taught. As he was leaving the synagogue, Christ Jesus looked up to the gallery and saw two unclean men still standing. He called to them to come down, but they were timid and ashamed. Through fear of the Pharisees they did not venture to obey at once. Then Christ Jesus commanded them to come down. To their own astonishment they found themselves able to descend the steps alone. The Pharisees were indeed upset when they saw the two poor despised sinners in their red mantles. The lepers sank down—trembling—on their knees before him. Christ Jesus laid his hand upon them, breathed upon the face of each, and said, "Your sins are forgiven you." And he admonished them to continence and the baptism of penance. They rose up. Their disfigurement had visibly decreased, their ulcers had dried, and the scales had fallen off. With tears they thanked their benefactor.

Many of the well disposed among the bystanders pressed around the cured, celebrating in words of praise their healing. The Pharisees protested loudly because he had healed on the Sabbath and questioned by what right

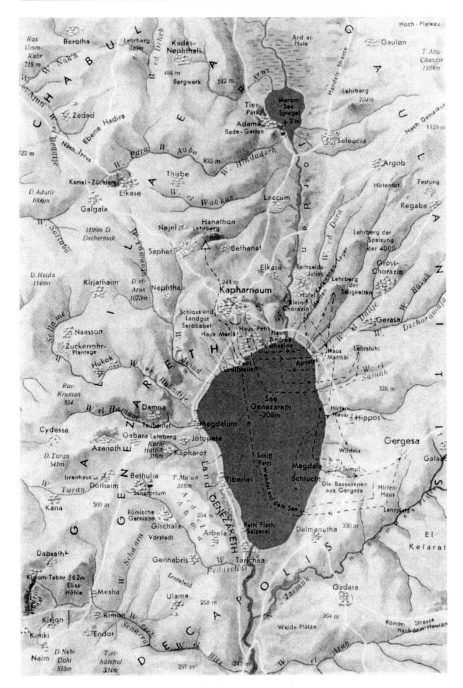

FIGURE 8: *The Sermons on the Mount*
November 6 – December 10, 30 CE

he could forgive sins. Without uttering a word, Christ Jesus passed through their midst. He went to the Blessed Virgin Mary's house. After consoling the holy women who had wept and lamented over the displeasure of the Pharisees, Christ Jesus went out again and spent the whole night in prayer.

The next morning, after healing some people at Peter's house, Christ Jesus instructed some fifty people waiting for baptism. These were then baptized by Andrew and Saturnin. Later, Christ Jesus went to the synagogue in Capernaum and healed a number of sick people who were waiting outside. Here he was approached by Jairus, the chief of the synagogue. Jairus pleaded with Christ Jesus to come and heal his daughter, Salome, who was on the point of death. On the way, a messenger arrived from Jairus' house and addressed him, "Your daughter has died. There is no further need to trouble the master." On hearing these words, Christ Jesus said to Jairus, "Fear not! Trust in me, and you shall receive help!" As they drew near Jairus' house, they saw minstrels and female mourners already assembled in the courtyard. Christ Jesus entered, taking with him only Peter, James the Greater, and John the son of Zebedee. In passing through the court, Christ Jesus said, "Why do you lament and weep? Go your way! The damsel is not dead, but only sleeping." At this the crowd of mourners began to laugh him to scorn, for they knew that she was dead. But Christ Jesus insisted on their retiring even from the court, which he requested be locked.

Then he entered the apartment where the grief-stricken mother with her maid was busy preparing the winding sheet. Christ Jesus, accompanied by the father, the mother, and the three disciples, passed on into the inner chamber in which the girl lay enveloped in a long garment. Christ Jesus raised her lightly in his arms, held her on his breast, and breathed upon her. Near the right side of the corpse was a luminous figure in a sphere of light. When Christ Jesus breathed upon the little girl, that figure entered her mouth as a tiny human form of light. Then Christ Jesus laid the body down upon the couch, grasped one of her wrists and said, "Damsel, arise!" The girl sat up in her bed. Christ Jesus still held her by the hand. Then she stood up, opened her eyes, and supported by the hand of Christ Jesus, stepped from the couch to the floor. Christ Jesus led her weak and tremulous, to the arms of her parents. They had watched the progress of the event at first coldly, though anxiously, then trembling with agitation, and now they were beside themselves with joy. Christ Jesus told them to give the child something to eat, and to make no unnecessary noise about the matter. After receiving the thanks of the father, Christ Jesus went down into the city.

On the way back, Christ Jesus spoke to his disciples on the subject of this miracle. He said that the father and mother had neither real faith nor an upright intention. If the child was raised from the dead, it was for her own sake and for the glory of God. The death from which she had just been roused, that is the death of the body, was a guiltless one, but from the death of the soul, she must now preserve herself. Christ Jesus spent part of that night retired in prayer.

After being present for the baptism of a number of people on the morning of November 19, Christ Jesus taught from the banks of the Sea of Galilee. As the throng of people grew, he and some of his disciples climbed aboard a ship placed at his disposal, and Christ Jesus taught from there. The other disciples boarded Peter's ship. After Christ Jesus finished teaching those on the shore, this second ship hooked up to the ship on which Christ Jesus was, towing it across the lake while Christ Jesus continued to teach those on board along the way. Around four o'clock that afternoon they reached the eastern shore and went to a nearby place where a number of tax collectors, including Levi, lived. He cast himself down before Christ Jesus, who said, "Levi, arise and follow me!" That night Christ Jesus stayed at an inn in the town of Bethsaida–Julias.

On the following day, Christ Jesus and the disciples visited Levi at his house and welcomed him as a disciple. Judas Thaddeus, Simon, James the Lesser, and Joses Barsabbas were especially pleased at this (Levi was their stepbrother), and they embraced him warmly. Christ Jesus spoke with Levi's wife and blessed the children. Then Levi knelt before him, and Christ Jesus, laying his hand upon him, blessed him and gave him the name Matthew. Following this there was a banquet in Matthew's home at which a large number of tax collectors and Pharisees were present. Christ

Jesus stayed overnight in Matthew's house, while the disciples slept on their boats.

On the next day, from the shore of the Sea of Galilee, Christ Jesus called Peter and Andrew, who were casting a net into the lake, "Come and follow me, I will make you fishers of people." A little further down the shore he called also to the brothers James and John, the sons of Zebedee. They abandoned their boat and their father then and there and followed him.

In the morning, Peter, Andrew, and Saturnin did the baptizing. That evening, when all were assembled at Matthew's house, the crowd was great and pressed around Christ Jesus. On that account, with the twelve disciples and Saturnin, Christ Jesus boarded Peter's boat and gave instructions to row toward Tiberius, which was on the opposite side of the lake in its greatest breadth. It seemed as if Christ Jesus wanted to escape from the crowd that pressed on him, for he was fatigued. Three platforms surrounded the lower part of the mast like steps, one above the other. In the middle one, Christ Jesus lay down, and he fell asleep. When the party put out from shore, the weather was calm and beautiful, but they had scarcely reached the middle of the lake before a violent tempest arose. The danger was imminent, and the disciples were in great anxiety when they woke up Christ Jesus with the words, "Master, have you no care for us? We are sinking!" Christ Jesus got up, looked out upon the water, and said quietly and earnestly, as if speaking to the storm, "Peace! Be still!" Instantly, all became calm. The disciples were struck with fear. They whispered to one another, "Who is this man who can control the waves?" Christ Jesus reproved them for their lack of faith and for their fear. Then he commanded them to sail back in the direction in which they had come, toward Chorazin (as the neighborhood was called because of the town Great Chorazin).

On the following day, Christ Jesus taught from the side of a mountain about one hour southwest of Great Chorazin. He healed numerous people and blessed the children who were brought to him. Many Gentiles were present, and all those seeking baptism were baptized. That evening in Matthew's house, Christ Jesus told a parable. He said, "The Kingdom of

Heaven is like a treasure that a man found hidden in his neighbor's field. Without disclosing the secret, he went and joyfully sold all that he owned to buy that field." Christ Jesus interpreted this parable as the Gentiles' longing for salvation.

On the next day, Christ Jesus did some teaching and healing on the shore of the lake. Among the numerous cures was a man with a completely withered arm and a shrunken and crooked hand. Christ Jesus stroked down the arm, took the hand into his own, and straightened out each finger one after the other, at the same time gently bending and pressing it. All this took place almost instantaneously, in a shorter time than one takes to say how it was done. The hand was restored to its proper shape, the blood began to circulate, and the man could move it, although it was still wasted and weak. However, its strength increased with each passing minute.

That afternoon, Christ Jesus and the twelve sailed back to Bethsaida, arriving there around four o'clock. They were met by the Blessed Virgin Mary, who was accompanied by Maroni, the widow of Nain, and her son Martialis, whom Jesus had raised from the dead on November 13.

On the following day, Friday, November 24, some twelve thousand people were gathered at Capernaum in the hope of seeing Christ Jesus. As the Sabbath began, he taught in the synagogue, and healed a possessed man who had been brought there.

That evening, some of the disciples, those who had formerly been engaged in fishing, obtained Christ Jesus' permission to go on their barks and pass the night at their old occupation, since there was a great need of fish to feed the multitude of strangers then present in Capernaum. The disciples spent the whole night in fishing, and the next morning rowed some who desired to cross to the other side of the lake. Meanwhile, Christ Jesus and the rest of the disciples distributed alms to the poor, to the sick that had been cured, and to needy travelers.

Later in the day at Peter's fishery, Christ Jesus gave a discourse that was attended by a very large crowd. The boats of Peter and Zebedee were lying not far from shore. The disciples who had been fishing the night before were on the shore a little distance from the crowd, cleaning their nets. Christ Jesus' little bark was lying near the larger ones. When the press of the crowd became too great, Christ Jesus made a sign to the fishermen, and they rowed his bark to where he was standing. The little bark was pushed up to the shore, and Christ Jesus entered it with some of his disciples. They rowed out a short distance from land, and then up and down, pausing sometimes here, sometimes there, as Christ Jesus instructed the crowd on the shore. He told them several parables relating to the Kingdom of Heaven, including one comparing it to a net cast into the sea.

As evening approached, Jesus instructed Peter to row his boat out upon the lake and to cast his nets to the fish. Peter, slightly vexed, replied, "We have labored all night and taken nothing, but at your word I will let down the nets." And he with the others entered their barks with their nets and rowed out into the lake. Jesus left the crowd and, in his own little boat, followed after Peter. Jesus continued to instruct the disciples. When out in deep water, Jesus told them where to let down the net. Then he left them and rowed back in his little boat to the landing place near Matthew's house.

By this time it was night, and on the edge of the boats near the nets, torches were blazing. The fishers cast out the net, and rowed toward Chorazin, but they were soon unable to raise the net. When at last, continuing to row eastward, they dragged the net out of the deep water and into shallow water, the net was so heavy that it gave way here and there. Then they called their companions in Zebedee's boat, who came and helped them empty part of the net.

They were actually terrified at the sight of the draft of fish! Never before had such a thing happened to them. Peter was confounded. He felt how vain were all the cares they had formerly bestowed upon their fishing—how fruitlessly they had labored, notwithstanding their troubles—and here at a word from Jesus, they had caught more fish in one effort than they had ever caught in months together. When the net was relieved of part of its weight, they rowed to shore, dragged it out of the water, and gazed awestruck at the multitude of fish it still contained.

At the sight of Jesus, who was waiting on the shore, Peter fell to his knees in front of him and said, "Have nothing to do with me, Master, for I am a sinful man!" Jesus said to Peter, "Do not be afraid; from now on you will be catching people." Then they brought their boats to shore, abandoned everything, and followed him.

On Tuesday, November 28, Jesus and the disciples sailed across the Sea of Galilee. After disembarking, they went to a mountain near Bethsaida-Julias, where many people were gathered to hear Jesus teach. Here began the "Sermon on the Mount" referred to in Matthew 5 and Luke 6. This sermon was actually preached in fourteen different sessions, and its conclusion was not delivered until some three months later, on March 15, 31. On that first occasion, Jesus spoke only of the first beatitude: "Blessed are the poor in spirit, for theirs is the kingdom of heaven."[1] The instruction lasted the whole day.

On the following day, Jesus began to teach concerning the second beatitude, "Blessed are those who mourn, for they will be comforted."[2] Five holy women were present, including the Blessed Virgin Mary, Mary Cleophas, and Maroni of Nain, as well as all the disciples who later became apostles. After the instruction was finished, Jesus and the disciples went back to the lake where he spoke to them about their mission in these words: "You are the light of the world." He illustrated his point by the similarities between a city sitting on top of a hill, a lamp stand, and the fulfillment of the Law. He also explained many of the sayings of the prophets.

On Friday, December 1, Jesus preached concerning the third beatitude, "Blessed are the meek, for they will inherit the earth."[3] Because the Sabbath was approaching, however, he broke off early and sailed back toward Capernaum. There he taught near the south gate, in a house that Peter had rented.

It was here that the healing of the paralytic occurred. As Jesus was developing an instruction on the forgiveness of injuries and loving one's enemies, a loud noise was heard on the roof of the house. Through the usual opening in the ceiling, a paralytic on his bed was lowered by four men who cried out, "Lord have pity upon a poor sick man!" He was let down on two cords into the midst of the assembly before Jesus. The friends

---

1   Matthew 5:3 NRSV.

2   Matthew 5:4 NRSV.

3   Matthew 5:5 NRSV.

of the sick man had tried in vain to carry the man through the crowd into the courtyard, and had at last mounted the steps to the roof of the hall whose trapdoor they had opened. All eyes were fixed upon the invalid. The Pharisees present were vexed at what appeared to them a great misdemeanor, a piece of unheard-of impertinence. But Jesus, who was pleased at the faith of the paralytic's companions, stepped forward, and addressed him who lay there motionless, "Be of good heart, son, your sins are forgiven!" These words were particularly distasteful to the Pharisees. They thought within themselves, "That is blasphemy! Who but God can forgive sins?" Jesus read their minds and said, "Why do you have such thoughts of bitterness in your hearts? Which is it easier to say to the paralytic, 'Your sins are forgiven'; or to say 'Arise, take up your bed and walk?'" And so he said to the man, "Arise, take up your bed, and go back to your home!" Immediately the man arose, cured. He rolled up the coverlets of his bed, laid the laths of the bed frame together, took them upon his shoulder, and accompanied by those who brought him and some other friends, went off singing canticles of praise while the whole multitude shouted for joy. The Pharisees, full of rage, slipped away, one by one. It was now the Sabbath, and Jesus and the multitude repaired to the synagogue in Capernaum, where he taught—this time without disruption.

Jairus, whose daughter, Salome, Jesus had raised from the dead on November 18, was also at the synagogue. As Jesus left, Jairus approached him to ask help for Salome, who was again close to death. Jesus agreed to go. On their way, the message of Salome's death reached them. But they continued on.

Then occurred the healing of the widow Enue from Cesarea Philippi, who had been suffering from a flow of blood for twelve years. It was already dark, and the crowd around Jesus was very great. Just then the widow, taking advantage of the darkness, made her way through the crowd while leaning on the arms of her nurses. She hoped in the dusk of the evening, and in the throng that would gather around Jesus on leaving the synagogue, to be able to touch him unnoticed. Jesus knew her thought and consequently slackened his pace. The nurses led her as close to him as possible. The sufferer knelt down. She leaned forward, supporting herself on one hand, and reached forward with the other hand to touch the hem of Jesus' robe. Instantly, she felt that she was healed.

Jesus at the same time halted, glanced around at the disciples, and inquired, "Who touched me?" To which Peter answered, "You ask, 'Who touched me?' The people throng and press upon you on every side as you can tell!" But Jesus responded, "Someone has touched me for I know that power has left me." He looked around and, as the crowd had fallen back a step, the woman could no longer remain hidden. Quite abashed, she approached him timidly, fell on her knees before him, and acknowledged in the hearing of those about them what she had done. She related how long she had suffered from the bloody flux, and she believed herself healed from the touch of his garment. Turning to Jesus she begged him to forgive her. Then he addressed to her these words, "Be comforted, my daughter, your faith has made you whole. Go in peace and remain free of your infirmity!" And she departed with her friends.

Then Jesus with rapid steps accompanied Jairus to his house. Peter, James, John the son of Zebedee, Saturnin, and Matthew were with him. In the forecourt, the mourners and weepers were gathered again, but this time they uttered no word of mockery, nor did Jesus say as he did before, "She is only sleeping," but he passed on straight through the crowd. Jairus' mother, his wife, and her sister came timidly forward to meet him. They were veiled and in tears; their robes, the garments of mourning. Jesus left Saturnin and Matthew with the people in the forecourt, while accompanied by Peter, James, John, the father, the mother, and the grandmother, he entered the room in which the dead girl lay.

It was a different room from the first time. Then she lay in a little chamber; now she was in the room behind the fireplace. Jesus called for a small branch from the garden and a basin of water, which he blessed. The corpse lay stiff and cold. It did not present so agreeable an appearance as on the former occasion. At that time, Jesus had said, "She is only sleeping," but now he said nothing. She was dead. Using the little branch, Jesus sprinkled her with the blessed water, prayed, and took her by the hand, and said, "Little maid, I say to you, arise!" She suddenly opened her eyes, obeyed the touch of Jesus' hand, arose and stepped from her couch. Jesus led her to her parents who, receiving her with hot tears and choking sobs, sank at Jesus' feet. He told them to give her something to eat, some bread and some grapes. The girl ate and began to speak.

Then Jesus earnestly exhorted the parents to receive the mercy of God thankfully, to turn away from vanity and worldly pleasure, to embrace the penance preached to them, and to beware of again compromising their daughter's life now restored for the second time. He reproached them with their whole manner of living, with the levity they had exhibited at the reception of the first favor bestowed upon them, and their conduct afterward, by which in a short time they had exposed their child to a much more grievous death than that of the body, namely, death of the soul. The little girl herself was much affected and shed tears. The parents were very moved and completely transformed. The father promised to break the bonds that bound him to worldliness, and to obey Jesus' orders. The mother and the rest of the family, who had now come into the room, also expressed their determination to reform their lives. Jairus, entirely changed, immediately made over a great part of his possessions to the poor.

Afterward, Jesus and his five disciples left Jairus' house by the rear in order to escape the crowd that pressed around the front of the dwelling. Jairus' house was in the northern part of Capernaum. On leaving it, Jesus and his disciples turned to the northwest toward the ramparts of the city. Meanwhile, two blind men with their guides were on the lookout for Jesus. It seemed almost as if they scented his presence, for they followed after him, crying, "Jesus, son of David, have pity on us!" At that moment, Jesus went into the house of a good man who was devoted to him. The house was built into the city wall and had on the other side a door opening into the country beyond the city precincts. The disciples sometimes stopped at this house. Its owner was one of the guards in this section of the city. The blind men and their guides, however, still followed Jesus, and even into the house, crying in beseeching tones, "Have mercy on us, son of David!" At last Jesus turned to them and said, "Do you believe that I can restore your sight?" And they answered, "Yes, Lord!" Then Jesus took from his pocket a little flask and poured from it some oil into a small, shallow dish. Holding the flask and the dish in his left hand, with his right hand he put a little earth into the dish. Then he mixed it up with the thumb and forefinger of his right hand, touched the eyes of the blind men with the same and said, "May it be done to you according to your desire." Their eyes were opened, they saw, they fell on their knees, and they gave thanks. To them also Jesus recommended silence as to what had just taken place. He did this to prevent the crowd from following him and to avoid exasperating the Pharisees. However, the two men could not forbear imparting their happiness to all that they met. Therefore a crowd soon gathered around Jesus.

Following this, some people from the region of Sephoris brought to Jesus a man who had recently been possessed by a dumb demon. He was one of the Pharisees that had formed a committee to spy on the actions of Jesus. His name was Joas, and he belonged to the group of those who, earlier at Sephoris, had disputed with Jesus on the subject of divorce. As he was led up to Jesus, the demon caused the man to attempt an attack on Jesus, but he, with a motion of his hand, commanded the demon to come out of him. The man shuddered, and a black vapor issued from his mouth. Then he sank to his knees before Jesus, confessed his sins and begged for forgiveness. Jesus pardoned him. The excitement produced by this cure was great, for it was considered a most difficult thing to do, to drive out a dumb demon. The Pharisees were indignant that one of their own had been helped by Jesus and openly avowed his sins, in which they themselves had a share. As the cured man was returning to his home, news of his deliverance spread throughout Capernaum, and people everywhere proclaimed that such wonders had never before been heard of in Israel.

On Saturday, December 2, Jesus visited the Centurion Cornelius. Then he went to Jairus' house and cautioned Salome to follow the word of God. At the close of the Sabbath, he taught in the synagogue. The Pharisees then returned with the intent of laying a snare for Jesus. They reproached him for making his appearance with a tax collector like Matthew. To this Jesus responded that he had come to console and convert sinners. Having set their trap, the Pharisees brought forth a poor creature with a withered hand, whom they had earlier intimidated and prevented from approaching Jesus. Then in a mocking retort, they said, "Master, here is one for whom you have come. Perhaps you will heal him also." Thereupon Jesus commanded the man with the withered hand to come forward and stand in the middle of the assembly. He did so, and Jesus said to him, "Your sins are forgiven!" The Pharisees, who scorned the man—his reputation was not of the best—cried out, "His withered hand has never prevented him from sinning!" Then Jesus grasped the hand, straightened the fingers, and said, "Use your hand!" The man stretched out his hand and found it cured. He went away giving thanks. Jesus justified the man against the defamations of the Pharisees; he expressed compassion for the man and declared him a good-hearted fellow. The Pharisees were covered with confusion and filled with wrath. They declared Jesus a Sabbath-breaker against whom they would lodge an accusation, and then departed.

On Monday, December 4, Jesus continued the Sermon on the Mount at another site near Bethsaida-Julias. He spoke the fourth beatitude, "Blessed are those who hunger and thirst for justice, for they will be filled."[4] After elaborating on this text, Jesus went with the twelve to a place on the east shore of the lake. There he gave them authority to cast out unclean spirits.

Jesus and the twelve, with about five other disciples, then rowed along the east bank of the Sea of Gallilee, down past Hippos, and landed near the small village of Magdala. As soon as Jesus stepped on shore, several who were possessed came running toward him with loud cries. Of their own accord, they asked him what he wanted there and cried out for him to leave them in peace. Jesus delivered them from the demons that possessed them. They gave thanks and went into the village. Now others came, bringing with them additional possessed persons. Peter, Andrew, James, John, and their cousins then went into Magdala where in the name of Jesus of Nazareth, they delivered the possessed and cured many sick, among them several women attacked by convulsions. Some that were cured by the disciples went to Jesus to hear his admonitions and instructions. Jesus continued the cures until twilight, and then spent the night on board the boat with the disciples.

On Wednesday, December 6, there occurred the healing of two possessed men from Gergesa. It was approaching ten in the morning; Jesus was climbing the northern side of the ravine, and the disciples joined

---

4   Matthew 5:6 NRSV.

him one after the other. While they were ascending, higher up on the mountain, the two possessed men were running about, darting in and out of the sepulchers, casting themselves on the ground, and beating themselves with the bones of the dead. They uttered horrible cries and appeared to be under the spell of some secret influence, for they could not flee. As Jesus grew nearer, they shouted out from behind the bushes and rocks that lay a little higher up the mountain, "You powers! You dominions! Assist us! Here comes one stronger than we!" Jesus raised his hand toward them and commanded them to lie down. They fell flat on their faces, but raising their heads again, cried out, "Jesus! You Son of God the most high. What have we to do with you? Why have you come to torment us before the time? We conjure you in the name of God to leave us in peace." By this time, Jesus and the disciples had reached the men as they lay trembling, their whole persons horribly agitated. Jesus asked, "How many are you?" They answered, "Legions!" The wicked spirits always spoke in the plural when they communicated from the mouths of these two possessed men. They indicated that the evil desires of these two men were innumerable. The wicked spirits now cried out from the mouths of the two possessed men, begging Jesus not yet to cast them into the abyss, not yet to drive them from this region. They ended their communication with this request: "Let us go into that herd of swine!" And Jesus replied, "You may go!" At these words the two miserable possessed men sank down in violent convulsions and a whole cloud of vapors issued from their bodies in numberless forms of insects, toads, worms, and mole crickets.

A few moments after, there arose from the herd of swine sounds of grunting and raging, and from the herdsmen shouts and cries. The swine, some thousand in number, came rushing from all quarters and plunged down through the bushes of the mountainside. It was like a furious tempest mingled with the cries and bellows of the animals. The scene was not the work of a few minutes only. It lasted more than an hour, for the swine rushed here and there, plunging headlong, and biting each other. Numbers precipitated themselves into the marsh at the foot of the mountain, and were swept down over a waterfall, and all went raging into the sea.

The disciples looked on disquieted, fearing that the waters in which they fished, as well as the fish themselves, would be rendered impure. Jesus divined their thoughts, and told them not to fear, since the swine would all go into the pool at the end of the ravine. This pool was a deep abyss, which through a sandbank had an inlet from the sea, but no outlet to the same. In it there was a whirlpool. It was into this cauldron that the swine plunged.

The herdsmen, who had at first run after the animals, now came back to Jesus, saw the possessed men who had been delivered, heard all that happened, and then began to complain loudly of the damage done to them. But Jesus replied that the salvation of these two souls was worth more than all the swine in the world. When the chief people of Gergesa had taken council together, they sent out a deputation to Jesus with instructions to hasten and beg him not to tarry in those parts, nor to do them greater injury.

On the next day, Jesus taught and healed. Then he instructed the disciples to sail back to Bethsaida, while he withdrew into the hills alone to pray. That night the disciples saw Jesus walking across the water toward them.[5]

On Friday, December 8, soon after Jesus and the disciples landed at Bethsaida, two blind men approached him. Jesus healed them. The people knew that he had come for the Sabbath. Indeed, so many came to him that he did not have time to eat. Not far from Capernaum, a person who was blind, dumb, and filled with demons was brought to Jesus. He healed him, evoking the crowd's astonishment. However, the Pharisees claimed that Jesus drove out demons with the help of Satan. That evening, as the Sabbath began, Jesus taught undisturbed in the synagogue, answering the Pharisees' accusation as follows. He knew their thoughts and said to them, "Every kingdom divided against itself shall fall. If Satan casts out Satan, he is divided against himself; how then will his kingdom stand?" With words like these Jesus silenced the Pharisees and without any further contradiction left the synagogue. That night, again, Jesus stayed at Peter's house.

The next day Jesus, accompanied by some of his disciples, visited Jairus' family, whom he consoled and exhorted to the practice of good.

---

5   This was not the walking on the water described in Matthew 14: 22–23, which took place later on January 29, 31.

They were very humble and entirely changed. They had divided their wealth into three parts, one for the poor, one for the community, and one for themselves. Jairus' old mother was especially touched and thoroughly converted to the good. The daughter did not make her appearance until called, and then came forward veiled, her whole deportment breathing humility. She had grown taller. She held herself erect, and presented the appearance of one in perfect health.

Jesus visited likewise the pagan centurion Cornelius, consoled and instructed his family, and then went with him to see Zorobabel, at whose house the conversation turned about King Herod's birthday and John the Baptizer. Both Zorobabel and Cornelius remarked that Herod had invited all the nobility, including themselves, to Machaerus for the celebration of his birthday, and they asked Jesus whether he would permit them to go. Jesus replied that if they dared to stand aloof from the evils that might there take place, it was not forbidden them to go, although it would be better if they could excuse themselves and remain at home.

Today there occurred—for the first time—the sending out of the disciples. At about ten o'clock in the morning, with the twelve and about thirty other disciples, Jesus left Capernaum and went in the direction of Saphet and Hanathon, accompanied by a large crowd. Around three in the afternoon, they approached Hanathon. Here Jesus and the disciples climbed a mountain used in former times by the prophets. Jesus had taught there less than one year ago, on January 5, 30. This time, however, the crowd did not go up the mountain. On the mountain, Jesus addressed the disciples, giving them instructions and sending them out into the world.

Each of the twelve had a small flask of oil, and Jesus taught them how to use it for anointing and also for healing. Afterward, the disciples knelt in a circle around Jesus, and he prayed and laid his hands upon the head of each of the twelve. Then he blessed the remaining disciples. After embracing one another, the disciples set off, having received indications from Jesus as to where they should go and when they should return to him. Peter, James the Lesser, John the son of Zebedee, Philip, Thomas, Judas, and twelve other disciples remained with him.

CHAPTER 9

THE DEATH OF JOHN THE BAPTIZER

JANUARY 1, 31 TO JANUARY 20, 31 CE

On Monday, January 1, Christ Jesus accompanied by Peter and John, the son of Zebedee, set off toward Samaria. They traveled quickly for the rest of the day and on through the whole night. On the way, Jesus told them that John the Baptizer would soon meet his end, and that he wanted to go to Hebron to comfort the Baptizer's relatives.

On January 3, Jesus taught in the synagogue at Thanat-Silo. Afterward, some people from Jerusalem told him of the sudden collapse of a wall and a tower in Jerusalem two days before. As a result, a crowd of laborers, including eighteen master workers sent by Herod, had been buried beneath the falling debris. Herod's workmen had engineered the accident to stir up the people against Pontius Pilate. But their plan had backfired, resulting in their own deaths. Jesus expressed his compassion for the innocent laborers, but added that the sin of the master workers was not greater than that of the Pharisees, Sadducees, and others who labored against the Kingdom of God. These later would also be buried one day under their own treacherous structures. After healing the sick, Jesus and the disciples made their way to Antipatris where they stayed overnight at an inn.

For the last two weeks Herod's guests had been pouring into Machaerus, most of them from Tiberius. It was one succession of holidays and banqueting. Near the castle there was an open, circular building with many seats. In it gladiators struggled with wild animals for the amusement of Herod's guests, and male and female dancers performed all kinds of

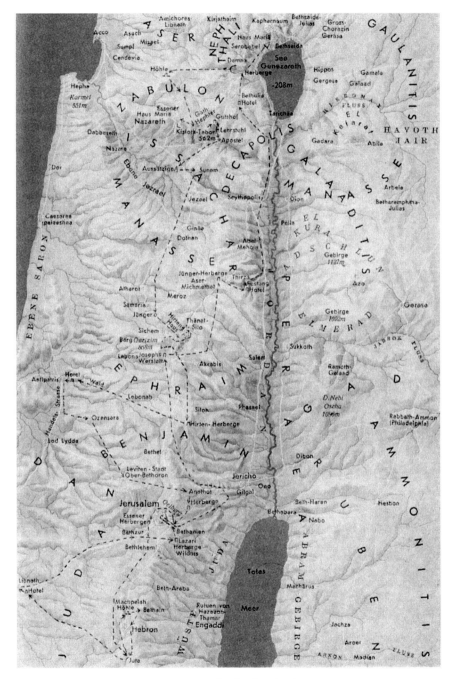

FIGURE 9: *Death of John the Baptizer*
January 1 to 20, 31 CE

voluptuous dances. Salome, the daughter of Herodias, had been trained by her mother, whose constant companion she had been throughout her earliest years. Herodias had her practicing before metallic mirrors. Salome was in the bloom of girlhood, her deportment bold, her attire shameless. For a long time Herod had looked upon her with lustful eyes. This the mother regarded with complacency, and laid her plans accordingly. That night, during the festivities to celebrate Herod's birthday at Machaerus, Salome danced for a while before Herod who, quite dazzled and enchanted, gave expression to his admiration, in which all his guests enthusiastically joined.

When all had eaten and wine had flowed freely, the guests requested Herod to allow Salome to dance again, and for this purpose, they cleared sufficient space. Salome appeared with some of her dancing companions. She was clothed in a light transparent robe and wore a crown. She was the central figure in the group of dancers. The dance consisted of a constant bowing, a gentle swaying and turning. The whole performance gave expression to the most shameful passions, and in it Salome excelled all her companions. Herod was completely ravished, perfectly entranced by the changing attitudes. After witnessing the spectacle of Salome's dancing before him, Herod said to her, "Ask what you will, and I will give it to you. Yes, I swear, even if you ask for half of my kingdom, I shall give it to you." Salome hurriedly conferred with her mother saying, "What should I ask for?" And her mother directed her to ask for the head of John the Baptizer on a dish. Salome hastened back to Herod and said, "I will that you give me at once the head of John the Baptizer on a dish!"

Only a few of Herod's most confidential associates who were nearest the throne heard the request. Herod looked like one struck with apoplexy, but Salome reminded him of his oath. Then he commanded one of the Herodians to call his executioner, to whom he gave the command to behead John the Baptizer and give his head on a dish to Salome. The executioner withdrew, and in a few moments Salome followed him. Herod, as if suddenly indisposed, soon left the hall with his companions. He was very sad. His confidential associates told him that he was not bound to grant such a request; nevertheless they promised the greatest secrecy, in order not to interrupt the festivities. Herod was exceedingly troubled. He paced the most remote apartments of his palace like one demented. Nevertheless, the feast went on undisturbed.

John the Baptizer was in prayer. The executioner and his servant took the two soldiers on guard at the entrance of John's prison into the cell with them. The guards brought torches, but the space around John was so brilliantly illuminated that their flame became dull like a light in the daytime. Salome waited in the entrance hall of the vast and intricate dungeon house. With her was a maidservant who gave the executioner a dish wrapped in a red cloth. The latter addressed John, "Herod the King sends me to bring your head on this dish to his daughter Salome." John allowed him little time to explain. He remained kneeling, and bowing his head toward him, he said, "I know why you have come. You are my guest, one for whom I have long waited. I am ready."

An iron ring was laid on his shoulders. The ring was provided with two sharp blades, which, being closed around the throat with a sudden pressure given by the executioner, in the twinkling of an eye severed the head from the trunk. The head bounded to the earth, and a triple stream of blood springing up from the body sprinkled both the head and body of the saint, as if baptizing him in his own blood. The executioner's servant raised the head by the hair, insulted it, and laid it on the dish that his master held. The latter presented it to the expectant Salome. She received it joyfully, yet not without secret horror. She carried the holy head covered by the red cloth on the dish. The maid went before, bearing a torch to light the way through the subterranean passages. Salome held the dish timidly at arm's length before her. Her head, still laden with its ornaments, was turned away in disgust.

Thus she traversed the solitary passages that led up to a kind of vaulted kitchen under the castle of Herodias. Here she was met by her mother, who raised the cover from the holy head, which she loaded with insult and abuse. Then taking a sharp skewer from a rack on the wall, she used it to pierce the tongue, the cheeks, and the eyes. After that, looking more like a demon than a human being, she hurled it away from her and kicked it with her foot through a round opening down into a pit in which the offal and refuse of the kitchen were swept. Then did that infamous woman together with her daughter return to the noise and wicked revelry of the feast, as if nothing had happened.

The holy body of the saint, covered with the skin that he usually wore, was laid by the two soldiers on his stone couch. The men were very much touched by what they had just witnessed. They were afterward discharged from duty and imprisoned that they might not disclose what they knew of John's murder. All that had any share in it were bound to the most rigorous secrecy.

The guests, however, gave John the Baptizer no thought. Thus his death remained concealed for a long time. The report was even spread that he had been set at liberty. The festivities went on. As soon as Herod ceased to take part in them, Herodias began to entertain. Five of those who knew of John's death were shut up in dungeons. They were the two guards, the executioner and his servant, and Salome's maid, who had shown some compassion for the saint. Other guards were placed at the prison door, and they in turn were at regular intervals replaced by others. One of Herod's confidential followers regularly carried food to John's cell, consequently no one had any misgiving of what had taken place.

On the morning of January 4, Jesus entered the town of Antipatris, and visited the house of the chief magistrate, whose name was Ozias. He had sent for Jesus because his daughter, Michol, about fourteen years old, lay on a couch, pale, wasted, and so paralyzed as to be unable to move any of her limbs. Jesus healed the girl, by anointing her with oil. She arose at Jesus' command, and she and her parents were filled with joy at this miracle. Jesus then proceeded to the forecourt of the house where he found numbers of people waiting for him with their sick. Here too were Peter and John the son of Zebedee. Jesus cured the sick of all kinds of maladies and, followed by a crowd, went into the synagogue where the Pharisees and a large number were awaiting his coming.

In the synagogue, Jesus told the parable of the good shepherd. He said, "I have a story to tell you. It has to do with a sheep pen. One who does not use the entrance of the pen, but climbs in over the fence, is an outlaw. The shepherd of the sheep enters by the gate. The one who tends the gate opens it for him. The shepherd calls each of his own sheep by name. The sheep hear his voice, and he leads them out. When he has brought all his own sheep out of the pen, he goes ahead of them and they follow him, because the sheep know his voice. They will not follow a stranger's voice. If they do not recognize the voice, the sheep will scatter.

Jesus told this simple parable, but his audience did not understand its meaning. So he tried again. "I am the gate for the sheep. Anyone who comes in through me will be cared for and find pasture. I am the good shepherd. I will put the sheep before myself and sacrifice myself for the sheep. A hired hand who does not own the sheep is not a real shepherd. When he sees the wolf come, he will run away, because the sheep do not matter to him. I am the good shepherd. I know my own sheep and the sheep know me. In the same way, I know the Father and the Father knows me. No one comes to the Father except through me."

Then speaking of his mission, Jesus related another parable. He said,

A [moneylender] owned a vineyard and rented it to some farmers, so they could work it and he could collect its produce from them. He sent his servant so the farmers would give him the produce from the vineyard. They seized him, beat him, and almost killed him, and the servant returned and told his master. His master said, "Perhaps he did not know them." He sent another servant, and the farmers beat that one as well. Then the master sent his son and said, "Perhaps they will show my son some respect." Because the farmers knew he was the heir to the vineyard, they seized him and killed him.[1]

After that, Jesus closed the story with a question, an answer, and an allusion to a part of Psalm 118. "What will the owner of the vineyard do? He will come in person, do away with those wicked farmers, and entrust the vineyard to others. Have you not read the scriptures: "The stone that the builders rejected has become the chief cornerstone. This is the Lord's doing: It is marvelous in our eyes."[2]

The next day, Jesus journeyed on from Ozensara to Bethoron, where he had already taught on July 24, 30. This evening at the start of the

1   Pagels 2003, Thomas 65.

2   Psalm 118:22–23 NRSV.

Sabbath, he spoke in the synagogue. Then he healed the sick, but the Pharisees objected to his healing on the Sabbath, saying that the Sabbath belonged to God. Jesus replied, "I have no other time and no other measure than the will of the Father in Heaven." Later when Jesus ate a meal with the Pharisees, they reproached him for allowing women of bad repute to follow him. They meant Mary Magdalene, Dina the Samaritan, and Mara the Suphanite. Jesus answered, "If you knew me, you would speak differently. I have come out of compassion for sinners."

Journeying on, Jesus passed through Anothor, the birthplace of the prophet Jeremiah. He then went on to Bethany, where Mary Magdalene was now living. She had moved into the living quarters of her sister, Silent Mary, who had died on April 9, 30. Mary Magdalene set off to meet Jesus, before he arrived at Bethany. She cast herself down at his feet, shedding tears of repentance and gratitude. Jesus raised her up and spoke tenderly to her, saying that she should follow in the footsteps of her departed sister who, although she had not sinned, had done penance. At Bethany, Jesus met with the Blessed Virgin Mary, who had traveled with some of the holy women to see him there. Jesus spoke with her privately about the death of John the Baptizer—about which she already knew by inner revelation.

On January 9, Jesus and his disciples spent the day in and around Juttah, teaching and healing. That evening, after the other women had retired, Jesus and the Blessed Virgin Mary, accompanied by Peter, John, and the three sons of Mary Heli (who had been disciples of John the Baptizer), went into the room where the Baptizer had been born. Kneeling together with the others on a large rug, the Blessed Virgin Mary recounted events from the Baptizer's life. Then Jesus told them that John had been put to death by Herod. Stricken with grief, they shed tears of lamentation on the rug. Jesus consoled them with earnest words. He said that silence should be maintained, at least for the time being. Apart from his murderers, no one knew of John the Baptizer's death.

Later that week, Jesus, with his disciples, visited the cave of Machpelah near Haim Mambre where Abraham, Sarah, Isaac, and Jacob were buried. All entered the cave barefoot and stood in reverential silence. Then they visited the town of Bethain, where Jesus taught and healed. He also alluded to John the Baptizer and spoke of the martyrdom of many of the prophets. A profound silence spread through the synagogue, affecting all deeply and causing many to shed tears. At this moment, too, several of the Baptizer's relatives received an interior revelation of his death, and many fainted from grief. Afterward, Jesus shared a meal with them and related the details of John's murder. Jesus spoke comforting words to all present.

On January 14, Jesus visited the grave of Zecharias, the father of John the Baptizer, in company with his disciples and the nephews of the murdered man. It was not like ordinary tombs. It was more like the catacombs, consisting of a vault supported on pillars. It was a most honorable burial place for priests and prophets. It had been determined that John the Baptizer's body should be brought from Machaerus and buried here, therefore the vault was arranged and a funeral couch erected. It was very touching to see Jesus helping to prepare a resting place for his friend. He also rendered honor to the remains of Zechariah. Then Jesus left, escorted by about twenty friends and disciples. That evening everyone went to an inn near Libnah. The next morning, Saturnin, Judas Barsabbas, and two other disciples arrived from Galilee at the inn. In the evening, a group of disciples left the inn and went to Machaerus to collect John's body.

When Saturnin, with the disciples, reached Machaerus, they climbed the mountain on which stood Herod's castle. They carried under their arms three strong wooden bars, about a hand in breadth, a leathern cover in two parts, leathern bottles, boxes in the form of bags, rolls of linen cloths, sponges, and other similar things. The disciples best known at the castle asked the guards to be allowed to enter. On being refused, they retraced their steps, went around the rampart and climbed upon one another's shoulders over three ramparts and two moats to the vicinity of John's prison. It seemed as if God helped them, so quickly did they enter and without disturbance.

After that they descended from a round opening above the interior of the dungeons. When the two soldiers on guard at the entrance to John's cell perceived them and drew near with their torches, the disciples went boldly on to meet them, and said, "We are the disciples of John the Baptizer. We are going to take away the body of our master, whom Herod put to death."

The soldiers offered no opposition but opened the prison door. They were exasperated against Herod on account of John's murder. As they entered the prison the torches went out, and the whole place filled with light. The disciples went about everything as quickly and as dexterously as if it were clear daylight. The disciples first hastened to John's body and prostrated before it with great reverence. Beside them in the prison, there was an apparition of a tall shining woman. She seemed so natural as she rendered all kinds of assistance. The corpse was still lying covered with the hairy garment. The disciples quickly set about making the funeral preparations. The apparition, who may well have been St. Elizabeth, took part in everything. Indeed she appeared to be the moving spirit of all: uncovering, covering, putting here, turning there, wrapping the winding sheets—in a word, supplying each one with whatever was wanted at the moment. Her presence seemed to facilitate matters in an incredible manner.

On January 17, Martha, Mary Magdalene, and the widow Mary Salome, who was living in Bethany as a guest of Martha, came to meet Jesus on his way to Bethany. That evening Jesus and his friends and disciples shared a meal in Bethany. After everyone had gone to bed, Jesus went alone to pray on the Mount of Olives.

The next morning Jesus and a group of disciples went to Jerusalem, first visiting the house of Joanna Chuza. Around ten in the morning, Jesus went to the Temple and taught there without arousing any opposition. After sharing a small meal with his disciples in the early afternoon at the house of Joanna Chuza, Jesus and the disciples went to the pool called Bethesda, where Jesus imparted instructions to the sick, healing a number of them.

By then the Sabbath had already begun. So Jesus went to the Temple and taught there again. Toward evening, the body of John the Baptizer was brought by the Essenes to the vault wherein Zecharias and many of the prophets were reposing, and which Jesus had recently prepared for its reception. The Baptizer's relatives, male and female, were assembled in the vault with the disciples and the two soldiers who had come with the latter from Machaerus. Several of the Essenes also were present, among them some very aged people in long, white garments. These latter had provided John with the means of subsistence during his first sojourn in the desert. Many lamps were burning in the vault. The body was extended on a carpet, the winding sheet removed, and amid many tears, anointed and embalmed with myrrh and sweet spices. Then the disciples, having reswathed the body, laid it in the compartment hewn out for it above that of his father.

On the morning of January 20, Jesus and the disciples healed the sick at the Coenaculum on Mount Zion. That afternoon they ate there, and then Jesus went to the Temple. Once again, he was able to teach there without encountering any opposition. That evening he and the disciples ate at the house of Simon the Pharisee in Bethany. Afterward, at Lazarus' castle, Jesus said goodbye to Lazarus, Martha, and Mary Magdalene.

CHAPTER 10

SECOND FESTIVAL OF THE PASSOVER

MARCH 20–31, 31 CE

O n Tuesday, March 20, Christ Jesus and the disciples split up into different groups for the journey to Bethany. Jesus was accompanied by Simon, Judas Thaddeus, Nathanael Chased, and Judas Barsabbas. They made rapid progress, arriving that night at Lazarus' estate near Ginnim. Continuing their journey, Jesus and his four traveling companions reached the town of Lebonah the next evening. On the next day, after healing some people in Lebonah, Jesus and the four disciples traveled on to Korea where he healed several people.

About three hours from Bethany, but still in the desert, stood a solitary shepherd's hut whose occupants depended for the most part on the charity of Lazarus. To this abode, Mary Magdalene with a single companion, Mary Salome a relative of Joseph, had come to meet Jesus. She had prepared for him some refreshments. On his approach, she hurried out and embraced his feet. Jesus rested here only a short time, and then set out for Lazarus's inn, one hour from Bethany. The two women returned home by another way.

When Jesus and the disciples arrived at Bethany, they were greeted by Lazarus. The Blessed Virgin Mary was also there, and other disciples and friends had already arrived. That evening, Jesus and all those gathered together in Bethany celebrated the Sabbath in the great hall of the castle. He spoke much about the Paschal lamb and his future suffering. On the following day, Jesus taught in the morning and afternoon. Then at the close of the Sabbath, all went for a walk in the gardens surrounding Lazarus'

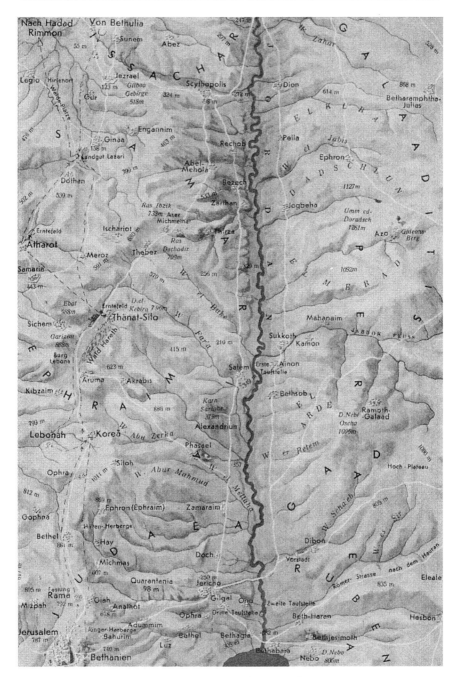

FIGURE 10: *Journey to the Second Passover*
March 20 to April 1, 31 CE

castle. Jesus spoke of his Passion and said in plain terms that he was the Messiah. His words increased his hearers' reverence and admiration for him. Mary Magdalene followed him everywhere, full of love and contrition. She sat at his feet to take in his words. Since her final conversion, she had changed greatly in her countenance and bearing. That evening there was a meal attended by all, including friends and disciples from Jerusalem.

Around ten o'clock the next morning, Jesus and the disciples crossed the Mount of Olives and went to the Temple. Here Jesus taught the disciples and a crowd of people who had gathered around. However, as there were several teaching chairs set up, Jesus did not arouse too much attention. After about an hour, he and the disciples returned to Bethany. That afternoon, about fifty Galileans—followers of Judas of Gamala— were seized by Roman soldiers, as Pontius Pilate had been informed they would try to start an insurrection. However, the people rebelled, attacking the soldiers, and managed to free the captives. Several people died in the ensuing scuffle.

News had spread that Jesus was in Jerusalem for the Festival of the Passover, and many sick people came to the Temple to be healed by him. As he was entering the Temple, Jesus caught sight of the man whom he had healed at the pool of Bethesda on January 19, 31. Jesus called out to him, "See, you are well! Sin no more, that nothing worse befall you." This person had not known who had healed him. But now he made it his business to tell the Pharisees that it was Jesus who had healed him on the Sabbath. Immediately, the Pharisees gathered around Jesus, charging him with breaking the Sabbath, but no great disturbance arose. Jesus continued to teach concerning the Paschal sacrifice. The Pharisees asked scornfully whether he—the prophet—would do them the honor of eating the Paschal lamb with them. Jesus replied, "The Son of Man is himself a sacrifice for your sins!" In the end, as Jesus continued teaching, the Pharisees became so exasperated that they created a great commotion. But Jesus managed to slip away and disappear into the crowd, returning to Bethany where preparations were underway for the feast on the following day.

On the evening of March 27, all Jesus' friends and disciples gathered in the great hall at Lazarus' castle to share the Passover feast. During the meal, Jesus taught and explained. He delivered a stirring instruction on the vine, its cultivation, the extermination of the bad shoots, the planting of better shoots, and the pruning of the same after every new growth. He then turned to the twelve and the other disciples and told them that they were the shoots of which he spoke. He asserted that the Son of Man was the true vine and that they must remain in him; that when he would be subjected to the wine press, they must continue to publish the knowledge of the true vine, namely himself, and plant all vineyards with the same. The guests did not separate until late in the night. All were deeply impressed and joyful.

Early the next morning, Jesus and the disciples went to the Temple. They stood among the crowd from sunrise until about eleven o'clock. Then there was a pause in the reception of the offerings. Jesus went up to the great teacher's chair in the court before the sanctuary. A large crowd gathered around, including many Pharisees and also the man who had been healed at the pool of Bethesda. The Pharisees accused Jesus of breaking the Sabbath because he had healed this man on the Sabbath. Jesus replied that the Sabbath was made for humanity, not humanity for the Sabbath.

He then recounted the parable of the rich man and poor Lazarus, who is not Lazarus of Bethany. The rich man was very wealthy. He lived high, held the first position among his fellows, and was a distinguished Pharisee. He was very strict in the outward observance of the Law; but, on the other hand, he was extremely severe and merciless to the poor. He harshly rebuked the poor of the place who applied to him, as to their chief magistrate, for help and support. There was a poor, wretched man in the place called Lazarus. He was full of misery and covered with ulcers, but at the same time humble and patient. Hungering for bread, he had himself carried to the house of the rich man, in order to plead the cause of the poor. The rich man was reclining at table carousing, but Lazarus was harshly repulsed as one unclean. He lay at the gate begging for only the crumbs that fell from the rich man's table, but no one gave him to eat.

The dogs, more merciful, licked his sores. After that, Lazarus died a beautiful and edifying death. The rich man also died, but his death was frightful. A wailing voice was afterward heard proceeding from his tomb, and the whole country was full of the report of it.

This parable was based on a true story. The glutton was well known until his death; the glutton and poor Lazarus really existed. They died in Jesus' early years, and they had been much spoken of in pious families of that time.

The parable so outraged the Pharisees that they pressed around Jesus and sent for the Temple guards to take him into custody. At the height of the uproar, it suddenly grew dark. Jesus looked up to heaven and said, "Father, render testimony to your Son!" A loud noise like thunder resounded and a heavenly voice proclaimed, "This is my beloved Son in whom I am well pleased!" Jesus' enemies were terrified. The disciples escorted Jesus from the Temple to safety. They then proceeded northward from Jerusalem until they reached Rama, where they stayed the night at an inn.

Leaving Rama early the next morning, Jesus and the disciples made their way to Thanat-Silo, where Jesus was given a warm reception. All the Pharisees were away in Jerusalem. On this day, Pontius Pilate issued an order forbidding all Galileans from leaving the city without his permission.

On the following day, Jesus and the disciples left Thanat-Silo and went on to Atharot, where Jesus taught on a hill outside of the town and healed the sick. Later, after the Sabbath had begun, Jesus taught in the synagogue. He had been teaching there for some time when he turned to where the women were standing and called to him a poor crippled widow. Her daughters had conducted her to the synagogue and put her into the place she usually occupied. It never entered her mind to ask for help, although she had been impaired for eighteen years. She was crippled at the waist. When she walked, the upper part of her body was so bent forward that her hands were at her feet. Jesus addressed her as her daughters were leading her to him, "Woman, be freed from your infirmity!" And he laid his hand on her back. She rose up straight as a candle and then said aloud, "Blessed be the Lord God of Israel!" Then she cast herself at Jesus' feet and all present praised God.

CHAPTER 11

THE TRANSFIGURATION

APRIL 1 TO 20, 31 CE

S tarting on Sunday, April 1, Christ Jesus and the disciples journeyed to
Hadad-Rimmon, where he healed the sick and taught concerning the
resurrection from the dead, the last judgment, and God's mercy. Today
it was learned that Pontius Pilate had forbidden the Galilean zealots to
leave Jerusalem under pain of death, although they were anxious to do so.
Many of them had been arrested as hostages. Shortly after, Pilate set the
latter at liberty and gave all of them permission to make their offerings
at the Temple and leave the city. It was customary on this day to bring all
kinds of gifts to the Temple. The Temple was tolerably crowded, yet not
to overflowing. In different places, little groups of Israelites bowed down
in adoration, or stood upright, or lay prostrate on the ground, their heads
wrapped in prayer mantles. Judas of Gamala was standing near one of the
alms boxes surrounded by his followers, the Galileans whom Pilate had
imprisoned and afterward released. Now when these people had made the
offerings of money and were lost in their devotions, armed Roman soldiers
in disguise stole upon them from all sides. They struck down and stabbed
all they met. There ensued carnage and desecration of the Temple.

On April 3, Jesus went to Kisloth at the foot of Mount Tabor. Here he
taught and healed. Around three o'clock in the afternoon, Jesus started
ascending Mount Tabor by a footpath. He took only Peter, John, and
James the Greater, with him. They spent nearly two hours in the ascent,
for Jesus paused frequently at the different sites made memorable by the
sojourn of the Prophets. There he explained to them manifold mysteries

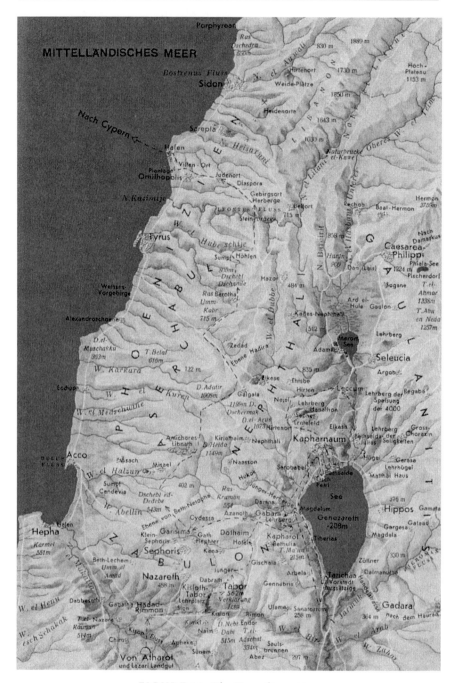

FIGURE 11: The Transfiguration
April 1 to 20, 31 CE

and united with them in prayer. The view from the summit extended far and wide; there Jesus continued his instruction. The sun had set and it was dark, but the disciples had not remarked the fact, so entrancing were Jesus' words and bearing. He became brighter and brighter, and apparitions of angelic beings hovered around him. Peter saw them, for he interrupted Jesus with the question, "Master, what does this mean?" Jesus answered, "They serve me!" Peter, quite out of himself, stretched forth his hands, exclaiming, "Master, are we not here? We will serve you in all things!" Jesus resumed his teaching. Meanwhile, he continued to shine with ever-increasing splendor, until he became as if transparent. The three disciples were so penetrated, so ravished that, when the light reached a certain degree, they covered their heads, prostrated themselves on the ground, and there remained lying. It was about midnight when the glory was at its height. There was a shining pathway reaching from heaven to earth, and on it angelic beings of different choirs, all in constant movement.

Then three figures approached Jesus in the light. Their coming seemed perfectly natural. They addressed Jesus and conversed with him. The first two were Moses and Elijah; the third spoke no word, was more spiritual, more ethereal. It was Malachi. When in describing his passion, Jesus came to his exaltation on the cross, he extended his arms at the words, "So shall the Son of Man be lifted up!" His face turned to the south. And now the prophets separated from Jesus. Moses and Elijah vanishing toward the east, and Malachi moving off toward the west into the darkness.

Then Peter, ravished with joy, exclaimed, "Master, it is good for us to be here! Let us make here three tabernacles: one for you, one for Moses, and one for Elijah!" Peter said this in the delirium of his joy, in his state of ecstasy, without knowing what he was saying.

When they had returned to their usual waking state, a cloud of white light descended upon them. The heavens opened above Jesus and there was a vision of God the Father seated on a throne. A stream of light descended on Jesus, and a voice pronounced the words, "This is my beloved Son in whom I am well pleased. Listen to him!" Fear and trembling fell upon them. Overcome by the sense of their own human weakness and the glory they beheld, the disciples cast themselves face downward on the earth.

Jesus went to them, touched them, and said, "Arise and do not be afraid!" They arose and beheld Jesus alone. He had permitted the disciples to have this experience in order to strengthen their faith, that they might not waiver when they saw him delivered, for the sins of the world, into the hands of evildoers.

Early in the morning of April 4, Jesus and the three disciples came down from the mountain top. While going down, Jesus spoke about what had taken place, and impressed upon the disciples that they should tell no one of the vision they had seen, until the Son of Man had risen from the dead. This command struck them. "What does that mean?" they asked one another, though they did not venture to ask Jesus about it.

They had not yet reached the foot of the mountain when Jesus was met by people coming to seek him with their sick. He healed and consoled. But the people were struck with awe at the sight of him, for there was something unusual, something supernatural and glorious in his appearance.

A little lower down the mount, he found assembled a crowd of people, including the disciples whom he had sent out into the environs the day before and several Doctors of the Law. Jesus saw that they and the disciples were having some kind of dispute. When they perceived Jesus, they ran forward to greet him, but they were amazed at his extraordinary appearance, for the rays of his glorification were still around him. The disciples guessed from the manner of the three returning disciples, who followed Jesus more gravely, more timidly than usual, that something wonderful must have happened.

When now Jesus inquired into the subject of dispute, a man from Amthar—a city on the Galilean mountain chain, the scene of the story of Lazarus and the rich man[1]—stepped forth from the crowd. He threw himself on his knees before Jesus, and implored him to help his only son. The boy was a lunatic and possessed of a dumb devil, who hurled him sometimes into fire, sometimes into water, and laid hold of him so roughly that he cried out with pain. The father had taken him to the disciples when they were in Amthar, but they had not been able to help him, and this was now the subject of dispute between them and the Doctors of the Law.

1   See March 28, 31.

Jesus addressed them, "O unbelieving and perverse generation, how long shall I be with you? How long shall I suffer you?" And he commanded the father to bring the boy to him. The father now led the boy up by the hand. As soon as the child saw Jesus, he began to tear himself frightfully, and the demon cast him to the earth, where he writhed in fearful contortions, foam pouring from his mouth. Jesus ordered him to be quiet, and he lay still. Then Jesus asked the father how long the boy had suffered in this way. He answered, "From early childhood. Ah, if you can, help us! Have mercy on us!" Jesus responded, "If you can believe, for all things are possible to him that believes." And the father, weeping, exclaimed, "Lord, I do believe! Help my unbelief!" Jesus raised his hand in a threatening manner toward the boy and said, "You dumb and impure spirit, I command you to leave him and never again return into him." The spirit cried out frightfully through the boy's mouth, convulsed him violently, and came out. This left the lad pale and motionless as one who was dead. They tried in vain to restore him to consciousness, and many from among the crowd called out, "He is dead! He is really dead!" But Jesus took him by the hand, and raised him up, well and joyous, and restored him to his father with some words of admonition. The latter thanked Jesus with tears and canticles of praise, and all the onlookers blessed the majesty of God.

After healing several more people, Jesus and the disciples continued on their way until they reached Dothaim. As they walked, the three disciples who had witnessed the transfiguration approached Jesus and questioned him upon the words, "Until the Son of Man is risen from the dead," which were still for them a subject of reflection and discussion. They argued, "The Scribes indeed say that Elijah must come again before the resurrection." Jesus responded, "Elijah indeed shall come and restore all things. But I say to you that Elijah has already come, and they did not recognize him, and they have done unto him whatever they had in mind, as it was written of him. So also, shall the Son of Man suffer from them." Jesus said several other things before the three disciples understood that he was speaking of John the Baptizer.

When all the disciples were again reunited around Jesus in the inn at Dothaim, they asked him why it was not in their power to free the possessed boy from the demon. Jesus answered, "Because of your unbelief. Truly I say to you, if you have faith the size of a mustard seed, and you say to this mountain, 'Move from here to there,' it shall move. Nothing shall be impossible for you. But this kind of demon is not cast out except by prayer and fasting." Then he instructed them on what was necessary to overcome the demon's resistance. Faith gives action to life and power, while at the same time it derives its own strength from fasting and prayer. He who fasts and prays is able to deprive the demon of its power by attracting it unto himself.

While Jesus was staying at Peter's house on April 6, some people from Capernaum said to Peter outside, "Does your Master pay the tribute, the two didrachmas?" Peter answered, "Yes." And when he went into the house, Jesus said to him, "What is your opinion, Peter? The kings of the earth, of whom do they receive tribute? Of their own children, or of strangers?" Peter answered, "Of strangers," and Jesus replied, "Then the children are free! But that we may not scandalize them, go to the sea and cast in a hook. The fish that comes up first, haul it in; and when you open its mouth, you will find a large coin. Take it to the tax collectors and give it to them for both you and me."

In simple faith, Peter went to his fishery, selected a line with a hook upon it, and threw it into the water. Soon he drew up a good-sized fish. He felt in its mouth and found an oblong, yellowish coin, with which he paid the tribute for Jesus and himself. The fish was so large that it gave the whole company a plentiful dinner.

After that, Jesus asked the disciples what they had been discussing on the way from Dothaim to Capernaum. They were silent, for they had been questioning who would be the greatest among them. Jesus, knowing their thoughts, said, "Let him that would be the first among you, become the last, the servant of all."

Then Jesus went with the disciples to Capernaum. At the start of the Sabbath on April 7, Jesus went to the synagogue and taught there. He visited the homes of the poor and many of his friends. At the marketplace, the schoolchildren and mothers with their little ones were assembled to honor Jesus. The disciples having asked again who would be the greatest in the Kingdom of Heaven, Jesus called to him a wealthy lady, the wife of a merchant, who was standing with her four-year-old boy at the door of her house close by. She drew her veil and stepped forward with her boy. Jesus took him from her, and she at once went back. Then Jesus embraced the child, had the boy stand before him in the midst of the disciples and the crowds of children standing around. Then Jesus said, "Whoever does not become like these children, shall not enter the Kingdom of Heaven! Whoever receives a child in my name, receives me. That is, receives him that sent me. And whoever humbles himself like this child, he is the greatest in the Kingdom of Heaven." After that, he blessed the boy, gave him some fruit and a little tunic, and beckoned to the mother. Jesus restored the child to her with some prophetic words. The child was named Ignatius; he became a disciple of the apostles. He was afterward a bishop and a martyr. There is a Saint Ignatius listed in *The Golden Legend* who became Bishop of Antioch and was martyred at Rome under the Emperor Trajan some time after 100 CE.[2] At the start of the Sabbath, Jesus went to the synagogue in Capernaum and taught there.

On the afternoon of the next day, Jesus was in Bethsaida and spoke with the disciples who had returned from their missionary journeys. Altogether about seventy disciples were gathered. As Jesus helped at the reception of the disciples, Peter said, "Lord, do you want to serve? Let us serve!" Jesus replied that he had been sent to serve. He spoke again of humility and said that whoever would be first must be the servant of all. Then he spoke of certain deeper mysteries. Also, he referred to the Fall and the ensuing separation from God. He said that now he had come to restore the relationship with God. His words were spoken with great solemnity and earnestness, so that the disciples were deeply moved.

Today, April 8, Jesus and the disciples walked in the region north of Capernaum. Jesus paused occasionally to teach the disciples or the laborers in the fields. That evening he stayed at a shepherd settlement where he told the parable of the lost sheep.

Jesus said, "The Kingdom is like a shepherd who had a hundred sheep. One of them, the largest, went astray. He left the ninety-nine

2   See de Voragine 1993, pp. 140–43.

and looked for the one until he found it. After his toil, he said to the sheep, 'I love you more than the ninety-nine.'"[3]

To the shepherds Jesus introduced his discourse in many ways, "Is this your own flock? Are these sheep of several flocks? How do you guard them? Why do your sheep wander about dispersed?" In this manner he put questions with which he linked his parables of the lost sheep and the good shepherd.

On April 11, there was talk of the murder of the Galileans that had occurred in the Temple at Jerusalem. Jesus then spoke in the following manner, "Do you imagine, because these Galileans suffered in this way, they were worse sinners than all Galileans? No, I assure you; unless you repent, you will all perish as they did. Or those eighteen who were killed when the tower of Siloam fell upon them—do you think that they were worse offenders than all the others living in Jerusalem? No, I assure you; unless you repent, you will all perish as they did."

He also told the story of the unfruitful fig tree. A man had a fig tree planted in his vineyard; and he came looking for fruit and did not find any. So he said to his gardener, "Look! For three years I have come looking for fruit on this fig tree and still I find none. Cut it down! Why let it waste the soil?" The gardener replied, "Sir, let it alone for one more year, until I dig around it and put manure on it. If it bears fruit next year, well and good; if not you can cut it down."

On Friday, April 13, after the evening Sabbath sermon in the synagogue, Jesus accepted the invitation of a well-to-do Pharisee to dine with him at his house not far from the dwelling of Cornelius the Centurion. There he found a man afflicted with dropsy, who begged for help. Jesus asked the Pharisees whether it was lawful to heal upon the Sabbath day. They gave him no answer, so he laid his hand upon the sick man and healed him. As the poor man was retiring with many thanks, Jesus remarked to the Pharisees, as he usually did on such occasions, that not one of them would hesitate on the Sabbath to draw out his ox or his ass that had fallen into a pit. The Pharisees were scandalized, but they could

---

3   Pagels 2003, Thomas 107.

make no reply. Jesus had, by means of the disciples, caused many of the poor to be assembled at the Pharisee's house. Now he asked the host whether the entertainment had been prepared for him. On receiving an answer in the affirmative, he enjoined that what was left after the guests had finished be distributed to the poor.

On the next day, as was usual on the Sabbath, Jesus and the disciples went for a walk. They went to a deserted region between Tiberius and Magdalum and were followed by a large crowd. Jesus took the opportunity to speak of renouncing all things, if one intended to follow him.

On the following day, Jesus sent out the disciples to invite the people to a sermon on the mountain near Gabara, which would begin on April 18, 31. The day after that as Jesus arrived at the outskirts of Tarichea, several lepers called out to him. He healed them and then went on to heal many sick people who were brought to him.

The next morning Jesus visited a sanitarium south of Tarichea and healed the sick there. Then he and the disciples went to a hostel close to the mountain where he would teach on the next day. Many people were already on their way to this event—so many, in fact, that the Pharisees complained to Jesus that the entire land was in disturbance. He answered them by saying that they too might, if they chose, come to hear his discourse the next morning. He also indicated that he had invited the multitude because he would not be among them much longer.

At about ten in the morning Jesus arrived at the mountain near Gabara where the continuation of the Sermon on the Mount was to take place. Many Pharisees, Sadducees, and Herodians were among the people gathered there to hear him. After beginning with a prayer, Jesus called the people to order. He bade them be attentive, because he was going to teach them what they would not learn from others, but at the same time was necessary for their salvation. What they could not then comprehend, would be repeated and explained later by his disciples whom he would send to them, for he himself would not be with them much longer. Then loudly and openly he warned the disciples gathered around him against the Pharisees and false prophets, and instructed the multitude upon prayer and love for one's neighbor. He also spoke about how to take care of personal money: not to lend it at interest, but to give it away! On another theme, introduced the idea of loving one's enemies in the same way that God showers blessings on all persons whether they are good or evil.

Because he had been so direct in his condemnation of Pharisees and false prophets, the Pharisees and those versed in the Law frequently interrupted Jesus with all kinds of contradictory remarks, but he paid no attention to them. He went on with his instruction, speaking very severely and warning the people against them until they were greatly incensed. He performed no cures on that day, but ordered that the weary sick on their beds be brought up in their turn and placed under awnings near him, so that they too might hear his teaching. He sent word to them to be patient until the close of his instruction.

Jesus taught until evening without intermission, the people taking refreshment by turns. No one saw Jesus eating. He taught the great multitude so unremittingly that toward evening his voice became weak. At last, he went down to the inn on the plain. It had once formed part of Mary Magdalene's property in Magdalum, and at its sale had been reserved for the use of the community. Among those who came to meet him there were the Apostle Lazarus, Martha, Dina the Samaritan, Mara the Suphanite, Maroni of Naim, and the Blessed Virgin Mary.

On April 19, Jesus continued his sermon on the mountain. The Pharisees began to proclaim Jesus as a "disturber of the peace," saying that they had the Sabbath, the festival days, and their own teaching, and that they did not need the innovations of this upstart. They threatened to complain to Herod—who would certainly put a stop to Jesus' activities. He answered that he would continue to teach and heal, in spite of Herod, until his mission was complete. Eventually, the pressure of the crowd forced the Pharisees to leave so that Jesus could continue his teaching undisturbed.

That evening, as Jesus and the disciples ate together, the Apostle Lazarus told of the journey that the women had made to Machaerus from Hebron and Jerusalem. As it had become known at Machaerus, through the domestics of Herodias, where John the Baptizer's head had been thrown, Joanna Chuza, Veronica, and one of the Baptizer's relatives journeyed there in order to make a search for it. However, until the vaulted sewer could be opened and drained, the head, which was resting on a stone projecting from the wall, could not be reached.

Two months flowed by. The sewers were cleaned out and repaired. There were many people engaged in carrying away the rubbish, and others gathered up the mud and slime from the sewers to enrich their fields. Among the latter were some women from Juttah and Jerusalem with their servants. They were waiting until the deep, steep sewer in which was the Baptizer's head, should be cleaned. While the workers went to take their meal, people who had been paid to do so introduced the women into the sewer. They prayed as they advanced that God would allow them to find the holy head, and they climbed the ascent with difficulty. Soon they perceived the head sitting upright on the neck upon one of the projecting stones, as if looking at them, and near it shone a luster like two flames. Were it not for this light, they might easily have made a mistake, for there were other human heads in the sewer. The head was pitiful to behold; the dark-skinned face was smeared with blood; the tongue, which Herodias had pierced, was protruding from the open mouth; and the yellow hair, by which the executioner and Herodias had seized it, was standing stiff upon it. The women wrapped it in a linen cloth and bore it away with hurried steps

Scarcely had they accomplished a part of their return when a company of Herod's soldiers, to the number of a thousand, came marching up to the castle. They had come to replace the couple of hundred already there on guard. The women hid themselves in a cave. When the danger had passed, they again set out on their journey through the mountains. On their way they came upon a soldier who, having by a fall received a severe wound on the knee, was lying on the road unconscious. Here, too, they came upon Zechariah's nephew and two of the Essenes who had come to meet them. They laid the head of the holy herald upon the wounded soldier, who instantly regained consciousness, arose, and spoke, saying that he had just seen John the Baptizer, and he had helped him. They bathed his wounds in oil and wine and took him to an inn without, however, saying anything to him about John's head. They continued their journey, always choosing the most unfrequented routes, just as had been done when John the Baptizer's body was conveyed to Juttah. The head was delivered to the Essenes near Hebron, and some of their sick, having been touched with it, were cured. The head was then washed, embalmed with precious ointments, and with solemn ceremonies laid with the body in the tomb.

On the morning of Friday, April 20, Jesus and the twelve healed the sick who were gathered at the foot of the mountain. The remaining disciples and the holy women dispensed food and clothing to the poor. This was the cause of much joy and thanksgiving. Afterward, the people dispersed to return to their hometowns in time for the Sabbath. Jesus and the disciples then made their way to Garisma. On the way, they passed through Kapharot where some Pharisees, who were well disposed to Jesus, warned him that Herod was out to imprison him and deal with him as he had done with John the Baptizer. Jesus replied that he had nothing to fear from "the fox," and that he would do what his Father had sent him to do. Reaching Garisma, Jesus and the disciples went to the synagogue for the start of the Sabbath.

On the following day, a number of Jews from the island of Cyprus, who were returning from the Feast of the Passover, listened with admiration at Jesus' teaching in the synagogue. They encouraged him to consider visiting Cyprus, where there were many Jews, all in a state of spiritual abandonment.

CHAPTER 12

JOURNEY TO CYPRUS

APRIL 26 TO MAY 30, 31 CE

On Thursday, April 26, the sea was calm, and the passage preceded so rapidly that the sailors called out, "Oh, what an auspicious voyage. This is thanks to thee, O prophet." Christ Jesus stood at the mast. He bid them to be silent and to give thanks only to God. Toward evening they landed at Salamis. Cyrinus, three elder brothers of Barnabas, and some elderly Jews in festive robes received Jesus and his followers, and conducted them to a lovely green terrace at some distance from the harbor. There they found carpets spread, washbasins filled with water, and on tables various dishes with refreshments. Cyrinus and his companions washed the feet of Jesus and his disciples, and offered them food. Then Jesus went to the synagogue in the Jewish quarter, where he healed some people who were suffering from dropsy.

The next morning, Jesus healed the sick at the local hospital. The newly cured followed him to the open square upon which, in the meantime, the other Jews had gathered, and where Jesus held an instruction first to the men. He took for his subject the collecting of manna by the Israelites in the wilderness, and said that the time for the true "Heavenly Manna" of doctrine and conversion of heart had come, and that a new "Bread from Heaven" was about to be given to them. This instruction over, the men withdrew and the women took their place. Jesus instructed the women in general terms; he spoke of the one Almighty God, the Father and creator of heaven and earth, of the folly of polytheism, and of God's love for humanity. After teaching in the open square, Jesus and

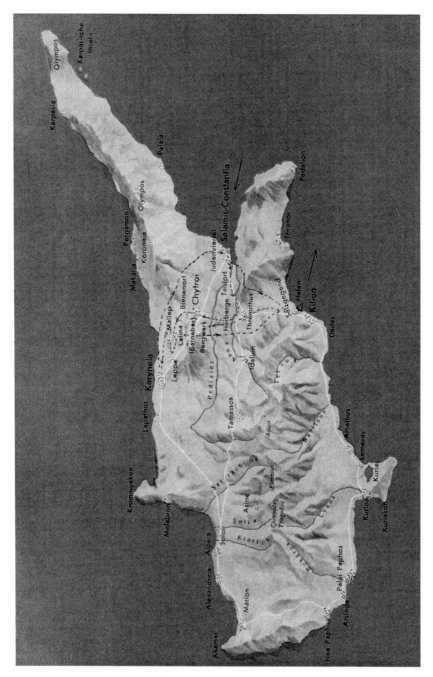

FIGURE 12: The Journey to Cyprus
April 26 to May 30, 31 CE

the disciples ate a meal held in his honor. At the start of the Sabbath, he taught in the synagogue.

The next morning he taught in the synagogue, which was completely full, and visited the hospital again. Then he dined as the guest of honor at the house of Cyrinus. At the end of the street and half within the walls of the pagan quarter was the magnificent home of Cyrinus, with its courts and side buildings. As soon as the house became visible in the distance, the wife and daughters of Cyrinus were seen approaching with their servants. They saluted Jesus and his disciples. Cyrinus had five daughters, along with nieces and other young relatives. All these children bore with them presents that, after bowing low before Jesus, they set down at his feet on carpets that they had previously spread. Besides the disciples, the guests numbered about twenty men. The women ate apart, and after dinner all took the customary Sabbath promenade out to the waterworks.

After that, all repaired to the synagogue for the closing exercises of the Sabbath. Jesus again taught upon sacrifice, taking his texts from Leviticus and from the Prophet Ezekiel. There was something impressive in his words as he showed that the laws of Moses were now realizing their most elevated signification. He spoke of the offering of a pure heart. Jesus, at the same time, prepared his hearers for baptism and exhorted them to penance, for the time was near.

On the following day, after healing some people who were then baptized by the disciples, Jesus taught on a hill. A large crowd gathered to hear him. The Roman Commandant of Salamis sent an invitation to Jesus, which he accepted. After his instruction, accompanied by the disciples and the elders, Jesus followed the messenger to the Commandant's residence. They had to go a distance of half an hour before reaching the principal gate of Salamis, a beautiful, high arch supported on pillars. As they advanced into the city, the crowd following Jesus constantly increased, and people were streaming from all sides toward the open square. In the center of the latter was a beautiful well. Opposite this well stood the Commandant's palace with its colonnade. On an open balcony over which was a pillared roof sat the Roman Commandant on a stone seat, watching Jesus approach.

The pagans were astonished at the marks of respect he showed to Jesus, for when the latter approached, the Commandant descended from the balcony, clasped his hand at the same time bowing low before him. Then he led Jesus up to the balcony, where he put to him, most graciously, question after question in a tone full of respect and earnestness. His profound sympathy and reverence for Jesus were visible. The latter answered all in vague and general terms. To the questions relative to his kingdom, to his army, he answered that his kingdom was not of this world. The kings of this world had need of warriors, but he gathered souls into the Kingdom of the Almighty Father, the creator of heaven and earth. In deeply significant words he touched, in passing, on many subjects. The Commandant was astounded at both his language and his bearing; he invited Jesus to come and speak again.

Around two in the afternoon, Jesus arrived at the home of the father of his disciple Jonas. Jonas' father was an Essene and lived a pious life. Here Jesus gave instruction to a number of people waiting to be baptized. Barnabas, James the Lesser, and Azor then baptized them.

On the following day, Jesus taught close to the place of baptism. Among the crowd—including both Jews and non-Jews—were some pagan philosophers. They questioned Jesus who took the occasion to speak of the pagan gods, the ideas entertained of them, the confusion existing in those ideas, the services rendered them, and all the cruelties related to them. Finally he mentioned and analyzed the various and contradictory attributes of these gods. Although Jesus spoke in a severe and conclusive manner, still his instruction was agreeable, and so suggestive of good thoughts to his hearers that it did not rouse displeasure.

Then in the afternoon, Jesus visited some private homes where he healed the sick. That evening, he dined with the rabbis as their guest of honor. Later, when he and the disciples had returned to their inn, a pagan woman—her name was Mercuria—came to speak with Jesus. Mercuria confessed her sins and Jesus spoke earnestly with her. He suggested she renounce her way of life and told her of God the Almighty. On the next day, the disciples continued to baptize, while Jesus taught and healed the sick. He then began to teach the pagan philosophers about the nature of their cults and the arising of false gods.

On May 2, Jesus set off, going from field to field, instructing the workers as he went. Jesus taught in parables of the harvest and the daily bread, and he cured several lame children who lay on sheepskins in a kind of cradle. When some of the people broke out in loud praise of his teaching, Jesus checked them with words something like these, "Whosoever has, to him shall be given; and whosoever has not, that also which he thinks he has, shall be taken away from him." That night Jesus stayed at an inn near the Roman way.

On the following day after a four-hour journey, Jesus reached an inn more than a half hour from Chytrus. Here he and his companions halted and the father of Barnabas, along with some other men, received Jesus and extended to him the usual acts of kindness. He rested here and taught, after which he took a light repast with his companions.

On the morning of Friday, May 4, Jesus visited an iron mine near Chytroi. He addressed the workers and spoke the following, "Here is a simple rule of thumb for behavior: ask yourself what you want people to do for you; then seize the initiative and do it for *them!*" He then entered the town and was greeted by the Jewish elders and also by two of the philosophers from Salamis. It was the start of the Sabbath, therefore Jesus taught in the synagogue. Many pagans listened from the terrace outside.

There was in the synagogue a pious old rabbi who had been for a long time afflicted by dropsy, and who, as usual, had caused himself to be carried to his customary place. As the literati were disputing Jesus on various points, he cried aloud, "Silence! Allow me a word." And when all were still, he called out, "Lord! You have shown mercy to others. Help me, too, and bid me come to you." Thereupon Jesus said to the man, "If you do believe, arise and come to me." The sick man instantly arose, exclaiming, "Lord, I do believe!" He was cured. He mounted the steps where Jesus stood, and thanked him, while the whole assembly broke forth into shouts of joy and praise. Jesus and his followers left the synagogue and went to Barnabas' dwelling. Then the master of the feast gathered together the poor and the laborers to partake of the dinner that Jesus had left for them. Afterward, Jesus stayed the night at the house of Barnabas' father.

On the next day, Jesus taught on a hill near Chytroi. In the afternoon, he healed the sick and then preached again in the synagogue for the close of the Sabbath. On the following day, accompanied by about one hundred people, Jesus went to a place near Chytroi where bees were kept. Jesus had come here principally to be able to instruct the pagans without interruption, without disturbance from visitors. This he did all the rest of the day in the gardens and arbors of the inn. His hearers stood or lay stretched on the grass, while he instructed them on the Lord's Prayer and the eight beatitudes. When addressing the pagans, he spoke especially of the origin and abomination of their gods, of the vocation of Abraham and his separation from idolaters, and of God's guidance of the children of Israel. He spoke openly and forcibly. There were about a hundred men listening to him. After the instruction, all took refreshments in the inn, the pagans apart. That evening, the pagans having retired, Jesus instructed the Jews and they prayed together. All spent the night at the inn.

Later Jesus taught at a well near Chytroi and prepared the listeners for baptism. The Jews and pagans were separated. Jesus spoke about circumcision, saying that it could not be demanded of pagans; pagan converts should be circumcised only if they themselves requested it. On the other hand, it could not be expected of the Jews that they should permit pagans to enter the synagogue. Trouble should be avoided, and one should thank God for those who renounced idolatry and sought salvation.

On the next day, Jesus continued to teach at the well while the disciples baptized. Around noon, he set off for Mallep, a village built by Jews for their colony. He was received there with much joy and celebration. In the synagogue Jesus taught concerning the petition "Thy Kingdom Come" of the Lord's Prayer. He spoke of the Kingdom of God as being within us and of its near approach. He explained to his hearers that it was a spiritual kingdom, not an earthly one, and he told them how it would fare with them that rejected it.

At the midday meal on the following day, when Jesus was taking dinner with the elders, three blind boys about ten to twelve years old were led in to him by some other children. The former were playing on flutes and another kind of instrument that made a buzzing, humming sound like a Jew's harp. At intervals they also sang in a very agreeable manner. Their eyes were open, and it seemed as if cataracts had obscured their sight. Jesus asked them whether they desired to see the light, in order to walk diligently and piously in the paths of righteousness. They answered most joyously, "Yes, Lord, and will you help us? We will do whatever you command." Then Jesus said, "Put down your instruments." And he stood them before him, put his thumbs to his mouth and passed them one after the other from the corner of the eyes to the temple above. Then he took up a dish of fruit from the table, held it before the boys, and said, "Do you see that?" Then he blessed them, and gave them its contents. They stared around in joyful amazement; they were intoxicated with delight, and at last cast themselves weeping at Jesus' feet. The whole company was deeply touched; joy and wonder took possession of all. Jesus took occasion from this circumstance to give a beautiful instruction on gratitude. He said, "Thanksgiving is a prayer that attracts new favors, so good is the Heavenly Father." That evening, Jesus taught again in the synagogue.

On Saturday, May 12, Jesus went with a large crowd of people to the bathing gardens on the outskirts of the town. Here he taught and prepared people for baptism. James the Lesser and Barnabas then baptized. Many people accompanied Jesus today for the Sabbath-day walk, which he took in the valley of Lafina, before returning to the synagogue for the close of the Sabbath.

On the following day, Jesus again taught at the place of baptism. Several bridegrooms were present. He gave them instruction concerning marriage. Then they received baptism. Afterward, Jesus accepted an invitation to dine at the house of a rabbi in the village of Leppe, west of Mallep. The bridegrooms were also invited, together with their brides-to-be. Both during and after the meal, Jesus spoke of the sanctity of marriage. He insisted on the point of each man having but one wife, for they had here the custom of separating on trifling grounds and marrying again. On this account, he spoke very strenuously, and related the parables of the wedding feast, the vineyard, and the king's son. It was already dark when he and the disciples returned to Mallep to sleep.

During the next two days, Jesus taught concerning the Feast of Weeks, which was approaching. He spoke of the Feast of Weeks as a festival of remembrance for the giving of the Law to Moses on Mount Sinai. On the evening that the Feast of Weeks began, there was a torch-light prayer procession, which Jesus joined. Afterward, he retired to pray alone.

The next morning, Jesus took part in the ceremonies to celebrate the Feast of Weeks in the synagogue. He walked at the head of the column of rabbis as they proceeded around the synagogue blessing the land, the sea, and all the regions of the earth. There then followed the reading. It had to do with the exodus from Egypt and the giving of the Law on Mount Sinai on the fiftieth day after the Passover.

On Friday, May 18, Jesus and the disciples visited various homes to teach, comfort, and heal. He spoke with several women about their marriage difficulties. That evening, with the beginning of the Sabbath, Jesus spoke in the synagogue with power and earnestness. He spoke of the breaking of the commandments and of adultery. Afterward, he prayed alone all night.

The next day, many came to visit Jesus at his inn. The husbands of the women who had complained of them to Jesus were also among the number, as well as others guilty of similar offenses, but against whom no charge had been made. They presented themselves individually as sinners before Jesus, cast themselves at his feet, confessed their guilt, and implored pardon. After hearing and exhorting these sinners individually, Jesus told them to send their wives to him. When they came, he related to each one separately the repentance of her husband, exhorted her to heartfelt forgiveness and entire forgetfulness of the past. The women wept, promised everything, and thanked Jesus. He reconciled several of these couples right away that same day. Everyone was astonished at the remarkable effect that Jesus had in helping people right their life situations. After dinner Jesus and all the people went to the synagogue for the closing exercises of the Sabbath. Jesus resumed his discourse of the day before, though not in terms so severe. He told his audience that God would not abandon them that called upon him.

On Sunday, May 20, Jesus spent the whole day visiting people at their homes. Everywhere he recommended to the Jews that they move from Cyprus to Palestine, prophesying future catastrophes that would take place on Cyprus.

On Monday, May 28, Jesus visited some farms east of Mallep. He taught there and healed the sick, including a blind child. Later, there was a festival meal in Mallep, to which Jesus invited the poor and needy. Afterward, he taught concerning the meaning of the word "Amen." He called it the beginning and end of everything. He spoke almost as if God had by it created the whole world. That night, he and the disciples left Mallep. Around two in the afternoon of the following day Jesus and the disciples arrived back at Salamis. Jesus met again with the Roman Commandant, who decided to convert.

At dawn of the following day, the Commandant bade farewell to Jesus, who then made his way to the harbor at Kition, about two hours from Salamis. After eating a meal at the harbor, Jesus and his traveling companions—now about twenty-seven in number—set off from Cyprus on board three ships.

CHAPTER 13

THIRD FESTIVAL OF THE PASSOVER

A RECONSTRUCTION OF THE PERIOD WITHOUT VISIONS

JULY 9, 31 TO MAY 16, 32 CE

The entry for Sunday, July 8, is the last of the daily accounts of Sister Emmerich's visions that Clemens Brentano recorded in his notebooks.[1] In Dr. Powell's *Chronicle of the Living Christ,* he details information about The Gap in Anne Catherine Emmerich's Account of the Ministry [of Christ Jesus]. He asks two relevant questions: where does the gap lie and why did it escape the notice of Clemens Brentano and others who have occupied themselves with Anne Catherine Emmerich's visions?[2] In an extended sequence of information, Dr. Powell details the exact timing of the missing periods and uses additional sources to confirm the validity of the dating.[3]

It has been possible to reconstruct much of the information from this period from *The Gospel According to John.* It is that reconstruction in ten elements that follows below.

(1) *Christ Jesus was in Galilee before the Feast of Tabernacles; his brothers advised him to go to Judea.*

After this Jesus went about in Galilee. He did not wish to go about in Judea because the Jews were looking for an opportunity to kill him. Now the Jewish Festival of Booths was near. So his brothers said to him, "Leave

---

1   See Powell 1996, p. 309.

2   Ibid., p. 41.

3   Ibid., pp. 42–55.

here and go to Judea so that your disciples also may see the works you are doing; for no one who wants to be widely known acts in secret. If you do these things, show yourself to the world." ... Jesus said to them, "My time has not yet come, but your time is always here." After saying this, he remained in Galilee.[4]

(2)   *Christ Jesus attended the Festival of Tabernacles in Jerusalem (September 19–26, 31 CE).*

But after his brothers had gone to the festival, then he also went, not publicly but as it were in secret. The Jews were looking for him at the festival and saying, "Where is he?" And there was considerable complaining about him among the crowds. While some were saying, "He is a good man," others were saying, "No, he is deceiving the crowd." Yet no one would speak openly about him for fear of the Jews.

About the middle of the festival Jesus went up into the temple and began to teach. The Jews were astonished at it, saying, "How does this man have such learning, when he has never been taught?" Then Jesus answered them, "My teaching is not mine but his who sent me. Anyone who resolves to do the will of God will know whether the teaching is from God or whether I am speaking on my own. Those who speak on their own seek their own glory; but the one who seeks the glory of him who sent him is true, and there is nothing false in him."

Then Jesus cried out as he was teaching in the temple, "You know me, and you know where I am from. I have not come on my own. But the one who sent me is true, and you do not know him. I know him, because I am from him, and he sent me." Then they tried to arrest him, but no one laid hands on him, because his hour had not yet come. Yet many in the crowd believed in him and were saying, "When the Messiah comes, will he do more signs than this man has done?"[5]

(3)   *On the last day of the Festival, September 26, 31, he spoke the words, "Let anyone who is thirsty come to me," and the Pharisees tried to have him arrested.*

---

4   John 7:1–6, 9 NRSV.

5   John 7:10–18, 28–31 NRSV.

On the last day of the festival, the great day, while Jesus was standing there, he cried out, "Let anyone who is thirsty come to me, and let the one who believes in me drink. As the scripture has said, 'Out of the believer's heart shall flow rivers of living water.'" Now he said this about the Spirit, which believers in him were to receive; for as yet there was no Spirit, because Jesus was not yet glorified. When they heard these words, some in the crowd said, "This is really the prophet." Others said, "This is the Messiah." But some asked, "Surely the Messiah does not come from Galilee, does he? Has not the scripture said that the Messiah is descended from David and comes from Bethlehem, the village where David lived? ... Search and you will see that no prophet is to arise from Galilee." [6]

(4)   *In the Temple, Christ Jesus pardoned*
        the woman who had committed adultery.

Early in the morning he came again to the temple. All the people came to him and he sat down and began to teach them. The Scribes and the Pharisees brought a woman who had been caught in adultery; and making her stand before all of them, they said to him, "Teacher, this woman was caught in the very act of committing adultery. Now in the law Moses commanded us to stone such women. Now what do you say?" They said this to test him, so that they might have some charge to bring against him. Jesus bent down and wrote with his finger on the ground. When they kept on questioning him, he straightened up and said to them, "Let anyone among you who is without sin be the first to throw a stone at her." And once again he bent down and wrote on the ground. When they heard it, they went away, one by one, beginning with the elders; and Jesus was left alone with the woman standing before him. Jesus straightened up and said to her, "Woman, where are they? Has no one condemned you?" She said, "No one, sir." And Jesus said, "Neither do I condemn you. Go your way, and from now on do not sin again." [7]

---

6   John 7:37–42, 52 NRSV.

7   John 8:2–11 NRSV.

(5)   *In the Temple, Christ Jesus referred to himself with the words,*
       "I am the light of the world." The Pharisees disputed with him
       and took up stones to throw at him, but Christ Jesus hid himself
       and left the Temple.

Again Jesus spoke to them, saying, "I am the light of the world. Whoever follows me will never walk in darkness but will have the light of life." Then the Pharisees said to him, "You are testifying on your own behalf; your testimony is not valid." Jesus answered, "Even if I testify on my own behalf, my testimony is valid because I know where I have come from and where I am going, but you do not know where I come from or where I am going. You judge by human standards; I judge no one. Yet even if I do judge, my judgment is valid; for it is not I alone who judge, but I and the Father who sent me. In your law it is written that the testimony of two witnesses is valid. I testify on my own behalf, and the Father who sent me testifies on my behalf." Then they said to him, "Where is your Father?"

Jesus answered, "You know neither me nor my Father. If you knew me, you would know my Father also." He spoke these words while he was teaching in the treasury of the temple, but no one arrested him, because his hour had not yet come.... He said to them, "You are from below, I am from above; you are of this world, I am not of this world. I told you that you would die in your sins, for you will die in your sins unless you believe that I am he." They said to him, "Who are you?" Jesus said to them, "Why do I speak to you at all? I have much to say about you and much to condemn; but the one who sent me is true, and I declare to the world what I have heard from him." They did not understand that he was speaking to them about the Father. So Jesus said, "When you have lifted up the Son of Man, then you will realize that I am he, and that I do nothing on my own, but I speak these things as the Father instructed me. And the one who sent me is with me; he has not left me alone, for I always do what is pleasing to him." As he was saying these things, many believed in him.

Then Jesus said to the Jews who had believed in him, "If you continue in my word, you are truly my disciples; and you will know the truth, and the truth will make you free." They answered him, "We are descendants of Abraham and have never been slaves to anyone. What do you mean by saying, 'You will be made free'?"

Jesus answered them, "Very truly, I tell you, everyone who commits sin is a slave to sin." Jesus said to them, "If God were your Father, you would love me, for I came from God and now I am here. I did not come on my own, but he sent me. Why do you not understand what I say? It is because you cannot accept my word.... Very truly, I tell you, whoever keeps my word will never see death." The Jews said to him, "Now we know that you have a demon. Abraham died, and so did the prophets; yet you say, 'Whoever keeps my word will never taste death.' Are you greater than our father Abraham, who died? The prophets also died. Who do you claim to be?" Jesus answered, ... "Your ancestor Abraham rejoiced that he would see my day; he saw it and was glad." Then the Jews said to him, "You are not yet fifty years old, and have you seen Abraham?" Jesus said to them, "Very truly, I tell you, before Abraham was, I am." So they picked up stones to throw at him, but Jesus hid himself and went out of the temple.[8]

(6)   Near the pool of Siloam in Jerusalem,
       Christ Jesus healed the man born blind.

As he walked along, he saw a man blind from birth. His disciples asked him, "Rabbi, who sinned, this man or his parents, that he was born blind?" Jesus answered, "Neither this man nor his parents sinned; he was born blind so that God's works might be revealed in him. We must work the works of him who sent me while it is day; night is coming when no one can work. As long as I am in the world, I am the light of the world." When he had said this, he spat on the ground and made mud with the saliva and spread the mud on the man's eyes, saying to him, "Go, wash in the pool of Siloam." ... Then he went and washed and came back able to see. The neighbors and those who had seen him before as a beggar began to ask, "Is this not the man who used to sit and beg?"... He kept saying, "I am the man." But they kept asking him, "Then how were your eyes opened?" He answered, "The man called Jesus made mud, spread it

---

8   John 8:12–20, 23–34, 42–43, 51–54a, 56–59 NRSV.

on my eyes, and said to me, 'Go to Siloam and wash.' Then I went and washed and received my sight." They said to him, "Where is he?" He said, "I do not know."

They brought to the Pharisees the man who had formerly been blind. Now it was a Sabbath day when Jesus made the mud and opened his eyes. Then the Pharisees also began to ask him how he had received his sight. He said to them, "He put mud on my eyes. Then I washed, and now I see.".... So [the Pharisees] said again to the blind man, "What do you say about him? It was your eyes he opened." He said, "He is a prophet."

The Jews did not believe that he had been blind and had received his sight until they called the parents of the man who had received his sight and asked them, "Is this your son, who you say was born blind? How then does he now see?" His parents answered, "We know that this is our son, and that he was born blind; but we do not know how it is that now he sees, nor do we know who opened his eyes. Ask him; he is of age. He will speak for himself."... So for the second time they called the man who had been blind, and they said to him, "Give glory to God! We know that this man is a sinner." He answered, "I do not know whether he is a sinner. One thing I do know, that though I was blind, now I see." They said to him, "What did he do to you? How did he open your eyes?" He answered them, "I have told you already, and you would not listen."

[The man continued,] "Here is an astonishing thing! You do not know where he comes from, and yet he opened my eyes. We know that God does not listen to sinners, but he does listen to one who worships him and obeys his will. Never since the world began has it been heard that anyone opened the eyes of a person born blind. If this man were not from God, he could do nothing."

Jesus heard that [the Pharisees] had driven him out, and when he found him, he said, "Do you believe in the Son of Man?" He answered, "And who is he, sir? Tell me, so that I may believe in him." Jesus said to him, "You have seen him, and the one speaking with you is he." He said, "Lord, I believe." And he worshiped him. Jesus said, "I came into this world for judgment so that those who do not see may see, and those who do see may become blind." Some of the Pharisees near him heard this and said to him,

"Surely we are not blind, are we?" Jesus said to them, "If you were blind, you would not have sin. But now that you say, 'We see,' your sin remains."[9]

(7)   [Christ] Jesus told the parable of the good shepherd.

"Very truly, I tell you, anyone who does not enter the sheepfold by the gate but climbs in by another way is a thief and a bandit. The one who enters by the gate is the shepherd of the sheep. The gatekeeper opens the gate for him, and the sheep hear his voice. He calls his own sheep by name and leads them out. When he has brought out all his own, he goes ahead of them, and the sheep follow him because they know his voice. They will not follow a stranger, but they will run from him because they do not know the voice of strangers." Jesus used this figure of speech with them, but they did not understand what he was saying to them. So again Jesus said to them, "Very truly, I tell you, I am the gate for the sheep. All who came before me are thieves and bandits; but the sheep did not listen to them. I am the gate. Whoever enters by me will be saved, and will come in and go out and find pasture. The thief comes only to steal and kill and destroy. I came that they may have life, and have it abundantly. I am the good shepherd. The good shepherd lays down his life for the sheep. The hired hand, who is not the shepherd and does not own the sheep, sees the wolf coming and leaves the sheep and runs away—and the wolf snatches them and scatters them. The hired hand runs away because a hired hand does not care for the sheep. I am the good shepherd. I know my own and my own know me, just as the Father knows me and I know the Father. And I lay down my life for the sheep. I have other sheep that do not belong to this fold. I must bring them also, and they will listen to my voice. So there will be one flock, one shepherd. For this reason the Father loves me, because I lay down my life in order to take it up again. No one takes it from me, but I lay it down of my own accord. I have power to lay it down, and I have power to take it up again. I have received this command from my Father." Again the Jews were divided because of these words. Many of them were saying, "He has a demon and is out of his mind. Why listen

---

9   John 9:1–15, 17–21, 24–27a, 30–41 NRSV. As this healing took place on the Sabbath (between Friday evening and Saturday evening), it must have taken place on one of the dates in 31 CE, between: Oct. 5/6 and Nov. 23/24.

to him?" Others were saying, "These are not the words of one who has a demon. Can a demon open the eyes of the blind?"[10]

(8)   *Christ Jesus attended the Festival of the Dedication of the Temple in Jerusalem, where the Pharisees tried to arrest him again. (November 28–December 5, 31 CE)*

At that time the festival of the Dedication took place in Jerusalem. It was winter, and Jesus was walking in the temple, in the portico of Solomon. So the Jews gathered around him and said to him, "How long will you keep us in suspense? If you are the Messiah, tell us plainly." Jesus answered, "I have told you, and you do not believe. The works that I do in my Father's name testify to me; but you do not believe, because you do not belong to my sheep. My sheep hear my voice. I know them, and they follow me. I give them eternal life, and they will never perish. No one will snatch them out of my hand. What my Father has given me is greater than all else, and no one can snatch it out of the Father's hand. The Father and I are one."

The Jews took up stones again to stone him. Jesus replied, "I have shown you many good works from the Father. For which of these are you going to stone me?" The Jews answered, "It is not for a good work that we are going to stone you, but for blasphemy, because you, though only a human being, are making yourself God." Jesus answered, "Is it not written in your law, 'I said, you are gods'? If those to whom the word of God came were called 'gods'—and the scripture cannot be annulled—can you say that the one whom the Father has sanctified and sent into the world is blaspheming because I said, 'I am God's Son'? If I am not doing the works of my Father, then do not believe me. But if I do them, even though you do not believe me, believe the works, so that you may know and that the Father is in me and I am in the Father." Then they tried to arrest him again, but he escaped from their hands.[11]

(9)   *He went to the place on the Jordan between Ainon and Salem, where John the Baptizer had first baptized.*

---

10   John 10:1–21 NRSV.

11   John 10:22–39 NRSV.

He went away again across the Jordan to the place where John [the Baptizer] had been baptizing earlier, and he remained there. Many came to him, and they were saying, "John [the Baptizer] performed no sign, but everything that John said about this man was true." And many believed in him there.[12]

(10) *Although not mentioned in the Gospel of Saint John, it is certain that Christ Jesus attended the Festival of the Passover in Jerusalem in the Hebrew month of Nisan 32 CE, which started on Nisan 15, equating historically to April 14/15, 32 CE, and lasted for one week.*[13]

---

12 John 10:40–42 NRSV.
13 Powell 1996, pp. 309.

Chapter 14

The Raising of Lazarus

July 9 to July 27, 32 CE

On Wednesday, July 9, Christ Jesus stayed at a little village in Samaria. The Blessed Virgin Mary, accompanied by her elder sister Mary Heli, and Mary Heli's daughter, Mary Cleophas, were on their way from Bethany to meet him so that they could urge him to come to Bethany and heal Lazarus. On the next day, three holy women came to Jesus and told him of Martha and Mary Magdalene's request that he come to Bethany, as Lazarus lay seriously ill. After having spoken with Jesus, the three holy women decided to stay in the little village to celebrate the Sabbath there. Jesus himself went to another place with a large synagogue. Here he taught, healed, and blessed some children.

During the following week, Jesus taught concerning the Good Samaritan and the lost coin. He also healed the sick and blessed many children. On Wednesday, July 16, Jesus, accompanied by some of the twelve, returned to the little village, where the three holy women were waiting for him. Together they received the news of Lazarus' death. It was here that Jesus said to the disciples, "Let us go to Judea again."

After saying this, he told them, "Our friend Lazarus has fallen asleep, but I am going there to awaken him."[1]

Toward evening on Thursday, July 17, Jesus, accompanied by the three holy women and those of the twelve, set off for Bethany. They traveled that night by moonlight to Lazarus' country estate at Ginnim. Here Martha and Mary Magdelene were waiting for him. On the next day the holy

---

1   John 11:11 NRSV.

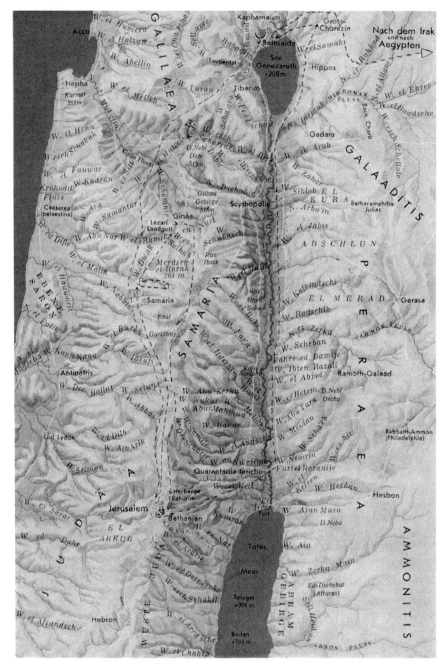

FIGURE 13: *The Raising of Lazarus*
July 9 to 27, 32 CE

women stayed at Lazarus' estate. Jesus and those of the twelve went to Ginnim for the Sabbath. Jesus taught in the synagogue. After the close of the Sabbath on the next day, Jesus and those of the twelve returned to Lazarus' estate. Mary Magdalene came to meet Jesus on the way. She lamented over the death of Lazarus, saying that if Jesus had been there her brother would not have died. Jesus replied that his time had not yet come. They then ate at Lazarus' estate and Jesus taught. He asked Martha and Mary Magdalene to allow all of Lazarus' effects to stay in Bethany, saying that he would come there in a few days. It was then that Jesus told them plainly, "Lazarus is dead."[2] On the next morning, the holy women set off back to Bethany. Jesus and the disciples returned to Ginnim.

On Monday, July 21, Jesus and the disciples journeyed toward Bethany. Toward evening of the next day, they reached the inn of a little place near Bahurin. Here Jesus taught concerning the laborers in the vineyard. On the following day, Jesus and the disciples made their way to Bethany. As he walked, Jesus taught. Mary Salome went on ahead, arriving in Bethany toward evening. She went first to Martha to tell her that Jesus was approaching. Mary Magdalene went with Mary Salome to greet him, but she returned without having spoken to him.

Lazarus had been dead for eight days. His sisters had kept him at home for four days in the hope that Jesus would come and raise him to life. But when they found that Jesus was still not resolved to go back with them, they returned to Bethany and buried their brother. Their friends, men and women from the city and from Jerusalem, were now gathered around them, lamenting the dead as was the custom.

On Friday, July 25, Jesus and the disciples made their way toward Bethany. As he walked Jesus taught. Mary Salome, the wife of Zebedee, went on ahead, arriving in Bethany toward evening. She went in to Martha and told her that Jesus was approaching. Martha told her sister, because through love for Mary Magdalene, she wanted her to be the first to meet Jesus. Although Mary Magdalene and Mary Salome went out to meet him, Mary Magdalene was not seen speaking to him. It was already growing

---

2   See John 11:14–15 NRSV.

dusk when Mary Magdalene returned and took Martha's place, who then went out to meet Jesus.

> Martha said to Jesus, "Lord, if you had been here, my brother would not have died. But even now I know that God will give you whatever you ask of him." Jesus said to her, "Your brother will rise again." Martha said to him, "I know that he will rise again in the resurrection on the last day." Jesus said to her, "I am the resurrection and the life. Those who believe in me, even though they die, will live, and everyone who lives and believes in me will never die. Do you believe this?" She said to him, "Yes, Lord, I believe that you are the Messiah, the Son of God, the one coming into the world."[3]

It was dusk. Martha hurried back and spoke with Mary Magdalene, who went up to Jesus, casting herself at his feet and saying, "Lord, if you had been here, my brother would not have died." Jesus wept. He then taught about death late into the night.

In the early hours of the morning of Saturday, July 26, Jesus went with the twelve to Lazarus' grave. They were accompanied by seven holy women and many other people. He went into the vault where Lazarus' tomb was. As Jesus instructed the disciples to remove the stone from the grave, Martha said, "Lord, by this time there will be an odor, for he has been buried for four days. Then the raising of Lazarus from the dead took place.

> There stood the rainbow of the Holy Spirit over the dark cleft of the grave, on which a stone was laid. At his word the stone was taken away.
>
> Thereupon the Son-made-flesh lifted up his eyes to the heavenly Father and thanked him, that he had heard him. Then he cried with a loud voice, which condensed the rainbow of Spirit into lightning, bearing within it the rolling thunder of the Father: "Lazarus, come forth!" And he that was dead came forth, his hands and feet bound with bandages, and his face wrapped with a cloth. Jesus said to them: "Unbind him, and let him go!"

3   John 11:20–27 NRSV.

Thus it happened that the soul of Lazarus, called out of the bosom of the Father by the Word of the Son, turned back through the portal of the rainbow of the Holy Spirit into the realm of earthly life. In Christ he had died, out of the Father he had been born, and through the Holy Spirit he was brought to new life. The three lines of the Rosicrucian verse—*Ex Deo nascimur; in Jesu morimur; per Spiritum sanctum reviviscimus*—take their power and their substance from the Mystery of the Raising of Lazarus.[4]

After the cloths and winding sheet had been removed, Lazarus climbed out of his coffin and came out from the tomb. He tottered on his feet and looked like a phantom. He went past Jesus through the door of the vault. His sisters and the other holy women stepped back, as if he were a ghost. Jesus followed him from the vault into the open air, went up to him, and took hold of both his hands in a gesture of friendship. A great crowd of people, who beheld Lazarus in fear and wonder, thronged around. Jesus walked with Lazarus to his house. The disciples and the holy women went with them. A great tumult arose among the crowd. Inside the house, the women went to prepare a meal, leaving Jesus and the disciples alone with Lazarus.

The disciples formed a circle around Jesus and Lazarus. Lazarus knelt before Jesus who blessed him, laying his right hand on Lazarus' head and breathing upon him seven times. Thus, he consecrated Lazarus to his service, purifying him of all earthly connections, and infusing him with the seven gifts of the Holy Spirit, which the disciples would receive only later at Whitsun. Afterward, all dined together. Jesus taught, and Lazarus sat next to him. Because there was a great commotion outside, Jesus sent the disciples to disperse the crowd. He continued to teach that evening.

Before daybreak on Sunday, July 27, Jesus, accompanied by John the son of Zebedee and Matthew, went to Jerusalem to the house on Mount Zion where later the Last Supper would take place. This house belonged to Nicodemus. Jesus remained there for the whole day and that night. Mary Mark, Veronica, and about a dozen other friends came to visit him. Meanwhile, a meeting of the Pharisees and high priests was being held to

---

4   Tomberg, *Lazarus, Come Forth!* pp. 87–88.

discuss the raising of Lazarus by Jesus. The Pharisees feared that Jesus might awaken all the dead and that this would lead to great confusion. In Bethany, a tumult arose. Lazarus was forced to hide and the disciples also left the city.

CHAPTER 15

JOURNEY TO THE TENT CITY OF THE KINGS

AUGUST 6 TO SEPTEMBER 30, 32 CE

At daybreak on Wednesday, August 6, Christ Jesus and three shepherd youths—Eliud, Silas, and Eremenzear—parted company with the twelve and the other disciples, who were saddened by their departure. This journey outside of Palestine, accompanied by only the three shepherd youths, was not recorded, as none of the twelve was present, and no one really knew where he was. Andrew, Peter, and Philip returned to their homes. The remaining disciples split up and went in various directions.

Meanwhile, Jesus and his traveling companions journeyed eastward, Jesus teaching as they went. That night they stayed at a house. Jesus did not say who he was; he was taken to be a traveling shepherd. He taught in parables but did not heal anyone.

On the next morning, Jesus traveled on in a southeasterly direction. He and the three young shepherds stayed the night with some shepherds they met on the way. There had been a great uproar in Jerusalem about the raising of Lazarus and some assumed that Jesus had left Judea in order to be forgotten.

Before the onset of the Sabbath on Friday, August 8, Jesus and the three youths reached the town of Cedar, one of the last towns east of Palestine where there was a Jewish settlement.

Cedar was divided into a heathen and a Jewish quarter. Jesus and the youths went to the synagogue for the celebration of the Sabbath. There Jesus was held to be a prophet. For the next two days Jesus taught in

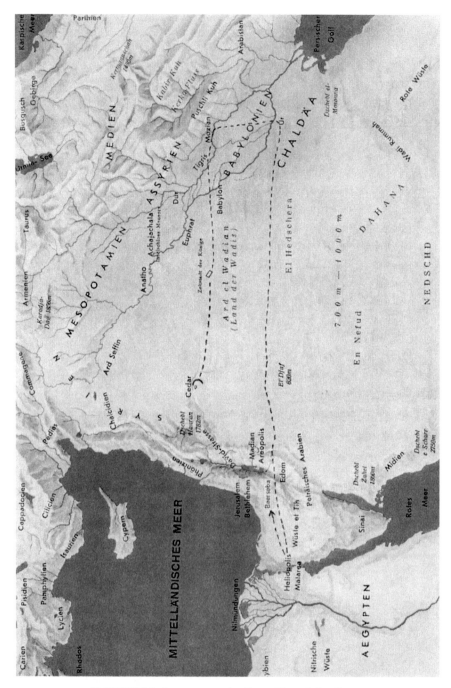

FIGURE 14: *Journey to the Tent City of the Kings*
August 6 to September 30, 32 CE

Cedar, where he was invited into various homes. He also taught in the open by the town well.

On August 13, Jesus and the three youths journeyed eastward toward Edon. On the way, Jesus visited a house that stood off by itself in which both the father and mother of the family had long been bedridden with incurable maladies. Several children were going and coming around the house. All were good. Here also they asked him about Jesus of Nazareth, of whom they had heard diverse reports. Jesus answered them by telling them a parable of a king and his son, in which he spoke of the one of whom they inquired. He told them that the son would be persecuted, and that he would return to his father's kingdom, which he would share with all those who had followed him. Then Jesus asked the bedridden couple whether they believed all that he had told them and whether they would follow the good king? They assured him of their belief and their willing-ness to follow the good king. Jesus then promised the two old people that God would reward them by curing them and allowing them to follow him to Edon. All of a sudden, they were restored to health and, to the astonish-ment of the beholders, were indeed able to follow Jesus to Edon.

On the afternoon, of the next day Jesus and his traveling companions reached Edon. They went to a wedding celebration to which Jesus had been invited. It was in progress when they arrived. News of Jesus had spread from Cedar and he was received as a prophet. At the wedding feast, Jesus taught, telling of a man who had changed water into wine at a wed-ding in Cana. The celebration lasted late into the night.

The next morning, in Edon, Jesus taught in front of the house where the wedding celebration had taken place. He spoke about marriage. Then he returned to Cedar for the Sabbath as he had promised. That evening, until about ten o'clock, he taught in an open place for prayer, a garden near to the synagogue. Then he went into the synagogue.

On the following day, Jesus taught in the synagogue and, that eve-ning, in the garden next to the synagogue. He spoke again about marriage. On the morning of Sunday, August 17, Jesus continued to speak in the synagogue about marriage. A divorced couple came to him. There were two groups: the husband and his relatives and the wife and her relatives.

Jesus spoke with each group separately. Then the estranged couple came together, held hands, and Jesus blessed them. On the evening of the next day, Jesus visited a shepherd settlement north of Cedar.

On the following day, Jesus and the three youths went further. In the evening, they arrived at Sichar, a little town north of Cedar. Jesus was received as a guest in the house of Eliud, whose wife had been unfaithful. Eliud knew nothing of it. Jesus spoke alone with the wife who confessed her guilt and sank down weeping at Jesus' feet. He blessed her and spoke words of consolation to Eliud, but without mentioning his wife's infidelity. The next morning Jesus took hold of Eliud's hands and spoke with him lovingly about the washing of the feet. Then he began to speak to Eliud of his destiny. Jesus told him that his children were not his, but had been conceived illicitly, and that his wife was expecting a child that was not his. He said that his wife regretted this and wanted to make amends. He said that Eliud should forgive his wife. Eliud then cast himself down on the ground, smitten with anguish. After a while, Jesus raised Eliud up, comforted him, and washed his feet. Eliud became quiet and still. Jesus instructed him to call his wife, who came into the room. She was wearing a veil. Jesus took her hand, placed it in Eliud's hand, blessed them, and comforted them. Jesus raised the wife's veil, and bid her send the children to him, whom he also blessed. From this time on, the couple remained true to one another. Afterward, Jesus went from house to house.

On the afternoon of August 21, Jesus taught beneath the porch of the town hall. He spoke in parables, referring to the bees, as there were many beehives kept by the people of the town. He spoke also of the vine and the vineyard, saying that he would produce the "wine of life" from the true vine. The next morning Jesus visited many people of the town, teaching about the cultivation of the vine and drawing analogies with marriage and alluding to his work of love, wherever it may bear fruit. That afternoon he attended a wedding that took place in the open air, in front of the synagogue. With nightfall, as the stars shone above, they held the Sabbath in the synagogue. On the following day, Jesus taught in parables. He also said, "Do not let your hearts be troubled. Believe in God, believe also in me. In my Father's house there are many dwelling places. If it were not so, would I have told you that I go to prepare a place for you? And if I go and prepare a place for you, I will come again and will take you there myself, so that where I am, there you may be also." He again spoke about marriage and of the importance of regarding marriage as a spiritual task, one that included the spiritual education of children. Moreover, he alluded to himself as the spouse of a bride on whom all those gathered together would be reborn.

On August 24, Jesus persuaded the people of Sichar to build a house for the newly-married couple close to the hill where the beehives were placed. He instructed the couple to cultivate a vineyard behind the house, in the area reaching up to where the bees were. Two days later the Feast of the New Moon began. It was celebrated in the evening in the synagogue. Afterward the people of Sichar gathered in the town hall to hear Jesus speak. He told them that he would not stay in Sichar, that he had no house, and that his kingdom would come later. First, he had to cultivate and water his Father's vineyard. He taught until late in the night.

On the evening of August 29, Jesus went to the synagogue for the Sabbath and taught there. He taught again in the synagogue on the next day. He spoke of the bridegroom's house, which was delicate in construction. The bridegroom's name was Salathiel. Jesus said that one should not become too attached to the earth. Why build a house for the body, when this itself was a fragile house. The house of the soul should be purified and sanctified as a temple, and should not be desecrated. He also spoke about the Messiah and how to recognize him.

On August 31, Jesus spoke with a couple who wanted to marry. He told them that their plan to marry was motivated by the desire for property. They were shocked that he could read their thoughts, for they had not spoken to anyone about their secret intentions. Then they gave up their plans and believed in Jesus. On the following day Jesus taught further concerning marriage. He spoke of David, who had fallen into sin on account of the superabundance of forces within him, which he should have consumed within himself. He added that nothing is lost through continence, but rather through wastefulness.

That afternoon he went about one hour east of Sichar to the house of a rich herd owner who had died suddenly in one of his fields. His wife and children were very sad and had sent for Jesus, begging him to come to the funeral. He came, accompanied by the three shepherd youths, by Salathiel and his wife, and about twenty-five people from Sichar. After sending away the people from Sichar, apart from Salathiel and his wife, Jesus spoke with the wife of the dead man, whose name was Nazor. He said that if she and her son and daughter would believe in his teaching and follow him, and if they would keep silence on the matter, Nazor would be raised to life again. For, he said, Nazor's soul had not yet passed on to be judged but was still present over the place in the field where he had died. Jesus then went with them to the field. Praying, he called Nazor back to his body, saying to those present, "When we return, Nazor will be alive and sitting upright." They then returned to the house to find Nazor sitting upright in his coffin, wrapped in linen cloths and with his hands bound. After being freed from the wrappings, Nazor climbed out of the coffin and cast himself at Jesus' feet. The latter told him to wash and purify himself, stay hidden in his room, and say nothing about being raised from the dead until after Jesus had left the region. Jesus and the five people with him then stayed there overnight.

The next morning, Jesus spoke with Nazor and washed his feet. He said that in the future he should think more of his soul and should put right the wrong he had done to some poor shepherds whose property he had unjustly confiscated. Jesus then blessed Nazor's wife and children. Afterward, he spoke with Salathiel and his wife, saying to Salathiel, "You have allowed yourself to be drawn by the beauty of your wife's body. But think how beautiful the soul must be, that God sends his Son to the Earth in order to save the soul through the sacrifice of his body." Jesus said that he wanted to teach on the Sabbath at the synagogue in Cedar, and that he would then leave this area and travel east through Arabia. They asked him why he wanted to go to those who worshiped the stars. He answered that he had friends there who had followed a star to greet him at his birth. He wanted to seek them out in order to invite them into the vineyard of the kingdom of his Father. That night, Jesus stayed at Nazor's house. The next day Jesus returned to Sichar, where a crowd of people had gathered. To the great astonishment of the crowd, Jesus publicly healed the sick. All were filled with joy at these miraculous healings.

At noon on Friday, September 5, Jesus taught in a house in Cedar. His theme was marriage. Salathiel and his wife were there. Jesus spoke of the conditions for living together in order to become the good vine. All things between husband and wife should be dealt with lovingly. They should remain free of desire and should consider their motivation for each action in their marriage. If motivated by desire alone, a couple would reap bitter fruit. Jesus warned those present concerning overindulgence and instructed them to pray, exercise restraint, and guard against intoxication of wine.

On the following day, throughout the Sabbath, Jesus taught concerning the vine, the grain, and the wine. He spoke of Melchizedek as a forerunner, whose sacrifice was bread and wine; in himself, however, the sacrifice was to become flesh and blood. Jesus indicated clearly that he was the Messiah, and said that they should follow him.

On September 9, Jesus and the three shepherd youths left Cedar. About twenty people accompanied them to a place some distance from the town. Here Jesus blessed those who had accompanied them and then that group returned to Cedar. This was about midday. Jesus and the young shepherds went eastward and toward evening came to a settlement where the people lived in tents. Jesus and his companions were invited to eat and stay there. There was a festival of star worship that took place there that night; it was the night after the full moon. The heathens cried out as the moon rose, or when other stars rose. Later that night Mars rose, then Jupiter, and later still Saturn. On the following morning Jesus taught the heathens, reprimanding them for their sacrificial practices, saying that they should pray to the Father who had created everything. He was well received. Then he left. As he was traveling further with the three shepherd youths, he remarked to them how well he had been received by the heathens.

Later that week, Jesus and his three young traveling companions had made rapid progress on their way. Around the onset of the Sabbath, they arrived at a well not far from a small shepherd settlement. Here they prayed together and held the Sabbath.

On the following day, some shepherds came to Jesus to hear him teach. He asked them if they had heard of the men who more than thirty years ago had been led by a star to greet the newborn King of the Jews? They replied, "Yes, yes!" Whereupon Jesus said that he was the King of the Jews and that he now wanted to visit these men again. That evening, after teaching, Jesus dined with the shepherds and blessed the meal they ate together.

On September 14, Jesus taught the shepherds again. He spoke of the creation of the world and of the Fall and of the promise of the restoration of all. Then Jesus appeared to catch a sunbeam with his right hand, and he made a luminous globe of light from it. It hung from the palm of his hand on a ray of light. While he was talking, the shepherds could see all the things he was describing in the globe of light. At the end of the discourse, the globe of light disappeared, and the shepherds cast themselves down in sorrow. Jesus later taught them the Lord's Prayer and how to worship God, the creator of all. On the following day, Jesus stayed with the shepherds, teaching them about their flocks and also about various herbs.

Then on September 15, Jesus and the three youths continued on their way. About twelve shepherds accompanied them. During the hottest part of the day, they rested. They made most rapid progress during the hours of darkness.

On September 18, Jesus and the three youths arrived at another settlement. They were led to a house where various fruits were brought to them. Meanwhile the other shepherds, who had received some food, made their way back home. Jesus asked the people in the house about the three kings. He was told that after they had returned from Judea, they had settled in a place not far away and had erected a "tent city" around a step-pyramid. They knew that the Messiah would visit them. Of the three kings, the eldest, Mensor, was alive and well. Theokeno, the next in age, was bedridden, while the third, Sair, had died about nine years before. His corpse lay undecayed in a tomb built in the form of a pyramid. The people, who believed Jesus to be an envoy of the King of the Jews awaited by the kings Mensor and Theokeno, sent a messenger to King Mensor to inform him of Jesus' arrival. The tent city where the two kings lived was only a few hours away. When the hour for the Sabbath approached, Jesus asked for one of the unoccupied cabins to be placed at his service and that of his disciples. As there were no lamps of Jewish style, they made one for themselves and celebrated their holy exercises. They remained until the close of the Sabbath on September 20. Afterward, Jesus taught the people of the place. On the following day, Jesus went to the tent city of King Mensor and King Theokeno. Meanwhile when the kings received the news of Jesus' arrival, they made great preparations for his reception. Trees were bound together so as to form covered walks, and triumphal arches erected. These latter were adorned with flowers, fruits, ornaments of all kinds, and hung with tapestry.

Seven men were dispatched to the pastoral region to meet Jesus and bear him a welcome. They were dressed in white and they had long gold-embroidered mantels. They wore white turbans on their heads ornamented with gold and high tufts of feathers. In their presence, Jesus delivered an instruction in which he spoke of right-minded pagans who, though ignorant, were devout of heart.

As Jesus approached, King Mensor came to greet him; he was riding on a camel and accompanied by about twenty men. They were filled with joy as they went up to Jesus. The king climbed down from his camel, handed Jesus his royal scepter, and cast himself down before him. King Mensor asked Jesus about the King of the Jews, believing Jesus to be an envoy of that king. They all went back to the tent city, where they dined together.

On the next day, King Mensor went with Jesus to King Thekeno, who on account of weakness and old age was no longer able to walk. He rested upon an upholstered bed. Jesus visited him daily with King Mensor. Both kings related how they had seen the star that led them to the newborn child in Bethlehem. They asked Jesus why they had lost sight of the star as they had approached Jerusalem. Jesus replied, "To test your faith, and because it should not come across Jerusalem." With this, Jesus told his hosts that he was not an envoy of the Messiah, but the Messiah himself. On hearing this, the kings fell prostrate on the ground in tears. King Mensor especially wept with emotion. He could not contain himself for love and reverence, and was unable to conceive how Jesus could have condescended to come to him. Jesus added that he had come for gentiles as well as for Jews; he had come for all who believed in him. When the two kings said they wanted to follow him back to Israel, Jesus said that his kingdom was not of this world. He said that they would be much upset and their faith sorely tried if they were to see how he would be despised and mistreated. These words they could not comprehend. And they inquired how it could be that things could go so well with the bad while the good had to suffer so much. Jesus then explained to them that they who enjoy on earth have to render an account hereafter, and that this life is one of penance.

On September 25, Jesus visited the temple in the tent city. The priests showed Jesus a representation of the crib that, after their return from Bethlehem, they had caused to be made. It was exactly like what they had seen in the star, entirely of gold, and surrounded by a plate of the same metal in the form of a star. Jesus drew for them on a plate the figure of a lamb resting on a book with seven seals, and a little standard over his shoulder. He requested them to make one using this design and place it on the column opposite the crib. Jesus also went to the tomb of King Sair. King Theokeno told Jesus how, according to their custom, they had placed a branch in front of the tomb; he said that a dove was often seen to settle on this branch and he asked Jesus what this meant. The latter asked King Theokeno about King Sair's faith. King Thekeno replied, "Lord, his faith was like mine. Right up to his death, since we went to worship the King of the Jews, King Sair always wanted to think and do his will." Jesus explained to the two kings that the dove on the branch revealed that King Sair had been baptized with the baptism of the Holy Spirit.

On Friday, September 26, King Mensor and King Theokeno told Jesus how they had first seen the star fifteen years before his birth. It was a vision of a virgin with a scepter in one hand and a pair of scales in the other, a beautiful ear of corn in one of the scales and a wine grape in the other.[1] Since returning from Bethlehem, for three days each year they had celebrated a festival in honor of the Solomon Jesus, the Solomon Mary, and the Solomon Joseph, who had welcomed them so lovingly. That evening as

---

1   Robert Powell confirms that the date for the beginning of this vision coincides with Dec. 8, 22 BCE,. and the conception of the Solomon Mary.

the Sabbath began, Jesus and the three shepherd youths separated themselves from the others and prayed together.

On the next day, at the close of the Sabbath, Jesus went into the temple where there was an idol of a dragon. As one of the women cast herself down before this idol to worship it, Jesus said, "Why do you cast yourself down before Satan? Your faith has been taken possession of by Satan. Behold whom you worship." Instantly there appeared before her, visible to all, a slender, red fox-colored spirit with a hideously pointed countenance. All were horrified. Jesus pointed to the spirit and indicated that it was this spirit that had woken the woman from sleep each morning before the break of day. Jesus said, "This awoke you. However, every person also has a good angel, who should wake you, and before whom you should cast yourself down and follow his advice. All then saw a radiant figure at the woman's side. At this approach of the good angel, the satanic spirit withdrew. Like the two kings, this woman later became baptized by the Apostle Thomas and received the name *Sarena*.

On the morning of September 28, Jesus went with King Mensor to visit King Theokeno. He bade King Theokeno to arise. Taking him by the hand, Jesus raised him up, and King Theokeno was able to walk. From this time on, he was no longer bedridden. Jesus then went with the two kings to the temple where he taught. After teaching the people, Jesus gave instruction to the two kings and the four priests of the temple. He explained that when the good angels withdraw, Satan takes possession of a temple service. He said that they should remove the various animal idols and teach love and compassion and give thanks to the Father in Heaven. Jesus promised them that he would send one who would more fully instruct them, and he directed them to remove the wheel with its starry representations. It was as large as a carriage wheel of moderate size and had seven consecutive rims, on the uppermost and the lowest of which were fastened globes from which streamed rays. The central point consisted of a larger globe, which represented the earth. On the circumference of the wheel were twelve stars, in which were as many different pictures, splendid and glittering.

Jesus now took bread and wine, which had been prepared beforehand. Having consecrated the bread and wine, he placed them upon a small altar.

He prayed and blessed everyone. The two kings and the four priests knelt before him with their hands folded across their chests. Jesus laid his hands upon their shoulders and prayed over them. He blessed the bread and wine and said that they should partake of it once every three months. He taught them the words of blessing to use and said that they should begin taking the communion of bread and wine on the anniversary of their adoration at the crib. On the next day, Jesus taught again in the temple. He gave instruction to the women concerning prayer, saying also how they should bring up their children. Afterward, he blessed the children.

Before daybreak on September 30, Jesus left the tent city of the kings. King Mensor begged him to remain with them, and wept profusely at Jesus' departure. Jesus and the three shepherd youths traveled far that day. In the evening, they reached a shepherd settlement where they stayed the night.

CHAPTER 16

JOURNEY TO THE BIRTHPLACE OF ABRAHAM

OCTOBER 1 TO 12, 32 CE

Christ Jesus and his three traveling companions—Eliud, Silas, and Eremenzear—left the shepherd settlement before daybreak on October 1. Once again they journeyed for the entire day. That night they slept in a hut made of earth and moss. The following morning Jesus and the three youths spoke with the people living at this place and accompanied them to their temple, where he taught. The name of the place was Atom and the chieftain of the people there was called Azaria. He was the son of one of King Mensor's brothers. Jesus stayed that night in Azaria's house.

On the evening of Friday, October 3, with the onset of the Sabbath, Jesus and the three shepherd youths went back to the hut where they had stayed on their arrival in Atom. Here they prayed together. Later, in the temple, Jesus healed one of Azaria's wives, who was afflicted with an issue of blood. He also healed a woman possessed by a devil that had made her fall hopelessly in love with a youth. The youth's name was Caisar, and he was exceptionally pure. He had long had a presentiment of the coming of salvation and joined Jesus and the three shepherd youths to accompany them on their further journey. Jesus taught in the temple throughout the night until the break of day. The following day Jesus and the four youths spent the entire day in prayer. At the close of the Sabbath, they went to the temple. Jesus taught the people and then gave instruction to the priests concerning the communion of bread and wine. He consecrated the bread and wine, and blessed the priests.

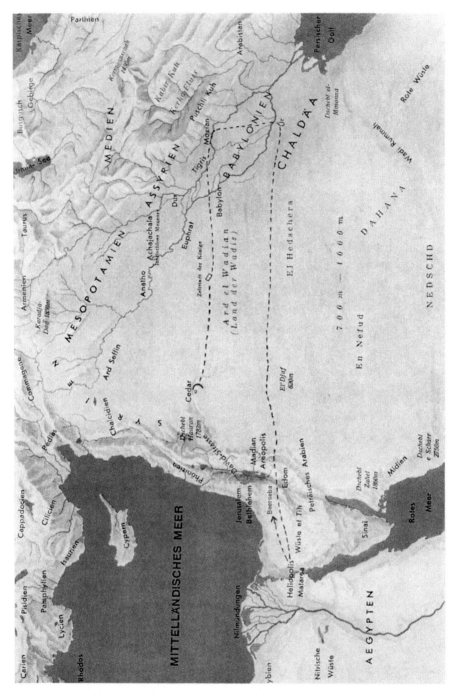

FIGURE 15: *Journey to the Birthplace of Abraham*
October 1 to 12, 32 CE

The next morning Jesus and the four youths left Atom, first traveling southward and then in an easterly direction. Toward evening they arrived at the Chaldean city of Sikdor. Here Jesus taught in the temple. He reproved them for their idolatry. He said that he was the vine whose blood would renew the world and that he was the grain of corn that would be buried in the earth and would rise again. The people here were very humble and believed that the Jews alone were the chosen people. Jesus comforted them and said that he had come for all human beings. He commanded them to destroy their idols and give alms to the poor.

The following day, Jesus and his four traveling companions left Sikdor. On the way, they stopped to eat bread and honey. They traveled all night. They journeyed on. Having already crossed the Euphrates River, they then crossed the Tigris River. In the evening, they arrived at the city of Mozian, where they stayed the night. In the morning, Jesus did not enter the temple. He taught at a well in front of the temple. He strongly reprimanded the people on account of their idolatry. He left the city and traveled through-out the night in a southerly direction, recrossing the Tigris. The next day, Jesus and his traveling companions continued their journey. Traveling on, Jesus and the four youths recrossed the Euphrates.

Toward the evening of October 10, as the Sabbath began, they arrived at Ur, the birthplace of Abraham. Here they stayed in a house and held the Sabbath together in prayer. On the next day Jesus and his companions continued to celebrate the Sabbath. After the sun had set, he taught in an open place where he spoke of Abraham. On the following day, the people of Ur accompanied Jesus and strewed branches on the street in front of him as he and the four youths left the city.

CHAPTER 17

THE LONG JOURNEY TO EGYPT

OCTOBER 12, 32 TO JANUARY 8, 33 CE

At daybreak on Sunday, October 12, Christ Jesus and the four youths—Eliud, Silas, Eremenzear, and Caisar—set off on the long journey to Egypt. They traveled toward the west for a long time, over a beautiful plain that, toward the end, became sandy, and was finally covered with underbrush. About noon they reached a well by which they sat down to rest. The remainder of the journey was made through a wood and over cultivated land. Toward evening they arrived at a great, round building encircled by a courtyard and a moat. All around were heavy-looking houses with flat roofs. That of the great building was covered with verdure and even trees, while in the massive wall of the courtyard were the abodes of some poor people. At the fountain in the courtyard, Jesus and the disciples washed their feet, as usual. Now, from the roundhouse came forth two men in long garments profusely trimmed with laces and ribbons, and wearing feathered caps on their heads. The elder of the two carried a green branch and a little bunch of berries, which he presented to Jesus, who with the disciples followed him into the building. In the center of the structure was a hall, lighted from the roof, whose fireplace was reached by steps. From this circular space, they proceeded around through irregularly shaped rooms opening one into the other, and whose end wall, concave in form, was hung with tapestry. The floor was level and, like the walls, covered with thick carpets. In one of these apartments, Jesus and his companions took a frugal repast and drank something from vessels never before used, but it was not obvious what the beverage consisted of. After the meal, the

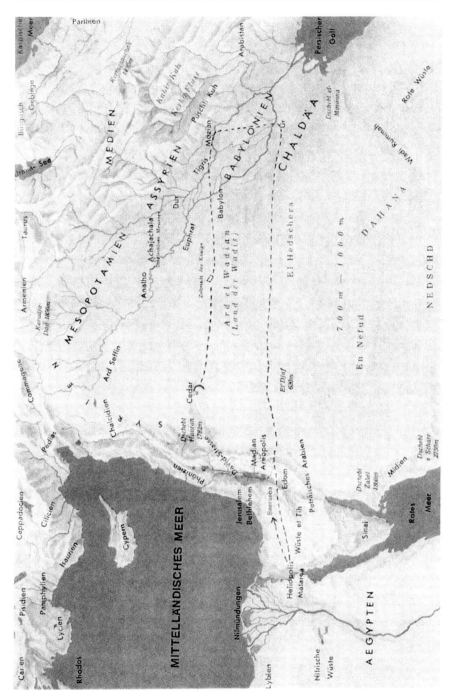

FIGURE 16: The Long Journey to Egypt
October 12, 32 to January 12, 33 CE

master of the house took them around and showed them everything. The whole castle was filled with beautifully wrought idols. There were figures of all sizes, large and small, some with a head like that of an ox, others like that of a dog, and others with a serpent's body. One of them had many arms and heads and into its jaws could be put all kinds of things. These people sacrificed animals, but they had an aversion to blood, which they always allowed to run off into the earth. They had, also, the custom of distributing bread, of which the more distinguished among them received a larger portion.

Jesus taught at the fountain in the courtyard, and strongly criticized the people's worship, though his words were not taken in good part. The chief of their settlement was particularly obstinate in his errors. He was irritated at Jesus, and became enraged, even contradicting him. Jesus then told the people that, on the night of the anniversary on which the star had appeared to the three kings, the idols would all break, the oxen idols would bellow, the dog idols would bark, and the bird idols would squawk. This would be the proof of his words. The people listened to him in disbelief. Jesus told them that this would take place throughout Chaldea in the places he had visited.

During this period, which lasted some two and one-half months, until the end of the year 32 CE, Anne Catherine Emmerich had a vision on Christmas night of the entire journey through Chaldea, from Cedar, to the tent city of the kings, to Atom, Sikdor, Mozian, Ur, and the last Chaldian settlement. Everywhere, as Jesus predicted, the idols were broken and animal idols of the various kinds cried out. Historically (in 32 CE) this was probably December 7 and 8, the anniversary of the immaculate conception of the Solomon Mary, the night when the three kings had first seen the star, fifteen years before the birth of the Solomon Jesus.[1]

---

1   At this point in Dr. Powell's record, there is a gap of approximately two and one-half months. While this can be presumed to be related to the journey across the desert from Ur in Arabia to the first Egyptian settlement, there is no explanation by Dr. Powell of why the daily journal was interrupted, nor is there any corresponding daily record in the English Translation of the 4th German edition.

Jesus and the four youths traveled quickly, pausing nowhere, but ever hurrying on. They traversed the Arabian Desert, approaching Egypt, and passed south of Mount Sinai, which they saw in the distance. They then crossed the Sinai desert. At first, they traversed a sandy desert, toiled slowly up a steep mountain ridge, pursued their way over a country covered with vegetation, then crept through low brush like juniper bushes, whose branches met overhead to form a covered path. After that, they came to a stony region overrun with ivy, thence through meadows and woods until they reached a river, not rapid but deep, over which they crossed on a raft of beams. It was still night on the evening of December 7, 32, when they arrived at a city built on both sides of a waterway. It was the first Egyptian city on their route. During the night, many idols fell to the ground.

In the morning of January 1, 33, there was an uproar in the town, when people discovered the broken idols. Jesus and the four youths hurriedly left the town, and as they did some children ran after them calling out, "These are holy people!" Jesus and his companions traveled further westward. They plunged into the deep ravines that traversed the sandy region. That evening, not far from a city, they rested and took food at the source of a brook, the disciples having washed Jesus' feet. When they entered the town, it was night. They made their way through the deserted streets, and then traveled on further. At a good distance from this city, the way led over an immense stone bridge that took them across the Nile River. The river flowed from south to north and divided into many branches that ran in different directions. The country was low and level, and off in the distance there were some high buildings in form like the temples of the star worshipers, though built of stone and much higher.

The next day when they were still an hour away from Heliopolis, Jesus took the same road by which he, as the Solomon Jesus, with the Solomon Mary and the Solomon Joseph, had entered it some four decades before. This road was situated on the first arm of the Nile River, which flows in the direction of Judea. Before entering Heliopolis, Jesus met some Jews who had been friends of the Solomon Holy Family during the time of their stay in Heliopolis. They conducted Jesus and his traveling companions into the city. Before the entrance lay a large, four-cornered, perfectly flat stone, on which, among other names, was inscribed the name Heliopolis. Inside the city, there was a very large temple surrounded by two courts, several high columns tapering toward the top and ornamented with numerous figures. There was also a row of large dogs with human heads, all in a recumbent posture. The city showed evident signs of decay. The people led Jesus under a projection of a thick wall opposite the temple, and called several citizens of the neighborhood. Among the women there was one, tall and advanced in years, who was especially distinctive. All welcomed Jesus respectfully, for they had been friends of the Solomon Holy Family at the time of their sojourn here. In the back of the projecting wall was a space, now ornamented in festal style, in which the Solomon Joseph had prepared an abode for the holy family. With the onset of the Sabbath, Jesus was escorted to the synagogue by an aged man. In the synagogue, Jesus taught and prayed. On the following day Jesus taught again in the synagogue at Heliopolis.

On Sunday, January 4, when Jesus, escorted by many of the inhabitants, left Heliopolis, he took with him a young man belonging to the city, and who now made his fifth disciple. His name was Deodatus, and that of his mother was Mira. She was that tall, distinguished woman who had, on the first evening of Jesus' arrival, been among those that welcomed him under the portico. During the Solomon Mary's sojourn in Heliopolis, Mira was childless; but on the prayer of the Solomon Mary, this son was given to her. He was tall and slender, and appeared to be about eighteen years old. When his escort had returned to the city, Jesus resumed his journey through the desert with his five disciples.

On the next day, the traveling party arrived at a small town in the desert, where some Jews were living. He went to the town well, where he was greeted and then escorted to a house. In this little town, Jesus was held by the Jews to be a prophet. There was no synagogue, so Jesus taught in a house. Before he left, Jesus blessed the children of this place.

On Thursday, January 8, Jesus and his disciples arrived at the town of Beersheba, where Jesus was received in a friendly manner.

CHAPTER 18

LAST JOURNEY TO JERUSALEM

JANUARY 26 TO FEBRUARY 19, 33 CE

On the evening of Monday, January 26, Christ Jesus, who had previously dismissed the additional disciples, arrived in Capernaum with, Silas, Eliud, and Eremenzear. Here they were met by Peter, Andrew, and James the Lesser. Also a young man called Sela was presented to Jesus. He was a cousin of the bridegroom of Cedar to whom Jesus had given the house and vineyard on the occasion of his journey to the star worshipers. It was the bridegroom who had sent Sela to Jesus, and he had been in Andrew's house awaiting his coming. Sela threw himself on his knees before Jesus, who placed his hands upon the young man's shoulders and admitted him to the number of his disciples.

Jesus made use of him at once, sending him to the superintendent of the synagogue to request the key and the roll of scriptures that had been found in the Temple during the seven years that it had stood dilapidated and deprived of divine service. The last time that Jesus taught here, he had made use of the same roll of scriptures, which were from Isaiah. When the youth returned, Jesus and his companions went into the synagogue and lighted the lamps. Jesus directed a space to be cleared and a pulpit with a flight of steps to be placed in it. A great crowd was gathered, and Jesus taught a long time from that roll of scriptures. The excitement in Capernaum was very great. Afterward, the people on the streets of Capernaum called out, "Joseph's son is here again!"

On the next day, Jesus left Capernaum before daybreak, traveling to Nazareth with several of the twelve and the other disciples. Arriving, he

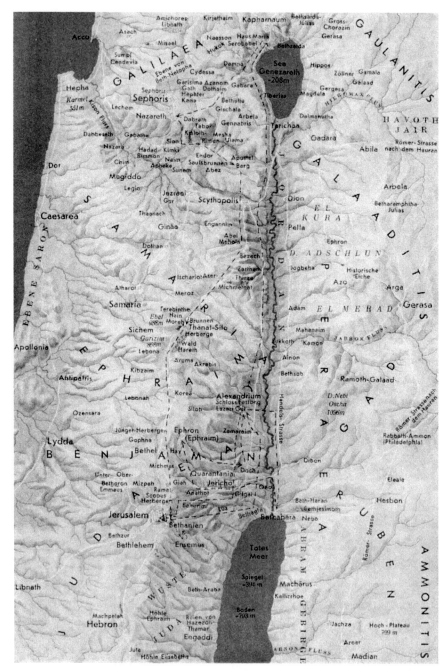

FIGURE 17: The Last Journey to Jerusalem
January 26 to February 19, 33 CE

went straight to the synagogue. Here his presence caused much commotion. After teaching, Jesus and those with him went to an inn and stayed the night there. The following morning Jesus went to various houses in Nazareth and healed. He also blessed the children. He sent the twelve on ahead to a mountain about sixteen miles south of Tiberius and then followed them there, accompanied by the remaining disciples. It was already night when he arrived at the "mount of the apostles." He found the twelve waiting for him at the top, grouped around a fire. Throughout much of the night, Jesus taught, giving the twelve and the other disciples instructions for the next period.

Around daybreak, Jesus and the disciples set off southward for Thanat-Silo, the twelve having gone on ahead. Jesus met up with the twelve at a well about one hour's distance from the town. They then proceeded together to Thanat-Silo. Here the Blessed Virgin Mary, Martha, Mary Magdalene, and some other holy women were waiting for them at an inn. In the evening, after a meal, Jesus taught.

On the morning of Friday, January 30, Jesus healed the sick and sent the twelve off to various places. The holy women left for Bethany. Jesus, accompanied by some disciples, followed in the same direction, arriving at an inn before the onset of the Sabbath. Here, the disciples who had returned with him from his great journey were waiting for him. At this inn, Jesus celebrated the Sabbath together with about twenty disciples. They remained at the inn until the close of the Sabbath on the following day. They prayed, and Jesus gave them instructions about what they should do.

Subsequently, Jesus and the disciples proceeded on the way toward Bethany. Jesus taught the disciples as they went. He said that he would go to Jerusalem to teach, after which he would return to his heavenly Father. They arrived at an inn about an hour from Bethany. Here the Blessed Virgin Mary, the holy women, and five of the twelve—Judas, Thomas, Simon, James the Lesser, and Judas Thaddeus—were waiting for him. There was a meal, and Jesus taught here.

The next morning, the five of the twelve and the sixteen disciples who had come with Jesus divided into three groups: one led by Judas Thaddeus, the second by James the Lesser, and the third by Jesus accompanied by the

three silent disciples. On this journey, Jesus cured a man possessed by a
devil. The parents of the young man ran after Jesus just as he was entering
a little village of scattered houses. He followed them into the court of
their house, where he found their possessed son who, at Jesus' approach,
became furious, leaping about and dashing against the walls. His friends
wanted to bind him, but they could not do it, as he grew more and more
rabid. Thereupon Jesus commanded all present to withdraw and leave him
alone with the possessed. When they obeyed, Jesus called to the possessed
to come to him. But he, not heeding the call, began to put out his tongue
and to make horrible grimaces at Jesus. He called him again, but he did
not come. Rather, with his head twisted over his shoulder, the possessed
one looked at him. Then Jesus raised his eyes to heaven and prayed. When
Jesus again commanded the possessed to come to him, he did so and cast
himself full length at his feet. Jesus passed over him twice first one foot
and then the other, as if treading him underfoot. A black spiral vapor rose
from the mouth of the possessed and then disappeared in the air. The
rising exhalation contained three knots, the last of which was the darkest
and strongest. The possessed now lay like one dead at Jesus' feet. He then
commanded him to rise. The poor creature stood up. Jesus led him to his
parents at the gate of the courtyard, and said to them, "I give you back
your son cured. Sin no more against him." They had sinned against him,
and it was on that account that he had fallen into so miserable a condition.
During the following two days Jesus again taught in the synagogue of
Bethany and healed in the town.

On Friday, February 6, having returned to Bethany, Jesus went to the
synagogue for the beginning of the Sabbath. The next day he continued
to teach in the synagogue. That evening Jesus did not pass the night in
Bethany, but outside in the disciples' inn. While at this inn, three men
came to Jesus from Jerusalem: Obed, the son of the old man Simeon, a
Temple servant and a disciple in secret; the second, a relative of Veronica;
and the third, a relative of Joanna Chusa. These disciples asked why he
had so long abandoned them, why he had in other places done so much of
which they knew nothing. In his answer to these questions, Jesus spoke of
tapestry and other precious things that looked new and beautiful to one

who had not seen them for some time. He said also that if the sower sowed his seed all at once and in one place, the whole might be destroyed by a hailstorm, so the instruction and cures that were scattered far and wide would not soon be forgotten. They also reported that the high priests and Pharisees wanted to send out spies, so that they could capture him as soon as he came to Jerusalem. Hearing this, Jesus took with him only his two latest disciples, Sela of Cedar and Silvaneus, and traveled the whole night with them to Lazarus' estate near Ginea.

On the morning of February 9, while it was still dark, Jesus and the two disciples arrived at Lazarus' property south of Alexandrium and knocked at the gate of the courtyard. It was opened by the Apostle Lazarus himself who, with a light, conducted them into a large hall where were assembled Nicodemus, Joseph of Arimathea, John Mark, and Jair, the younger brother of Obed. They ate a meal together.

On Monday, February 16, Jesus went to a little place about an hour north of Jericho. Here there was a retreat house for the sick and needy. At that site, Jesus restored sight to an old blind man. This was the man whom once before, when engaged in healing, he had sent away. At that former time, he had restored sight to two others by anointing their eyes with a salve made of clay mixed with spittle. He now cured this man by his word alone. Later that week, Jesus returned to Lazarus' estate near Alexandrium.

On the morning of February 19, Jesus, accompanied by the Apostle Lazarus, left Alexandrium and went to Bethany. The holy women came to meet him as he approached Bethany. In the evening, Jesus went to the Temple in Jerusalem. He was accompanied part of the way by the Blessed Virgin Mary. He was preparing her for his approaching Passion, and he told her that the time for the fulfillment of Simeon's prophecy, that a sword would pierce her soul, was near at hand. They would, he said, cruelly betray him, take him prisoner, maltreat him, put him to death as a malefactor, and all would take place under her eyes. Jesus spoke long upon this subject, and the Blessed Virgin Mary was grievously troubled. Jesus stayed overnight in Jerusalem in the house of Mary Mark, the mother of John Mark.

CHAPTER 19

FOURTH FESTIVAL OF THE PASSOVER

FEBRUARY 20 TO APRIL 3, 33 CE

O n Friday, February 20, Christ Jesus went to the Temple for the celebration of the Sabbath. After the Pharisees had left, Jesus taught from the teacher's chair in the portico of Solomon, where Jesus of Nazareth had taught when he was twelve years old. All of the twelve were present, and many people came to hear him. He spoke with great seriousness. For Jesus, the start of this Hebrew month of Adar signified the beginning of his public teaching in the Temple and of the way leading to the Cross. Inwardly, he was torn with sorrow at humanity's corruption. On the following day, Jesus taught again in the Temple, beginning his teaching after the Pharisees had ended theirs.

For all of the following week, Jesus taught in the Temple each day. On one of those days he set forth the parable of the field overgrown with weeds that had to be carefully uprooted so that the good grain would ripen and not be uprooted by the weeds—meaning the Pharisees.

On Friday, February 27, Jesus was in Bethany and spoke at length with the Blessed Virgin Mary about his approaching suffering. This evening he went to the Temple in Jerusalem for the onset of the Sabbath. After the Pharisees had left, Jesus taught late into the night.

The next morning Jesus taught in the Temple. Around three o'clock, he shared a meal with about twenty of his disciples at the house of Mary Mark. On Sunday, March 1, Jesus taught again in the Temple. He spoke of John the Baptizer, and many pupils of John were present, but they did not display themselves openly. That evening he went to Bethany and spoke with the holy women. Afterward, he retired to sleep at Lazarus' castle.

On Wednesday, March 4, Jesus left Bethany and went to the Temple in Jerusalem and taught there. He said that many did not believe in him but followed him only because of the miracles he performed. He added that they would forsake him in the hour of decision and that it would be better for them to leave him now. At this many left. About one hundred people remained. Jesus wept over this defection on his return to Bethany. Shortly before sunset on the next day Jesus went to the Temple. He was accompanied by six disciples. He taught that he would be leaving them soon.

On the afternoon of Friday, March 6th, Jesus came from Bethany to Jerusalem before the onset of the Sabbath. He ate at the home of John Mark. The holy women and the Apostle Lazarus were also present, but the Apostle Lazarus did not go with Jesus to the Temple when the Sabbath began. Later, Jesus returned to Bethany. The following day Jesus taught again in the Temple and, after a short pause around midday, he continued teaching. He said that one should not hoard up perishable treasures. He spoke, too, of prayer and fasting and the danger of hypocrisy with regard to these practices. He referred to his approaching end, indicating that he would make a triumphal entry into Jerusalem beforehand.

Addressing the twelve, he revealed to them something of their future tasks. Peter, John the son of Zebedee, and James the Lesser would remain in Jerusalem; the others were to spread out and teach in various lands, e.g., Andrew in the region of Galaad, and Philip and Bartholomew around Gessur. Jesus told them that they would all meet again in Jerusalem, three years after his death, and that John the son of Zebedee and the Blessed Virgin Mary would then go to Ephesus. In this instruction he made some allusion, though without naming it particularly, to the house in which the Last Supper was to be eaten and in which later on they were to receive the Holy Spirit. He spoke of their assembling in it and of their partaking of a strengthening and life-giving food in which he himself would remain with them forever. The Pharisees were enraged by what they heard and wanted to stone Jesus as he made his way out of the Temple. Jesus, however, managed to elude them and return to Bethany.

After this, he did not teach in the Temple again for about three days but remained hidden in the castle of the Apostle Lazarus in Bethany. The twelve came to him and asked him about what he had taught in the Temple on the Sabbath. Three Chaldeans arrived to see him, having heard of his teaching in Chaldea. Jesus spoke to them only briefly but he directed them to Cornelius, the Centurion of Capernaum, who had been a heathen like themselves, and who would instruct them. The youths went to the Centurion, who related to them the cure of his servant. The three Chaldeans returned from Capernaum to Bethany and thence to Sikdor, where they gathered together the other converts, and with them and their treasures went to join King Mensor.

Early on the morning of March 11, Jesus went to the Temple with about thirty disciples. He taught concerning his approaching suffering. Later, he returned to Bethany. On the next day, he taught again in the Temple and stayed in Jerusalem overnight. The next morning, all the disciples accompanied Jesus as he went to the Temple. There were several selling their wares in one of the forecourts to the Temple. Jesus commanded them to leave. As they hesitated, he himself began to gather their things together, and some people carried them away. Later, in the afternoon, Jesus went to the house of John Mark. As the Sabbath began, he returned to the Temple. After the Jews had finished their sacred services, Jesus again taught in the Temple and prolonged his instruction late into the night. In it he made frequent allusions to his journey among the pagans, so that it could be easily understood how good they were and how willing they were to receive his teachings. In support of his words, he noted the recent arrival of the three Chaldeans. They had not seen Jesus when he was in Sikdor, but they had heard of his doctrine, and were so impressed by it that they had journeyed to Bethany for more instruction. He taught until late and stayed in Jerusalem that night.

The following day, March 14, Jesus cordoned off part of the teaching hall in the Temple for himself, the twelve, and his disciples. He taught them concerning their future tasks. During the last part of his discourse, he placed the twelve in pairs before him. With Judas Iscariot, he spoke but few words. Treason was already in Judas' heart. He was becoming angry, and had already had an interview with the Pharisees. On the next day, Jesus taught again in the Temple concerning his approaching suffering. The disciples were downcast.

On March 16, Jesus taught for about four hours in the Temple. Once again, he described what would happen to him and how many of the disciples would forsake him. He spoke of his forthcoming triumphant entry into Jerusalem and said that he would then remain with them for fifteen days. The disciples did not understand the "fifteen days" and believed that he meant a longer period. Jesus repeated "three times five days."

On the following day, the Scribes and Pharisees, having been greatly disturbed by Jesus' teaching in the Temple, met at the house of Caiaphas, the high priest. They proclaimed that henceforth it was forbidden for anyone to harbor Jesus or the disciples in their homes or anywhere else. Jesus went to Bethany to stay with the Apostle Lazarus.

On the next day, in a basement room in the Apostle Lazarus' castle, Jesus told the Apostle Lazarus, Peter, James, and John the son of Zebedee that tomorrow would be the day of his triumphant entry into Jerusalem. The remaining of the twelve came and when all were gathered together, Jesus spoke with them at length. Then he went to a room where the Blessed Virgin Mary and six other holy women were gathered. He began his instruction by speaking of the Garden of Eden, the Fall of Adam and Eve, the Promise of a Redeemer, the progress of evil, and the small number of faithful laborers in the garden of God. From this, he went on to the parable of a king who owned a magnificent garden. A splendidly dressed lady came to him, and pointed out near his own garden a second garden of aromatic shrubs, which belonged to a good, devout man. She said to the king: "Since this man has left the country, you should purchase his garden and plant it with aromatic shrubs. But the king wanted to plant garlic and similar strong smelling herbs in the poor man's garden, although the owner looked upon it as a sacred spot in which he desired to see only the finest aromatics. The king caused the good man to be called, and proposed that he should remove from the place or sell his garden to him. The good man cultivated his garden carefully and was desirous of keeping it. But he had to suffer great persecutions. His enemies went even so far as to attempt to stone him in his own garden, and he fell quite sick. But at last the king with all his glory came to naught, while the good man, his garden, and all belonging to him prospered and increased. Jesus explained this parable as having reference to paradise, the fall of man, redemption, the kingdom of this world, and the Lord's vineyard in it. The parable signified also that as sin and death had begun in a garden, so the passion of him who had taken upon himself the sins of the world would begin in a garden, and after satisfying for the same, the victory over death would be gained by his resurrection in a garden. After this they all had a meal together.

Early on the morning of March 19, Jesus instructed Silas and Eremenzear to go to Jerusalem, not by the main road, but along a secondary route via Bethphage. They were commissioned to make the road passable by opening the hedges and removing the barriers. The two set out on their journey, opening the hedges and removing all obstructions from the way. In Jerusalem, the vendors and people, whom Eremenzear and Silas had told that morning to clear the way because the Lord would be coming, began straightaway and most joyfully to adorn the road. They tore up the pavement and planted trees, the top branches of which they bound together to form an arch, and then hung them with all kinds of yellow fruit like very large apples.

Jesus said that they would find a donkey and a foal in front of an inn at Bethphage and that they should tether the donkey to a fence. If asked what they were doing, they should reply that the Lord had need of these animals.

After the youths had been gone for some time, Jesus divided the disciples into two groups. Sending the older disciples on ahead, Jesus followed with the twelve and the younger disciples. The Blessed Virgin Mary, accompanied by six other holy women, followed at a distance. As soon as the two disciples that were waiting near Bethphage spied the procession coming, they hurried forward to meet it, taking with them the two animals. The she-ass was covered with trappings that hung to its feet, the head and tail alone being visible. Jesus now put on the beautiful, festal robe of fine white wool that one of the disciples had brought with him for that purpose. He took his seat on the larger donkey. The twelve and the disciples bore branches from palm trees.

As the procession moved forward, all began to sing, and the people of Bethphage, who had gathered around the two disciples while they were awaiting Jesus' coming, followed after like a swarm. Jesus reminded the disciples of what he had previously told them to notice, namely, those that would spread their garments in his path, those that would break off branches from the trees, and those that would render him the double honor, for these last would devote themselves and their worldly goods to his service. Crowds came pouring out of the city to meet the twelve and the disciples, who were approaching with songs and canticles. At this juncture, several aged priests in the insignia of their office stepped out into the road and brought the procession to a standstill. The unexpected movement silenced the singing. The priests called upon Jesus to say what he meant by such proceedings on the part of his followers, and why he did not prohibit this noise and excitement. Jesus answered that if his followers were silent, the stones on the road would cry out. At these words, the priests retired.

Many among the crowd that followed Jesus to the Temple not only broke off branches from the trees, but snatched off their mantles and spread them down, singing and shouting all the while. The road was so quickly covered with branches, garments, and carpets that the procession moved on quite softly through the triumphal arches that spanned the space between the walls on either side. The news spread quickly of the procession of Jesus and the disciples into the city, and people came from everywhere to see it. There was great jubilation.

As Jesus came near Jerusalem and he beheld the city, he wept. When he arrived at the city gate, the jubilation grew. Jesus rode up to the Temple and dismounted there. To move from the city gate to the Temple, although a distance of about a half an hour, the procession took three hours. By this time the Pharisees had ordered all of the houses, as well as the city gate, to be closed, so that when Jesus dismounted before the Temple, and the disciples wanted to take the animals back to where they had found them, they were obliged to wait inside the gate until evening. The holy women returned to Bethany that evening, followed later by Jesus and the twelve.

The next day, Friday, March 20, as Jesus and the twelve made their way to Jerusalem, Jesus was hungry. This was a hunger to convert the people and to fulfill his mission. As he passed by a fig tree, he cursed it because it had no fruit.[1] The fig tree symbolized the old law and the vine the new law. Then Jesus said, "Those who would not acknowledge him would no longer bear fruit." After that Jesus went to the Temple. Many vendors were again selling their wares in the forecourt. Jesus drove them all out.

He taught in the Temple. At this time, some travelers from Greece told Philip that they wished to see Jesus. Philip spoke with Andrew, who told Jesus. The latter replied that he would meet them on the road between the city gate and the house of John Mark when he should have left the Temple to return to Bethany. After this interruption, Jesus continued his teaching. He was very much troubled and then, with folded hands, he raised his eyes to heaven. A flash of light descended upon him from a resplendent cloud, and a loud report was heard. The crowd standing there heard it and said that it was thunder. Others said, "An angel has spoken to him." Jesus answered, "This voice has come for your sake, not for mine." Later, Jesus left the Temple and disappeared into the crowd.

He went to John Mark's house, where he met and spoke with the travelers from Greece. They were good and well-respected people. Hearing Jesus' words, they were converted. In fact, these Greeks were among the first to become baptized by the disciples after Pentecost. Jesus then went to Bethany for the beginning of the Sabbath. On reaching Bethany, Jesus and the twelve went to the public house of Simon, the healed leper, where a meal awaited them. Mary Magdalene, filled with compassion for Jesus' fatiguing exertions, met the Lord at the door. She wore a penitential robe and girdle, her flowing hair concealed by a black veil. She cast herself at his feet and with her hair wiped from them the dust. She did it openly before all, and many were scandalized at her conduct. After Jesus and the disciples had prepared themselves for the Sabbath, that is, put on the garments prescribed and prayed under the lamp, they stretched themselves at table for the meal. At the end of the meal, Mary Magdalene came up to Jesus from behind and poured a vial of costly ointment upon his head

---

1   There are two interpretations of this particular action. The gospel versions in Mark and Matthew focus on Jesus's physical hunger, whereas the visionary record describes the hunger as related to his earthly mission.

and feet. She then dried his feet with her hair. Judas was incensed by this, but Jesus excused Mary Magdalene on account of her love. That night, Judas, full of chagrin, hurried back to Jerusalem. He was torn by envy and avarice, running in the darkness over Mount Olivet, and a sinister glare surrounded him, as if the devil were lighting his steps. He hurried to the house of Caiaphas, and spoke a few words at the door. He could not stay long in any one place. Then he ran to the house of John Mark. The disciples frequently lodged there, so Judas pretended that he had come from Bethany for that purpose.

While Jesus was teaching in the Temple on the morning of Saturday, March 21, some priests and Scribes came up and asked him, "By what authority are you doing these things?" Jesus answered, "I will also ask you a question; and if you tell me the answer, then I will also tell you by what authority I do these things." Then he asked them by what authority had John the Baptizer baptized. When they would not answer him, he replied that neither would he tell them by what authority he acted.

In the afternoon instruction, Jesus introduced the parable about the vineyard owner who had two sons. Later he told the parable concerning the rejection of the cornerstone by the builders. The Pharisees were enraged at Jesus' words and wanted to capture him, but they did not do so because of the people. That evening after the close of the Sabbath, Jesus returned to Bethany.

The next day Jesus taught in Bethany in the morning. Later he went to the Temple, where he taught for about three hours. He told the parable of the king who gave a marriage feast. That evening, after the close of the Sabbath, Jesus returned to Bethany.

On the following day, after teaching in Bethany, Jesus went to the Temple to teach there. As he mounted the teacher's chair in the Circular Hall, five men who were in league with the Pharisees and the Herodians, pressed up through the aisle from the door to the chair and asked him if they ought to pay tribute to Caesar. Jesus, aware of their malice, replied, "Why are you putting me to the test? Show me the coin of tribute." Where-upon one of them drew a large yellow coin from his breast pocket. Jesus said to them, "Whose head is this?" They answered, "Caesar's." Then

Jesus told them that they should render to Caesar the things that are Caesar's, and to God the things that are God's. Upon hearing his reply, they were amazed and they withdrew from him.

That afternoon, seven Sadducees came to him and questioned him about the resurrection of the dead. They brought forth the case of a woman who had had seven husbands and asked, "In the resurrection whose wife would she be?" Jesus answered that after the resurrection there would no longer be any sexual relations or marrying. He added that God is the God of the living and not of the dead. His hearers were astounded at his teaching.

The Pharisees left their seats and conferred together. One who was named Manasses and who held an office in the Temple modestly asked Jesus to tell him which one of the ten commandments is the greatest. Jesus responded that *love* is the highest commandment. Whereupon Manasses highly praised him. Then Jesus indicated that the Kingdom of God was not far from him. Jesus closed his discourse by asking the Pharisees two questions: "What do you think of the Messiah? Whose son is he?" They said to him, "David's son." He said to them, "How is it then that David in composing a psalm calls the Messiah Lord? If David calls the Messiah Lord, how can he be his son?" All were dumbfounded; they had nothing to reply. Nor from that time forward did any have the temerity to ask him any more questions.

When Jesus left the Temple, one of the disciples asked him, "What did you mean when you said to Manasses, 'You are not far from the Kingdom of God'?" Jesus answered that Manasses would become a follower of him, but that the disciples should be silent on this subject. From that hour Manasses took no part against Jesus. He lived in retirement until the Ascension, when he declared himself a believer and joined the disciples. That evening, Jesus and the twelve dined with the Apostle Lazarus, and Jesus taught until late that night.

On Tuesday, March 24, Jesus taught in Bethany and then went to the Temple. This morning the Pharisees were not present and he was able to teach the twelve and the disciples undisturbed. They asked him about the meaning of the words, "Thy kingdom come." Jesus spoke at length about this. He also said that he and the Father were one. And that he would be going to the Father. The disciples asked, "Why, if he and the Father were one, did he need to go to the Father?" Jesus spoke of his mission, saying that he would withdraw from humanity, from the flesh, and that whoever—with him, through him, and in him—separated himself from his own fallen nature, would at the same time commend himself to the Father. The twelve were deeply moved by these words and cried out joyfully and full of enthusiasm, "Lord! We will spread your Kingdom to the end of the world!" Jesus responded that whoever spoke like this would accomplish nothing. They should never boast, "I have driven out devils in your name!" or "I have done this and that!" In addition, they should not carry out their work publicly.

Then he told them that the last time he had left them, he had done many things in secret, but that they had at the same time insisted he should go to Nazareth although the Jews there, on account of the raising of Lazarus, wanted to kill him. But how then would all things be accomplished?

After midday, the Scribes and Pharisees crowded in such numbers around Jesus that the disciples were pushed to some distance from him. He spoke severely against the Pharisees. He added during his stern lecture, "You shall not arrest me now, because my hour has not yet come." At this the Pharisees left the Temple. It was already dark when Jesus made his way back to Bethany

On Wednesday, March 25, Jesus spent the whole day with the Apostle Lazarus, the holy women, and the twelve. During the morning, he taught the holy women. Then around three o'clock in the afternoon a great repast was served in the subterranean dining room, after which they prayed together. Jesus spoke of the nearness of the time of delivery of the Son of Man, saying, too, that he would be betrayed. Peter asked why he always spoke as if one of them would betray him, as he, Peter, could testify for the twelve that they would not betray him. Peter spoke boldly, as if his honor had been attacked. Jesus replied with more warmth than usual, more than had appeared when he said to Peter, "Get thee behind me, Satan!" Jesus answered that if they were not to receive his grace and prayer, they would all fall, and in his hour of reckoning they would all forsake him. Jesus also said that he would send them the Holy Spirit who would open up their understanding. He spoke of the coming of a time of tribulation, when all would be filled with fear, and he referred to a woman in the pangs of giving birth. He spoke of the beauty of the human soul, created in God's image, and how wonderful it is to save souls and lead them to their salvation. He taught until late into the night. That night, Nicodemus and one of Simeon's sons came secretly from Jerusalem in order to see him.

Early on the morning of Thursday, March 26, Jesus went to the Temple. Today was a day of sacrifice for all who wanted to purify themselves for the Feast of the Passover. Jesus and the twelve waited in the Temple and watched the people coming with their contributions for the treasury. The last person was a poor widow. It was not possible to see what the people contributed, but Jesus knew what she had given. He said to the disciples that she had given more than anyone else had, for she had given all that she had.

That afternoon Jesus taught in the Temple. Addressing some Pharisees, he said that they should not expect a peaceful Passover this year; they would not know where they should hide themselves; all of the blood of the prophets they had murdered would be upon their heads. He also said that the prophets would rise from their graves and that the earth would quake. Later, Jesus went with the disciples to the Mount of Olives. On the way, a disciple showed him the Temple and spoke of its beauty. Jesus answered that not one stone would be left upon another. On the Mount of Olives, Jesus sat down and some of the twelve asked him when the Temple would be destroyed. He spoke of his second coming. The last words he spoke here were, "Blessed are they who persevere until the end."

On Friday, March 27, Jesus, the twelve, and the disciples returned to the Mount of Olives early in the morning. He spoke of the destruction of Jerusalem and the end of the world. He also referred to his betrayal, saying that the Pharisees were longing to see the betrayer again. Judas listened with a smile. Jesus also warned the twelve not to be burdened with worldly cares. Later, he taught in the Temple, employing the parables of the ten virgins [see April 21, 31] and of the talents [see May 21, 32]. He also repeated his words to the Pharisees concerning the shedding of the blood of the prophets [see March 26, 33]. Jesus then spent the night at a place near the foot of the Mount of Olives.

Early on the morning of Saturday, March 28, Jesus taught the twelve and the disciples at the place at the foot of the Mount of Olives where he had spent the night. Then he went to the Temple. There he spoke of his departure, saying that he was going to the Father. He described how the Fall into sin had begun in a garden and that it would end in a garden. His enemies would lay their hands on him in a garden. They had wanted to kill him, following the raising of Lazarus. He had gone away in order that everything could be fulfilled. He characterized the journey he had made after the raising of Lazarus by dividing it into three parts: to the tent city of the kings, to the birthplace of Abraham, and to Egypt. He spoke also of Eve and said plainly that he was the savior who would free human beings from the power of sin.

On Sunday, March 29, Jesus went with the disciples across the Kidron Brook to Gethsemane. He pointed out to the twelve where he would be seized and added that here they would forsake him. Jesus was very downcast as they went toward Bethany. That evening, they took a meal together at the house of the Apostle Lazarus.

Early on the morning of Monday, March 30, Jesus went with the disciples to Jerusalem. In the Temple, he spoke of union and separation. He used the analogy of fire and water, which cannot be mixed. When water does not overpower fire, the flames become greater and more powerful. He spoke of persecution and martyrdom. By the flames of fire, he was referring to those disciples who would remain true to him, and by water he meant those that would leave him and seek the abyss. He spoke also of the mingling of milk and water; this symbolizes an inner union that cannot be separated. With this he meant his union with them. He referred to the mild and nourishing power of milk. He also spoke of the union of human beings in marriage. He said that there are two kinds of marriage: that of the flesh, in which the couple is separated at death; and that of the spirit, in which they remain united beyond death. He also spoke of the bridegroom and of the church as his bride and went on to refer to the union with them through the Last Supper, which could never be dissolved. He spoke also of the baptism of John the Baptizer, which would be replaced by the baptism of the Holy Spirit. He promised he would soon send the Holy Spirit, and he gave instructions to the disciples to baptize all who came to them to be baptized. That evening he returned to Bethany.

Tuesday, March 31, was the last time Jesus taught in the Temple. He spoke of the truth and of the necessity of fulfilling what one teaches. He wished to bring his teaching to fulfillment. It was not enough to believe; one must practice one's faith. Thus, he would bring his teaching to fulfillment by going to the Father. Before leaving his disciples, however, he wished to bestow on them all that he had; not money or property, which he did not have, but his power and his forces. These he wanted to give them, and also to found an intimate union with them to the end of the world, a more perfect union than the present one. He asked them to become united with one another as limbs of one body. By this, Jesus referred to what was to be accomplished through the Last Supper, but without mentioning it. He also said that the Blessed Virgin Mary would remain with them for a number of years after his ascension to the Father. As he left the Temple that evening, he took leave of it, saying that he would never enter it again in this body. This was so moving that the twelve and the disciples cast themselves down on the ground and wept. Jesus also wept. It was dark as he made his way back to Bethany.

Early on the morning of Wednesday, April 1, many disciples assembled at the home of the Apostle Lazarus in Bethany to hear Jesus teach. In all, about sixty people were gathered together. Toward three o'clock that afternoon, tables were prepared for a meal at the house of Simon the leper. At the meal, Jesus and the twelve served. Jesus passed from one table to the other, exchanging words with the disciples as he went. The Blessed Virgin Mary was indescribably sad, as Jesus had told her that morning of the nearness of his approaching death. Jesus also spoke with the disciples of this, saying that one of them would betray him to the Pharisees for a sum of money. The disciples wept bitterly and were so downcast that they could no longer eat. But Jesus bid them to partake of the food. He also gave instructions as to what they should do and where they should go after his death.

At the end of the meal, while Jesus was teaching, Mary Magdalene entered the room bearing an ointment that she had bought in Jerusalem that morning. She cast herself down at Jesus' feet, weeping, and anointed his feet with the costly ointment. Then she dried his feet with her hair. Some of the disciples were irritated by this interruption. Jesus broke off what he was saying, and said, "Do not take offense at this woman!" Then he spoke quietly with her. Mary Magdalene took the remaining ointment and poured it upon his head and the fragrance filled the room. Some of the disciples muttered at this. Mary Magdalene, who was veiled, wept as she made her way from the room. As she was about to pass Judas, he held out his arm and blocked the way. He scolded her on account of the waste of money, saying that it could have been given to the poor. However, Jesus said that she should be allowed to go, adding that she had anointed him in preparation for his death and burial, and that afterwards she would not be able to do so again. He said that wherever the Gospel would be taught, her deed and also the disciples muttering would be remembered.

Judas was furious and thought to himself that he could no longer put up with this kind of thing. He withdrew quietly and then ran all the way to Jerusalem. It was dark, but he did not stumble. Satan was with him all the time, red, thin-bodied, and angular. He was before him and behind him, as if lighting the way for him.

In Jerusalem the High priests and the Pharisees were still gathered together. Judas did not enter their assembly. Two of them went out and spoke with him in the courtyard below. When he told them he was ready to deliver Jesus and asked what they would give for him, they showed great joy, and returned to announce it to the rest of the council. After a while, one came out again and made an offer of thirty pieces of silver. Judas wanted to receive them at once, but they would not give them to him. They offered hands as a pledge of the contract, on both sides tearing something from their clothing. Judas then ran back to Bethany and rejoined the others. That night Nicodemus came from Jerusalem to speak with Jesus, and he returned to Jerusalem before the break of day.

Thursday, April 2, being Nissan 13 in the Jewish calendar, was the day prior to the Day of Preparation for the Festival of the Passover. Shortly before daybreak Jesus called Peter and John the son of Zebedee and gave them instructions concerning the preparation for the Passover feast in the Coenaculum. Heli showed Peter and John the room for the Last Supper. The two then went to the house of the deceased priest Simeon, and one of Simeon's sons accompanied them to the market place, where they obtained four lambs to be sacrificed for the meal. They also went to Veronica's house and fetched the chalice to be used that evening for the institution of the Holy Communion. This chalice was a very wonderful and mysterious vessel that had lain in the Temple for a long time among other old and precious things, whose use and origin had even been forgotten. It was stowed away in a chest along with other objects no longer in use, and when discovered was sold to some antiquaries. The chalice and all the vessels belonging to it were afterwards bought by Veronica.

When Jesus made known to the Blessed Virgin Mary what was about to happen to him, she besought him in touching terms to let her die with him. But he exhorted her to bear her grief more calmly than the other women, telling her at the same time that he would rise again, and he named the spot upon which he would appear to her. This time she did not shed so many tears, though she was sad beyond expression. There was something awe-inspiring in her deep gravity.

The other holy women, the Apostle Lazarus, and Jesus went to Jerusalem with the remaining nine of the twelve and a group of seven disciples. The disciples went to the Coenaculum to help with the preparations there, while Jesus walked with the nine of the twelve, teaching as he went, from the Mount of Olives to Mount Calvary and back again to the Valley of Josaphat. During the whole walk, Jesus gave uninterrupted instructions. Among other things, he told them that until now he had given them his bread and his wine, but that today he would give them his flesh and his blood. He would bestow upon them all that he had. His disciples did not comprehend his words—they thought that he was speaking of the Paschal lamb.

Here they were met by Peter and John, who summoned them to the Passover feast. Judas arrived just before the meal began. Jesus dined with the twelve in the main hall of the Coenaculum; two groups of twelve disciples, each with a "house father," ate in separate side rooms. The housefather of the first group, comprising the older disciples, was Nathanael, and that of the second group was Eliachim, the son of Cleophas and Mary Heli and the brother of Mary Cleophas. He had been a disciple of John the Baptizer. In one of the side buildings of the Coenaculum, the holy women took their meal.

At the start of the Paschal Feast, Simeon's son held the lamb's head up, and Jesus struck it in the neck with a knife, which he handed to Simeon's son that he might complete the slaughter. Jesus appeared timid in wounding the lamb, as if it cost him pain. His movement was quick, his manner grave. The blood was caught in a basin, and the attendants brought a branch of hyssop, which Jesus dipped into it. Then stepping to the door of the hall, he signed the two posts and the lock with the blood, and stuck the bloody branch above the lintel. He then uttered some solemn words, saying among other things, "The destroying angel shall pass by here. A new era and a new sacrifice are now about to begin. They shall last till the end of the world."

They then proceeded to the Paschal hearth at the end of the hall. There they found a fire already lighted. Jesus sprinkled the hearth with blood and consecrated it as an altar. Then followed by the disciples, Jesus walked around the Coenaculum singing psalms and consecrated it as a new temple. Meanwhile, Simeon's son had prepared the lamb. It along with the other three lambs that had been brought from the Temple were placed in the oven to be roasted.

Jesus ordered some water to be brought him in the anteroom. Standing in the midst of the twelve, he spoke to them long and solemnly. When the discourse was ended, Jesus sent John and James the Lesser to bring the water from the anteroom, and directed the others to place the seats in a half-circle. In the meantime, Jesus retired to the anteroom to lay aside his mantle, gird up his robe, and tie around himself a towel, one end of which he allowed to hang.

While these preparations were being made, the twelve got into a kind of dispute as to who among them should have the first place. Jesus, still in the anteroom, commanded John to take a basin, and James the Lesser a leathern bottle of water. Entering the hall, Jesus in a few words reproved the twelve for the strife that had risen among them. He said that he himself was their servant, and that they should take their places on the seats for him to wash their feet. Jesus went from one to another and, from the basin held under them by John, with his hand scooped up water over the feet presented to him. During the whole of the Paschal Supper, Jesus' demeanor was most touching and gracious, and at this humble washing of his disciples' feet, he was full of love. He did not perform this action as if it were a mere ceremony, but like a sacred gesture of love springing straight from the heart. By doing so, he wanted to give expression to the love that burned within him.

In profound recollection and prayer, Jesus next broke the bread into several morsels and laid them one over another on the plate. With the tip of his finger, he broke off a scrap from the first morsel and let it fall into the chalice. At that same moment, the Blessed Virgin Mary received it, although she was not present in that room. Again Jesus prayed. His words, glowing with fire and light, came from his mouth and entered all of the twelve, excepting Judas. Jesus then took the plate and said, "Take and eat. This is my body, which is given for you." While saying these words, he stretched forth his right hand over the plate, as if giving a blessing; and as he did so, a brilliant light emanated from him. His words were luminous as was also the bread, which as a body of light entered the mouths of the disciples. All of them were penetrated with light; Judas alone remained in darkness. It was at this point that Jesus said to Judas, "What you are about to do, do quickly." Soon after this, Judas left the Coenaculum.

Jesus now gave to the eleven disciples an instruction full of mystery. He told them how they were to preserve the Blessed Sacrament in memory of him until the end of the world. He taught them the necessary forms for making it, communicating it, and in what manner they were by degrees to teach and publish this mystery.

Then he instructed them upon the priesthood, the sacred unction, and the preparation of the chrism. After that, Jesus anointed Peter and John, on whose hands at the institution of the Blessed Sacrament he had poured the water that had flowed over his own, and who had drunk from the chalice in his hand. Then Jesus communicated to the eleven that after they had received the Holy Spirit, they were to consecrate bread and wine for the first time, and anoint the other disciples.

CHAPTER 20

THE PASSION OF CHRIST JESUS

APRIL 3, 33 CE

When Christ Jesus left the Coenaculum with the eleven, his soul was already troubled and his sadness on the increase. He led the eleven to the Mount of Olives by an unfrequented path through the Valley of Josaphat. It was about nine o'clock when Jesus reached the Garden of Gethsemane with the disciples. Darkness had fallen upon the earth, but the moon was lighting up the sky. Jesus was very sad. He announced to the eleven the approach of danger, and they became uneasy. Jesus asked eight of the disciples to remain in the Garden. He took Peter, John the son of Zebedee, and James the Greater with him, crossed the road, and went on for a few minutes, until he reached the Garden of Olives farther up the mountain. He said to the three disciples, "Remain here and watch with me. Pray so that you do not enter into temptation!" And they stayed in that place. He turned to the left from the disciples and plunged down into a grotto formed by an overhanging rock.

When Jesus left the disciples, a large number of frightful figures surrounded him in an ever-narrowing circle. He withdrew trembling into the back of the cave, like one seeking shelter from a violent tempest, and there he prayed. To make satisfaction for the origin and development of all kinds of sin, Jesus, through love for us sinners, received into his own heart the root of all atonements. Thus entirely given up to his humanity, he fell on his face, calling upon God in unspeakable sorrow and anguish. From that point in the heavens in which the sun appears between ten and eleven in the morning, a narrow path of light streamed toward Jesus, and on it a file of angels come down to him imparting fresh strength and vigor. The rest of the grotto was filled with the frightful and horrible visions of sin, and with evil spirits mocking and tempting him. Jesus took all upon himself. At first Jesus knelt calmly in prayer, but after a while his soul shrank in affright at the multitude and heinousness of humanity's sins and ingratitude against God. So overpowering was his sadness, the agony of heart that fell upon him that, trembling and shuddering, he prayed imploringly, "Abba, Father, if it be possible, remove this chalice from me. My Father, all things are possible for you. Take this chalice from me!" Then recovering himself, he added, "But not what I will, but what you will." His will and that of the Father were one. Now that through love he had delivered himself to the weakness of his human nature, however, he shuddered at the thought of death.[1]

It was about half past ten o'clock when Jesus staggered to his feet, bathed in sweat and often falling, tottered rather than walked to where the three disciples were awaiting him. When he found the disciples sleeping, he clasped his hands and, sinking down by them from grief and exhaustion, he said, "Peter, are you asleep?" At these words, they awoke and raised him up. In his spiritual dereliction, he said, "What! Could you not watch with me one hour?" When they found him so terrified, so pale, trembling, and saturated with sweat, shuddering and shaking, his voice feeble and stammering, they were altogether at a loss what to think. Had he not appeared surrounded by the light so well known to them, they would not have recognized him as Jesus. John the son of Zebedee said to him, "Master! What has befallen you? Shall I call the other disciples? Shall we take flight?" Jesus answered, "Were I to live, teach, and work miracles for another thirty-three years, it would not suffice for the accomplishment of what I have to fulfill before this time tomorrow. Do not call the other eight disciples. I have left them where they are, because they could not

---

1   Dr. Rudolf Steiner has a different interpretation of this event. He states, "Why does Jesus become distressed? He does not tremble before the cross. That goes without saying. He is distressed above all in the face of this question, 'Will those whom I have with me here stand the test of this moment when it will be decided whether they will accompany me in their souls, whether they will experience everything with me until the cross?'" See Steiner, *The Gospel of St. Mark*, pp. 168–69.

see me in this suffering state without being completely overcome. But you, who have seen the Son of Man transfigured, may also see him in this hour of darkness and complete dereliction of soul; nevertheless, watch and pray, so that you do not fall into temptation. For the spirit is willing but the flesh is weak." In his overpowering sorrow, he said other things to them, and remained with them about a quarter of an hour.[2]

Jesus returned to the grotto. The three disciples, seeing him leave them thus, stretched out their hands after him, wept, threw themselves into one another's arms, and asked, "What does this mean? What is the matter with Him? He is perfectly desolate!" Then covering their heads, they began in great anxiety to pray. The eight disciples however, who had remained at the entrance, did not sleep. The anxiety that marked all of Jesus' last actions on that evening greatly disquieted them, and they wandered around Mount Olivet seeking a place to hide.

When Jesus went back into the grotto carrying his load of sadness with him, he cast himself face downward on the ground, his arms extended, and prayed to his Father in Heaven. Now began for his soul a new struggle, which lasted three quarters of an hour. Angels came and showed him in a long series of visions and in all its extent what he would have to endure for the atonement of sin. He understood not only the consequence of every species of concupiscence, but also its own peculiar expiatory chastisement, the significance of all the instruments of torture connected with it; so that not only the thought of the instrument made him shudder, but also the sinful rage of him that invented it, the fury and wickedness of all that had ever used it, and the impatience of all, whether innocent or guilty, who had been tortured with it. All these afflictions Jesus perceived in an interior contemplation, and the sight filled him with such horror that a bloody sweat started from this pores. Now these visions disappeared, however, and the angels with their soothing compassion retired from him, to whose soul a new sphere of agony, more violent even than the last, opened up.

---

2   The actual circumstances may well be more complicated. For a contemporary view by a stigmatic who became so in 2004 CE, consult von Halle *And if He Has Not Been Raised...*, pp. 92–120.

Now, he beheld the sufferings, temptations, and wounds of the future church, and he saw the ingratitude of humanity. The scandals of the ages, down to our own day and even to the end of the world, passed before Jesus' soul in an immense succession of visions: all forms of error, proud fallacies, mad fanaticism, false prophecies, obstinate heresies, all kinds of wickedness. Satan was present under many frightful forms, dragging away and strangling under the eyes of Jesus those redeemed by his blood. While these visions were passing before him, the voice of Satan was constantly heard whispering, "See! Can you undergo such suffering in the sight of such ingratitude?"

Jesus saw and felt in this distressing vision the whole weight of the poisonous tree of disunion with all its branches and fruits, which will continue to rend itself asunder until the end of time when the wheat will be gathered into the barn and the chaff cast into the fire. It was after this last vision, in which the armed bands had lacerated his flesh, that he turned as if fleeing out of the grotto, and went again to his disciples. But his step was far from secure. He walked bowed, like one tottering under a great burden. He was covered with wounds, and he fell with every step.

When he reached the three disciples, he did not, as on the first occasion, find them lying on their side asleep; they had sunk back on their knees with covered heads. Worn out with grief, anxiety, and fatigue, they had fallen asleep; but when Jesus approached, trembling and groaning, they awoke. They gazed on him with their weary eyes, but they did not at once recognize him, for he was changed beyond the power of words to express. The disciples sprang up, grasped him under the arms, and supported him tenderly. On the morrow, he said that he was going to die. In another hour, he continued, his enemies would seize him, drag him before the courts of justice, abuse him, deride him, scourge him, and put him to death in the most horrible manner. He begged them to console the Blessed Virgin Mary. He recounted to them in bitter anguish all that he would have to suffer until evening of the next day, and again begged them to comfort the Blessed Virgin Mary and Mary Magdalene.

When he wanted to return to the grotto, he had not the power to do so. John and James had to lead him. When he entered it, the disciples left him and returned to their own place. It was then a quarter past eleven. Again Jesus prayed in the grotto. He had conquered the natural repugnance to suffer. Now the abyss opened before him and, as if on a pathway of light, he saw a long flight of steps leading down to limbo. There he beheld Adam and Eve, all the patriarchs and prophets, the just of the Old Law, the parents of the Nathan Mary, and the parents of John the Baptizer. They were with longing so intense, awaiting his coming into that nether world, that at the sight of his loving heart they grew strong and courageous. His death was to open Heaven to these languishing captives. For him they were sighing! After Jesus had with deep emotion gazed upon these worthies belonging to former ages, the angels pointed out to him the multitudes of future saints who, joining their labors to the merits of his passion would through him be united to his Father in Heaven.

Now, however, these consoling pictures disappeared, and the angels displayed before his eyes all the scenes of his approaching passion. At the close of these visions of the passion, Jesus sank prostrate on his face like one in the throes of death. It was now dark in the grotto. At this point an angel swept down toward him. In stature he was taller, in figure more distinct, and more like a human being. He carried in his hands, and before his breast, a small vessel shaped like a chalice. Just above it floated a small oval morsel, about the size of a bean, which glowed with a reddish light. The angel hovered over the place where Jesus was lying and stretched forth his hand to him. When Jesus arose, the angel placed the shining morsel in his mouth and gave him to drink from the little luminous chalice. After that the angel disappeared.

Jesus had now voluntarily accepted the chalice of his Passion, and he received new strength. When Jesus returned to the disciples, he found them, as at first, lying on their sides near the wall of the terrace, their heads covered, and asleep. Jesus said to them, "This is not the time to sleep. You should arise and pray, for behold the hour is at hand, and the Son of Man shall be betrayed into the hands of sinners." After that, he said, "Let us go to meet them. I shall deliver myself without resistance into the hands of my enemies."

Judas arranged with the soldiers that he would enter the Garden of Gethsemane before them, kiss, and salute Jesus as a friend and disciple coming to him on some business; then they were to step forward and take him into custody. He wanted to make it appear as if their coming coincided accidentally with his own. He thought that, after the betrayal, he would take flight like the other disciples and be heard of no more. In addition, Judas was desirous that the soldiers should not carry chains and fetters. The soldiers pretended to accede to his wishes. In reality, they regarded him as a dishonorable traitor of whom they had need. Judas was not to be trusted and would be cast off when no longer of use. The twenty soldiers accompanied Judas in a friendly manner until they reached the place where the road divided between the Garden of Gethsemane and the Garden of Olives. Here they refused to allow him to advance alone. They adopted quite another tone, and acted toward him insolently and without respect.

When Jesus with the three disciples went out upon the road between the Garden of Gethsemane and the Garden of Olives, there appeared at the entrance, about twenty paces ahead, Judas and the band of soldiers, between whom a quarrel had arisen. Judas wanted to separate from the soldiers and go forward alone to Jesus. Nevertheless, they would not agree to his proposal. They held him fast, exclaiming, "Not so, friend! You shall not escape us until we have the Galilean!" When Jesus and the three disciples, by the light of the torches, distinguished the armed and wrangling band, Peter wished to repel them by force. However, Jesus told him to hold his peace, and took a few steps with them back to a green plot next to the road. Then Jesus took some steps toward the band and said in a loud and distinct voice, "Whom do you seek?" The leaders answered, "Jesus of Nazareth," whereupon Jesus said, "I am he." But scarcely had he uttered the words when, as if attacked by convulsions, the soldiers crowded back and fell to the ground one upon another. Judas, who was still standing by the soldiers, became more and more embarrassed. Meanwhile the soldiers had risen and approached Jesus and his disciples, awaiting the traitor's sign, the kiss. Peter and the other disciples gathered around Judas and called him a thief and a traitor. He tried to free himself by all kinds of excuses, but just at that moment up came the soldiers with offers of protection, thus openly witnessing against him. Jesus again inquired, "Whom do you seek?" Turning toward him, the leaders again said, "Jesus of Nazareth." Jesus replied once more, "I am he." Then he added, "I have already told you that I am he. If you seek me, let these go." At the words, "I am he," the soldiers fell to the ground a second time. They writhed as if struck with epilepsy, and Judas was again surrounded by the disciples, for they were exasperated with him. Judas was still struggling with the disciples, who were pressing up against the soldiers. The latter turned upon the disciples and freed the traitor, urging him anew to give them the sign agreed upon. They had been ordered to seize none but the one whom Judas would kiss. Judas now approached Jesus, embraced him, and kissed him with the words, "Hail Rabbi." Jesus replied, "Judas, would you betray the Son of Man with a kiss?" The soldiers instantly formed a circle about Jesus and the archers, drawing near, laid hands upon him. Judas wanted at once to flee, but the disciples would not let him. They rushed upon the soldiers, crying out, "Lord, shall we strike with the sword?" Peter, more impetuous that the rest, seized his sword and struck at Malchus, the servant of the high priest, and cut off a piece of his ear. Malchus fell to the ground, thereby increasing the confusion. Jesus said, "Peter, put up your sword. For whoever takes up the sword, shall perish by the sword. Are you not aware that I can ask my Father to send me more than twelve legions of angels? Shall I not drink from the chalice that my Father has given me? How will the scriptures be fulfilled if we do not permit this to be done?" Then he added, "Suffer me to heal this man." Going to Malchus, he touched his ear and prayed. At that moment the ear was healed.

Then Jesus addressed them, "You have come out with spears and clubs, to apprehend me as if I were a murderer. I have daily taught among you in the Temple, and you dared not lay hands upon me; but this is your hour and the hour of darkness." They bound Jesus' hands upon his breast in a cruel manner. They put around his waist a broad girdle armed with sharp points. Around his neck they laid a collar in which were points and other instruments to wound, and from it descended two straps, which were bound to the girdle so tightly that the neck was not free to move. At four points of this girdle were fastened four long ropes, by means of which the executioners could drag the prisoner hither or thither according to their will. Now, after several more torches had been lighted, the pitiable procession was set in motion. First went ten of the guards, then followed the executioners, dragging Jesus by the ropes; next came the scoffing Pharisees, and the ten other soldiers closed the procession. The disciples were still straying about wailing and lamenting, as if bereft of their senses. John the son of Zebedee, however, was following rather closely behind the last of the guards. The Pharisees, seeing him, ordered him to be seized. At this command, some of the guards turned and hurried after him. But he fled from them, and when they laid hold of the linen scarf he wore around his neck, he loosened it quickly and thus effected his escape.

The procession moved on at a hurried pace. When it left the road between the Garden of Olives and the Garden of Gethsemane, it turned for a short distance to the right on the west side of Gethsemane, until it reached a bridge that there crossed the Kidron brook. Even before the procession reached the bridge, Jesus had fallen to the earth twice, owing to the pitiless manner in which he was dragged along and the jerking of the executioners at the ropes. However, when they reached the middle of the bridge, the executioners pushed the fettered Jesus, whom they held fast with the ropes, from the bridge into the Kidron brook, accompanying their brutality with abusive words, as for instance, "Now he can drink his fill." But when pushed into the Kidron, he attempted to drink but was unable because of how he was bound. Jesus had repeatedly fallen to the earth, and he now appeared unable to proceed farther. Taking advantage of this, a compassionate soldier said, "You see for yourselves that the poor man can go no farther. If we are to take him alive before the High priests, we must loosen the cords that bind his hands, that he may be able to support himself when he falls. While the procession halted for the executioners to loosen the cords, another good-hearted soldier brought him a drink of water from a neighboring well. Peter and John the son of Zebedee, who were following the procession at some distance, ran hurriedly when it entered the city to some of the good acquaintances whom John had among the servants of the High priests, to find some way an opportunity of entering the judgment hall into which their master would soon be brought.

As soon as Jesus was taken into custody, Annas and Caiaphas were informed of the fact and they began actively to arrange their plans. The High priests now selected from the lists in their possession those whom they knew to be Jesus' most bitter enemies. These they summoned with the command to gather up, each in his own circle, all the evidence and proofs against Jesus they possibly could, and to bring them to the judgment court. All these now gathered, one after another, in the judgment hall of Caiaphas. There, too, assembled the mass of Jesus' enemies from among the haughty Pharisees and Scribes, along with their suborned witnesses from Jerusalem itself. These emissaries of Satan were brimful of rage against everything holy. All quarters of the city, however, were not aroused, only those parts to which the messengers had brought the invitation to the trial and those in which the Pharisees sought their false witnesses.

It was toward midnight when Jesus was led through the brilliantly lighted courtyard into the palace of Annas. Jesus, still surrounded by a body of the soldiers by whom he had been arrested, was dragged forward several steps by the executioners that held the cords. Jesus stood before Annas pale, exhausted, silent, his head bowed. Annas was full of irony and Jewish pride. He put on a half-laughing appearance, as if he knew nothing of what had taken place, and as if he were greatly surprised to find Jesus in the person of a prisoner brought before him. He addressed him in the following manner, "Ha, look there—Jesus of Nazareth. It is you! Where now are your disciples, your crowd of followers? Where is your kingdom? It appears that things have taken another turn with you! Now, are you silent! Speak, seditious man! Who has given you authority to teach? Speak! What is your doctrine?" At these words, Jesus raised his head, looked at Annas, and replied, "I have spoken openly before the entire world where the Jews have gathered together. I have said nothing in secret. Why do you question me? Ask those who have heard what I have spoken unto them. They know what I have said." The countenance of Annas during this reply of Jesus betrayed scorn and rage. A base menial standing near Jesus remarked this, and he struck Jesus with his open mailed hand! The blow fell full upon Jesus' mouth and cheek, while the scoundrel uttered the words, "Do you answer the high priest so?" Jesus, trembling under the violence of the blow and jerked at the same time by the executioners, one pulling this way, another that, fell sideways on the steps, the blood flowing from his face. With renewed ill-usage, they dragged Jesus up. Annas, still more enraged by Jesus' calm demeanor, summoned the witnesses to come forward and declare whatever they had heard him say. Thereupon the rabble set up a storm of cries and abuse. Annas now called for some writing materials, and with a reed pen wrote a list of words in large letters, each of which contained some accusation against Jesus. Then turning to the soldiers, he said, "Bind his hands and conduct the king to the high priest."

To reach the judgment hall of Caiaphas, one had to pass through a gateway into a spacious exterior court, then through a second gateway into an inner court that, with its walls, surrounded the whole house. Shortly before the arrival of the procession bringing Jesus to the high priest, Peter and John entered the outer court of the house. Through the influence of a servant known to him, John was fortunate enough to make his way through the gate of the great inner court, which because of the crowd was at once closed behind him. When Peter, who had been kept back a little by the crowd, reached the closed gate, the maidservant in charge would not let him pass. John interposed, but Peter would not have gotten in had not Nicodemus and Joseph of Arimathea, who just then sought admittance, said a good word for him. Caiaphas and his counselors were already a long time assembled; many of them had even remained since the departure of Judas and the soldiers. The rage and impatience of Caiaphas had reached such a pitch that, magnificently attired as he was, he descended from his lofty tribunal and went into the outer court, angrily asking whether Jesus would soon come. At last the procession was seen approaching, and Caiaphas returned to his seat.

Scarcely had Jesus passed through the colonnaded entrance and appeared before the Council, when Caiaphas cried out to him, "Have you come, you blasphemer of God, you who disturbs this our sacred night!" When the writing containing the accusations of Annas was read, Caiaphas poured forth a stream of reproaches and abusive epithets against Jesus, while the soldiers standing nearby dragged and pulled him from side to side, crying, "Answer! Open your mouth! Can you not speak!" All this went on while Caiaphas, even more enraged than Annas, vociferated question after question to Jesus who, calm and suffering, kept his eyes lowered, not even glancing at him.

Now began the interrogation of the witnesses. It consisted of nothing but the disorderly cries, the enraged shouts of the bribed populace, or the disposition of some of Jesus' enemies belonging to the exasperated Pharisees and Sadducees. Notwithstanding all their efforts, they were unable to prove any one of their charges. The crowd of witnesses seemed to come forward more for the purpose of deriding Jesus to his face than to render testimony. They contended hotly among themselves, while Caiaphas and some of the counselors did not cease their raillery and taunting expressions.

Nicodemus and Joseph of Arimathea were then called upon to explain how it happened that they had allowed Jesus to eat the Pasch in a supper room belonging to them. Having taken their places before Caiaphas, they proved from written documents that the Galileans, according to an ancient custom, were permitted to eat the Pasch one day earlier than other Jews. The rage of the Pharisees against Nicodemus became still greater when the latter closed his remarks by saying that the members of the Council must feel greatly aggrieved at being called upon to preside over a trial instituted by prejudice so evident, carried on with haste so violent on the night preceding the most solemn of their festivals; and that the gross contradictions of all the witnesses in their presence and before the assembled multitude were to them a positive insult. Caiaphas was now thoroughly exasperated. In spite of the ill treatment bestowed upon Jesus, the contradictory statements of the witnesses and the incomprehensibly silent patience of the accused were beginning to make an impression on many of those present. Some of the witnesses were laughed to scorn. Finally, Caiaphas rose from his seat, went down a couple of steps to Jesus, and said, "Do you have no answer to the testimony against you?" He was vexed that Jesus would not look at him. Then Caiaphas angrily raised his hands and said in a tone full of rage, "I adjure you by the living God that you tell us whether you are the Messiah, the Son of the Most Blessed God." A solemn silence fell upon the clamoring crowd. Jesus, strengthened by God, said in a voice that struck awe into all hearts, "I am! You yourself have said it. And I say to you, soon you shall see the Son of Man sitting on the right hand of the power of God, and coming in the clouds of Heaven!" Caiaphas exclaimed in a loud voice, "He has blasphemed! What need have we of further witnesses? Behold, you have heard the blasphemy, what do you think?" At these words, the whole assembly rose and cried out in a horrid voice, "He is guilty of death! He is guilty of death!" The high priest, addressing the executioners, said, "I deliver this king to you. Render the blasphemer the honors due to him!" After these words, he retired with his council to the round hall behind the tribunal, into which no one could see from the vestibule.

Peter could not remain standing any longer in the judgment hall, for his deep emotion would have betrayed him, nor could he leave without attracting notice. Therefore, he returned to the atrium and took a place in the corner near the fire, around which soldiers and people of all kinds were standing in groups. Peter kept silence; but already the interest he manifested in the proceedings, joined to the expression of deep grief depicted on his countenance, drew upon him the attention of Jesus' enemies. Just at that moment, the woman who had been in charge of the entrance, approached the fire; and as all were prating and jesting at Jesus' expense and that of his disciples, she put in her word and, fixing her eyes upon Peter, said, "You are one of the Galilean's disciples!" Peter, startled and alarmed, and fearing rough treatment from the rude crowd, answered, "Woman, I do not know him! I do not know what you mean. I do not understand you!" With these words, wishing to free himself from further remark, he arose and left the atrium. At that moment, a cock somewhere outside the city crowed.

As Peter was making his way out, another maidservant caught sight of him, and said to the bystanders, "This man, also, was with Jesus of Nazareth." They at once questioned him, "Are you also one of his disciples?" Peter, greatly troubled and perplexed, answered with an oath "Truly, I am not! I do not even know the man!" He hurried through the inner to the exterior court to warn some of his acquaintances whom he saw looking over the wall.

Peter, being allowed to go out, found among them a number of disciples whom anxiety had forced hither from their caves on Mount Hinnom. They went straight up to Peter, and with many tears questioned him about Jesus. However, he was so excited and so fearful of betraying himself that he advised them in a few words to go away, as there was danger to them where they were.

Peter could not rest anywhere. His love for Jesus drove him back into the inner court that surrounded the house. They let him back in again, on account of Nicodemus and Joseph of Arimathea, who had in the first instance procured his admittance. He did not, however, return to the court of the judgment hall, but turning went along to the right until he reached the entrance to the circular hall behind the tribunal. In that hall Jesus was being dragged about and abused by the vile rabble. Peter drew near, trembling. Although he felt himself an object of remark, his anxiety for Jesus drove him through the doorway, which was beset by the crowd watching the outrages heaped upon Jesus. Just then they were dragging Jesus, crowned with straw, around the circle. He cast a glance full of earnest warning upon Peter, a glance that pierced him to the soul. However, still struggling with fear, when he heard from some of the bystanders the words "What fellow is that?" he reentered the court. There, sad and distracted with compassion for Jesus and anxiety for his own safety, he wandered about with loitering steps. At last seeing that he was attracting notice upon himself, he went again into the atrium and took a seat by the fire.

Here he sat a considerable time when some that had seen him outside and noticed his preoccupied and excited manner entered and again directed their attention to him, while referring in slighting terms to Jesus and his affairs. One of them said, "Truly, you also belong to his adherents! You are a Galilean. Your speech betrays you." Peter began to evade the remark and to make his way out of the hall, when the brother of Malchus stepped up to him and said, "What! Did I not see you with him in the Garden of Olives? Did you not wound my brother's ear?" Peter became like one beside himself with terror. While trying to free himself, he began in his impetuous way to curse and swear that he knew not the man, and ended by running out of the atrium into the court that surrounded the house. The cock crowed again. Just at that moment, Jesus was being led from the circular hall and across this court down into a prison under it. He turned toward Peter and cast upon him a glance of mingled pity and sadness. Forcibly, and with terrifying power, the words of Jesus fell upon his heart, "Before the cock crows twice, you will deny me three times!"

When John went to the Blessed Virgin Mary at the residence of the Apostle Lazarus in Jerusalem, he confirmed what she already knew from interior contemplation. She ardently desired to be conducted to where she might be near her suffering Jesus. When now they reached the outer court of Caiaphas' Judgment Hall, the Blessed Virgin Mary, accompanied by John, withdrew into a corner under the gateway leading into the inner court. Her soul, filled with inexpressible sufferings, was with Jesus. She felt that this door alone separated her from Jesus, who was to be led out of the house and into the prison below. Longing to be near her beloved son, the Blessed Virgin Mary asked to be conducted to the door in front of his prison. When the door did open, it was Peter who came through weeping bitterly. This led to a less than ideal exchange between the Blessed Virgin Mary and Peter in which he acknowledged having denied Jesus three times. Then, Peter, like one crazed by grief, hurried out of the court, and fled from the city.

The prison cell into which Jesus was introduced lay under the Judgment Hall of Caiaphas. It was a small, circular vault. Even in this prison, the executioners allowed Jesus no rest. They bound him to a low pillar that stood in the center of the prison, though they would not permit him to lean against it. He was obliged to stagger from side to side on his tired feet, which were wounded and swollen from frequent falls and the strokes of the chains that hung to his knees. They ceased not to mock and outrage him, and when the two executioners in charge were wearied, two others replaced them and new scenes of villainy were enacted.

Standing in his prison, Jesus prayed uninterruptedly for his tormentors. Day was dawning, the day of his infinite sufferings and atonement. Jesus raised his manacled hands to greet the dawning light and clearly and audibly pronounced a prayer to his Father in Heaven. How touchingly Jesus thanked his heavenly Father for this day, which was to accomplish the aim of his life: the salvation of humanity and the fulfillment of his Father's will.

As soon as it was clear daylight, Caiaphas, Annas, the elders and scribes assembled in the great hall to hold a trial that would be perfectly lawful. Trial by night was not legal. It was a large assembly, and business was conducted in a very hurried manner. When they held council against Jesus in order to condemn him to death, Nicodemus, Joseph of Arimathea, and a few others opposed his enemies. The High priests even went so far as to exclude from the Council all those who were in any way well disposed toward Jesus. Caiaphas now ordered poor, abused Jesus, who was drained from want of rest, to be brought from the prison and presented before the Council, so that after the sentence he might without delay be taken to Pilate. Jesus was dragged by the executioners into the judgment hall through the rows of soldiers assembled in front of the house. Caiaphas, full of scorn and fury for Jesus standing before him in so miserable a plight, addressed him thus: "If you are the Anointed of the Lord, the Messiah, tell us!" Then Jesus raised his head and with divine forbearance and solemn dignity said, "If I shall tell you, you will not believe me. And if I shall also ask you, you will not answer me, nor let me go. But hereafter, the Son of Man shall be sitting on the right hand of the power of God."

The members of the Council glanced from one to another and, smiling scornfully, said to Jesus with disdain; "So then, *you* are the Son of God?" With the voice of eternal truth, Jesus answered, "Yes, it is as you say. I am he!" At this word of Jesus all looked at one another saying, "What need is there for further testimony? We ourselves have heard it from his own mouth." They ordered the executioners to bind him again, to place the chain around his neck, and to lead him as a condemned criminal to Pilate.

Judas, the traitor, lurking at no great distance, heard the noise of the advancing procession, and words such as these dropped by stragglers hurrying after it, "They are taking him to Pilate. The Sanhedrin has condemned him to death. The wretch that sold him was one of his own disciples. I should not like to have a share in that deed. Whatever the Galilean may be, he has never delivered a friend for money. In truth, the wretch that sold him deserves to hang!" Then anguish, despair, and remorse began to struggle in the soul of Judas, but all too late. Satan instigated him to flee. Like one bereft of his senses, he rushed into the Temple, where several of the Council and some of the Elders had gone directly after the condemnation of Jesus. Judas tore the bag of silver pieces from his girdle and held it toward the priests with his right hand, while in a voice of agony he cried, "Take back your money. Release Jesus. I recall my contract. I have sinned by betraying innocent blood." Raising their hands, they stepped back before the offered silver, as if to preserve themselves from pollution and said, "We know what we have bought from you, and we find him deserving of death. You have your money. We want none of it!" Their treatment inspired Judas with such rage and despair that he became as one insane. His hair stood on end, with both hands he rent asunder the chain that held the silver pieces together, scattered them in the Temple, and fled from the city. Satan whispered into Judas' ear all manner of torments and incitements for him to kill himself. Overcome by despair, Judas took his girdle and hung himself on a tree.

Pilate, the governor, summoned the high priests to bring forward their accusations. They laid three principal charges against him, for each of which they produced ten witnesses. The first charge they alleged was, "Jesus is a seducer of the people, a disturber of the peace, an agitator." Their second accusation was, "Jesus stirs up the people not to pay tribute to the Emperor." Here, Pilate interrupted them angrily. As one whose office it was to know about such things, he retorted with emphasis, "That is a great lie! I know better than that!" Then the Jews shouted out their third accusation, "Let it be so! This man of low, obscure, and doubtful origin puts himself at the head of a large party and cries woe to Jerusalem. He made a tumultuous entrance into Jerusalem, causing regal honors to be shown to him. Besides this, he teaches that he is the Christ, the Anointed of the Lord, the Messiah, the promised King of the Jews."

The accusation that Jesus, standing before him so poor, so miserable, so disfigured, should give himself out for that Anointed of the Lord, for that King, appeared to Pilate truly ridiculous. However, because the enemies of Jesus had brought forth the charge as injurious to the rights of the Emperor, Pilate caused Jesus to be conducted in his presence for an examination. Pilate regarded Jesus with astonishment as he addressed him, "Are you the King of the Jews?" Jesus answered him solemnly, "My kingdom is not of this world."

Pilate went out again to the terrace. He could not comprehend Jesus, but he knew this much about him, that he was not a king who would prove mischievous to the Emperor, and that he laid no claim to any kingdom of this world. Pilate therefore called down to the High priests below, "I find no kind of crime in this man!" But the accusers, whose rage was on the increase, cried out, "What! You find no guilt in Him? Is it no crime to stir up the people? He has spread his doctrine throughout the whole country, from Galilee up to these parts." When Pilate caught the word *Galilee*, he reflected a moment and then called down, "Is the man from Galilee a subject of Herod?" The accusers answered, "Yes." Pilate then said, "Since he is a Galilean and subject to Herod, take him to Herod. He is here for the feast, and he can judge him at once."

While Jesus was being taken to Herod, Pilate went to see his wife, Claudia Procla. They met at a summerhouse in a terraced garden behind Pilate's palace. Claudia was trembling and agitated. She had a long conversation with Pilate and implored him, by all that was sacred to him, not to injure Jesus. Then she related to him some things she had experienced in a vision she had concerning Jesus the night before. She identified the following elements in that vision: the annunciation to the Solomon Mary, the birth of the Solomon Jesus, the visitation of the magi to the Solomon Holy Family, the flight into Egypt, the massacre of the innocents, the adoration of the Nathan Jesus by the shepherds, the presentation of the Nathan Jesus to the Temple, the prophecies of Simeon and Anna, the temptation of Jesus in the wilderness, and other scenes from the life of Jesus. She endured anguish and sadness as a result of this vision. Besides being something very unusual for her, the vision was impressive and convincing. Pilate was greatly astonished and somewhat troubled by what she related. He wavered uneasily in his mind, but soon yielded to his wife's representations and said, "I have already declared that I find no guilt in Jesus. I shall not condemn him, for I know the utter wickedness of the Jews." He spoke at length of Jesus' bearing toward himself, quieted his wife's fears, and even went so far as to give her a pledge of assurance that he would not condemn him.

Jesus' enemies were much annoyed at this going backward and forward, and they did not cease insulting him and encouraging the executioners to drag him and push him about. Pilate's messenger had announced the coming procession; consequently, Herod was awaiting it. He was seated on a cushioned throne in a large hall surrounded by courtiers and soldiers. He was in an extraordinarily good humor at the thought of being able to institute, before his courtiers and the High priests, a grand judicial inquiry concerning Jesus, in which he might show forth his knowledge before both parties. Herod was very affable to Jesus, he even flattered him and repeated all that he knew of him. At first he asked him several questions, and wanted to see a sign from him. Nevertheless, Jesus answered not a syllable, and quietly kept his eyes cast down. Herod became very much vexed and ashamed before those present. Wishing, however, to conceal his embarrassment, he poured forth a torrent of questions and empty words. To all these questions Herod received no answer from Jesus. The suggestion was made that Jesus would not speak to Herod because of his adulterous connection with Herodias and the murder of John the Baptizer. Herod, although greatly vexed at Jesus' silence, did not permit himself to lose sight of his political ends. He did not wish to pass sentence on one whom Pilate had declared to be without guilt. He ended by overwhelming Jesus with words of scorn and contempt, and said, "Take this fool away!"

When the High priests and enemies of Jesus saw that Herod would in no way comply with their wishes, they dispatched some of their number with money to Acre, a section of the city where at present many Pharisees were stopping. A large sum of money was put into the hands of these Pharisees for distribution among the people as bribes, that with furious and vehement clamoring they might demand Jesus' death. From this insolent and godless rabble Jesus had to suffer the most shameful mockery and the most barbarous ill treatment. There was no one to pity Jesus; he sank to the earth three times under the blows from their clubs. Weeping angels hovered over him and anointed his head. Those blows would have proved fatal, were it not for the divine assistance.

Pilate, still hoping to carry out his first resolve not to condemn Jesus to death, commanded him to be scourged after the manner of the Romans. Then the executioners, striking and pushing Jesus with their short staves, led him through the raging multitude on the Forum to the whipping pillar. These barbarous men had often scourged poor offenders to death at this same pillar. The terrible scourging had lasted fully three quarters of an hour when an obscure man, a stranger, rushed indignantly to the back of the pillar, a sickle shaped knife in his hand, and cried out, "Hold on! Do not beat the innocent man to death!" The drunken executioners, startled for a moment, paused, while with one stroke the stranger quickly cut the cords that bound Jesus. The man then fled back and disappeared into the crowd; covered with blood and wounds, Jesus sank at the foot of the pillar and lay unconscious in his own blood.

They again led Jesus, the crown of thorns upon his head, the mock scepter in his fettered hands, the purple mantel thrown around him, into Pilate's palace. He was unrecognizable on account of the blood that filled his eyes and ran down into his mouth and beard. His body, covered with swollen welts and wounds, resembled a cloth dipped in blood. His gait was bowed down and tottering. When he reached the lowest step of the flight that led up to Pilate, even that hard-hearted being was seized with a shudder of compassion and disgust. Jesus was wearily dragged up the steps, and while he stood a little back, Pilate stepped to the front of the balcony. The trumpet sounded to command attention, for Pilate was going to speak. Addressing the high priests and the people, he said, "Behold, I bring him forth to you that you may know that I find no cause in him." Then Jesus was led forward by the executioners to the front of the balcony where Pilate was standing, so that he could be seen by all the people in the forum. Oh, what a terrible, heart-rending spectacle! Silence, awful and gloomy, fell upon the multitude as the inhumanly treated Jesus appeared and, from his eyes swimming in blood, cast a glance at the surging crowd. Nearby stood Pilate, pointing to him with his finger and crying to the Jews, "Behold the Man!" And the cry, "To the cross with him!" resounded furiously on all sides.

Pilate saw that he could do nothing with the raging multitude. Then Pilate called for water. The servant that brought it poured it from a vase over his hands before the people, while Pilate called down from the balcony, "I am innocent of the blood of this just man. From now on it is in your hands." Then went up from the assembled multitude the horrible, unanimous cry, "His blood be upon us and upon our children!"

Pilate, who was not seeking the truth but only a way out of his difficulty, became more undecided than ever. At the threat of the emperor, Pilate yielded to the will of the multitude, although against the promise he had pledged to his wife, against right and justice, and against his own conscience. Thus did Pilate leave his palace and proceed to the Forum where, opposite the scourging place, there was a high, beautifully constructed judgment seat. The sentence had full weight only when delivered from that seat. Now Jesus, in the scarlet cloak, the crown of thorns upon his head, his hands bound, was led by the soldiers and executioners through the mocking crowd and placed between the two murderers in front of the judgment seat. Pilate began the sentence of condemnation. He first spoke some words in which, with high-sounding titles, he named the Emperor Claudius Tiberius. Then he set forth the accusation against Jesus; that, as a seditious character, a disturber and violator of the Jewish laws, who had allowed himself to be called the Son of God and the King of the Jews, he had been sentenced to death by the High priests, and by the unanimous voice of the people given over to be crucified. Furthermore Pilate, who had in these last hours so frequently and publicly asserted the innocence of Jesus, now proclaimed that he found the sentence of the High priests just, and ended with the words, "I also condemn Jesus of Nazareth, King of the Jews, to be nailed to the cross." The unjust sentence was pronounced at about ten o'clock in the morning.

When Pilate left the judgment seat, part of the soldiers followed him and drew up in file before the palace. A small band of soldiers remained with the condemned. The executioners led Jesus into the center of the Forum. Several slaves, dragging the wood of the cross, entered through the gate on the western side, and threw it noisily at Jesus' feet. Meanwhile, some of the other executioners placed on the backs of the two thieves the arms of their two crosses and tied their upraised arms upon them by means of a stick around which they twisted a cord.

Pilate's horsemen were now ready to start, and the trumpet sounded. They jerked Jesus to his feet at which point the whole weight of his cross fell upon his shoulders. The procession of the crucifixion was headed by a trumpeter, who sounded his trumpet at every street corner and proclaimed the execution. Some paces behind him, a crowd of boys and other rude fellows followed, carrying drink, cords, nails, wedges, and baskets of tools of all kinds. Then sturdy men approached, bearing poles, ladders, and the trunks of the crosses for the two thieves. Finally, there was Jesus, bowed under the weight of his entire cross, exhausted, and tottering. With his right hand he grasped the heavy load on his right shoulder, and with his left hand he wearily tried to raise the flowing garment that was impeding his uncertain steps. Jeers and malicious words resounded on all sides. The procession was flanked by soldiers bearing lances. The procession wound through a very narrow back street, in order not to block the way of the people going to the Temple as well as to prove no hindrance to Pilate and his escort.

Toward the end of that narrow street, the way turned again to the left, becoming broader and somewhat steep. Just where the street begins to ascend, there was a hollow place often filled, after a rain, with mud and water. In it, as in many such places in the streets of Jerusalem, lay a large stone to facilitate crossing. Jesus, on reaching this spot with his heavy burden, could go no farther. He fell full-length on the ground by the projecting stone, his burden at his side. With supernatural help, Jesus was able to raise his head. The executioners restored the crown of thorns upon his head. Thus Jesus, with increasing disability continued up the steep street with his burden.

The Blessed Virgin Mary, who shared the sufferings of Jesus, had left the Forum about an hour previously with John the son of Zebedee and the holy women in order to venerate the places consecrated by Jesus' passion. Now, however, when the running crowd, the sounding trumpet, and Pilate's cavalcade announced the start of the bitter way to the cross, the Blessed Virgin Mary could no longer remain at a distance. She felt that she must behold her divine son in his suffering, and she begged John to take her some place where Jesus would pass. This he was able to do. They stepped out from under a gateway and looked to the right down the street. The procession at this moment was not more than eighty paces away from them. As they came closer, the Blessed Virgin Mary trembled, sobbed, and wrung her hands. One of the men said to the bystanders, "Who is that woman in such distress?" And someone answered, "She is the mother of the Galilean." Wringing her hands, she gazed on Jesus and, in her anguish, leaned for support on one of the pillars of the gate. Bowed down, his thorn-crowned head painfully bent over one shoulder on account of the heavy cross he was carrying, Jesus staggered forward. From his sunken eyes full of blood, he cast a look full of tenderness upon the Blessed Virgin Mary. Then for the second time, faltering under the weight of the cross, Jesus sank on his hands and knees to the ground. The most sorrowful Blessed Virgin Mary, in the vehemence of her love and anguish, saw neither soldiers nor executioners—she saw only her beloved and maltreated Jesus. Wringing her hands, she sprang over the couple of steps between the gateway and, rushing to Jesus, fell on her knees with her arms around him. The executioners obliged her to retire. John and the holy women led her away. She sank, like one paralyzed, on one of the cornerstones that supported the wall near the gateway.

After going some distance up the broad street, the procession passed through a gateway in an old inner wall of the city. In front of this gate was a wide open space at which three streets met. There was a large stepping-stone here, over which Jesus staggered and fell, the cross by his side. He lay on the ground, leaning against the stone, unable to rise. The Pharisees leading the procession cried out to the soldiers, "We shall not get him to Calvary alive. You must hunt up someone to help him carry the cross." Just appeared then, coming straight along the middle of the street, Simon of Cyrene. The crowd was so great that he could not escape, and as soon as the soldiers saw that he was a poor pagan laborer, they laid hold of him and dragged him forward to help carry the Galilean's cross. He resisted and showed great unwillingness, but they forcibly constrained him.

The procession had still a good distance to go before reaching the gate, and the street in that direction was somewhat declining. The gate was strong and high. Close to the gate there was a large puddle of muddy water in the uneven road, cut up by vehicles. Simon of Cyrene tried to step sideways for the sake of convenience, thereby moving the cross out of its place, and poor Jesus, for the fourth time, fell so heavily under his burden in the muddy pool that Simon could scarcely support the cross. The executioners beat Jesus and pushed him; raising him to his feet, they dragged him out of the rut. Just outside the gate there branched from the highroad northward to Mount Calvary a rough, narrow road several minutes in length. At this point, Jesus again sank fainting. He did not fall to the ground, because Simon, resting the end of the cross upon the earth, drew nearer and supported his bowed form. Jesus leaned on him. This was the fifth fall of Jesus while carrying his cross.

The procession again moved onward. With blows and violent jerking at the cords that bound him, Jesus was driven up the rough, uneven path between the city wall and Mount Calvary toward the north. At a spot where the winding path in its ascent turned toward the south, poor Jesus fell again for the sixth time. Nevertheless, his tormenters beat him and drove him on more rudely than ever until he reached the top of the rock, the place of execution, when with the cross he fell heavily to the earth for the seventh time. While being busy in setting up the cross, the executioners did not want Jesus to be in their way, so they imprisoned him in a nearby cave cut in the rock. They closed the door above him, and set guards before it.

The executioners next laid Jesus' cross on the spot where they intended to crucify him, so that it could be conveniently raised and deposited in the hole they made to receive it. They nailed on the foot block, bored the holes for the nails, and hammered in wedges under the arms. Then they made hollow places here and there along the trunk. These were intended to receive the crown of thorns and Jesus' back, so that his body might stand rather than hang, thus preventing the hands from being torn by the weight and hastening death. In the earth behind the little eminence, they sank a post with a cross beam around which the ropes for raising the cross could be wound.

Four executioners now went to the prison cave, seventy steps north-ward, and dragged Jesus out. They pulled him along with pushes, blows, and insults. The people stared and jeered; the soldiers, cold and grave, stood proudly erect, keeping order; the executioners snatched him from the hands of the guards and dragged him violently into the circle.

And now the executioners tore from Jesus the mantle they had flung around his shoulders. They next removed the fetter-girdle, and dragged the white woolen tunic over his head. When they wanted to remove the brown, seamless robe, they could not draw it over his head on account of the projecting crown of thorns. They consequently tore the crown again from his head, opening all the wounds afresh, tucked up the woven tunic, and with words of imprecations and insult, pulled it over his wounded and bleeding head. At last they tore off his girdle. As he appeared about to swoon in their hands, they set him upon a stone that had been rolled nearby, thrust the crown of thorns back on his head, and offered him a drink of gall and vinegar. However, Jesus turned his head away in silence.

At that same instant a man rushed into the circle of the executioners and handed Jesus a strip of linen, which he accepted with thanks and wound around himself. There was something authoritative about this benefactor. With an imperious wave of the hand toward the executioners, he said only the words, "Allow the poor man to cover himself with this!" and without further word to any other, hurried away as quickly as he had come.

Jesus was now stretched on the cross by the executioners. They rudely drew his right hand to the hole for the nail in the right arm of the cross and tied his wrist fast. One knelt on his breast and held the closing hand flat; another placed the long, thick nail, which had been filed to a sharp point, upon the palm of the hand and struck furious blows with an iron hammer. The muscles and ligament of the hand had been torn by the three-edged nail and driven into the narrow hole. When hammered in, the point of the nail could be seen projecting a little on the opposite side of the arm of the cross.

After nailing Jesus' right hand, the crucifiers found that his left hand, which was being fastened to the left arm of the cross, did not reach the hole they had made for the nail. In fact, they had bored the hole a good two inches from his fingertips. They consequently unbound Jesus' left arm from the crosspiece and wound cords around it. Then with their feet supported against the trunk of the cross, they pulled on the arm until the hand reached the hole. Both arms had been torn from their sockets, the shoulders were distended and hollow, and at the elbows one could see the disjointed bones. As they had done before, they fastened the arm again on the cross beam and hammered the second nail through the left hand.

The whole body of Jesus had been contracted by the violent stretching of the arms to reach the holes for the nails, and his knees were forcibly drawn up. The executioners now pulled on his legs and, winding ropes around them, fastened them to the cross; but on account of the mistake made in locating the holes on the cross arms, the feet of Jesus did not reach even to the block. When the executioners saw this, they gave vent to curses and insults. Then they tied ropes around the right leg and with horrible violence, pulled Jesus' foot to the block, and tied the leg fast with cords. His body was thus horribly distended. His abdomen was entirely displaced, and it seemed as though the ribs broke away from the breastbone.

With similar ferocity the left foot was drawn down and fastened tightly with cords over the right foot. Because the left foot did not rest firmly enough over the right foot for nailing, a hole was made in the left foot with an augur. Then, seizing the most frightful-looking nail of all, which was much longer than the others were, they drove it through the wounded instep of the left foot into the right foot below. With a cracking sound, the nail passed through Jesus' feet and into the hole prepared for it in the foot block and through that into the trunk of the cross. The nailing of the feet was the most horrible of all, on account of the distention of the whole body.

After the crucifixion of Jesus, the executioners passed ropes through a ring in the back of the cross, and they drew the cross into the center of the circle. Then they threw the rope over the transverse beam they had raised on the opposite side. By means of this rope, several of the executioners lifted the cross upright, while others supported it with blocks around the trunk, and guided it to the hole prepared for it. They pulled the top somewhat forward until it came into a perpendicular line, and its whole weight with a tremulous thrust shot down into the hole. The cross vibrated with the shock. Jesus moaned out loud.

The position of the sun at the time of Jesus' crucifixion showed it to be about a quarter past twelve, and at the moment that the cross was lifted, the trumpet of the Temple resounded. The Paschal lamb had been slaughtered.

While Jesus was being nailed to his cross, the two thieves were still lying on the eastern side of the mount, their hands bound to the crosspiece fastened on their shoulders, and guards keeping watch over them. When Jesus' cross was raised, the executioners dragged the thieves up to it with the words, "Now it's your turn." They unbound them from their crosspieces and proceeded with great hurry, for the sun was being clouded over, and all things suggested that a storm was forthcoming.

The executioners placed ladders against the trunks that had already been erected, and they fastened the curved crosspieces to the top of the trunks. Two ladders were placed against each of the two crosses, and executioners mounted them. Meanwhile the mixture of myrrh and vinegar was given to the thieves to drink, their doublets were taken off, and by means of ropes passed under their arms and thrown up over the arms of the cross, they were drawn into place. Their ascent was rendered more painful by the shocks they received and the striking of wooden pegs that had been inserted into the trunk of the crosses. On the cross beams and the trunks the ropes were knotted. The arms of the thieves were bent and twisted over the crosspieces. Around the wrists and elbows, as well as the knees and ankles, cords were wound and twisted so tightly that blood burst from the veins and their joints cracked. The poor creatures uttered frightful shrieks of pain.

After the crucifixion of the thieves and the distribution of Jesus' garments, the executioners gathered up their tools, addressed some mocking and insulting words to Jesus, and went their way. The Pharisees still present spurred up their horses, rode around the circle in front of Jesus, outraged him with many abusive words, and then rode off. The hundred Roman soldiers with their commander also descended the mount and left the neighborhood, for fifty others had come to take their place.

Now Jesus, raising his head a little, exclaimed, "Father, forgive them, they do not know what they are doing!" Then he prayed in a low tone. The thief on the right, by virtue of Jesus' prayer, received an interior enlightenment. He then confessed his crime to Jesus, saying, "Lord, if you condemn me, it will be just. But have mercy on me!" Jesus replied, "You shall experience my mercy."

A great change was taking place in the souls of most of the spectators. For even as the penitent thief was speaking, fearful signs were beheld in nature, and all present were filled with anxiety. To the east of the sun, something like a dark mountain arose and soon entirely hid the sun. The center appeared pale yellow, and around it was a red circle like a ring of fire. The sky became perfectly dark, and the stars shone out with a reddish gleam. Terror seized upon man and beast. The cattle bellowed and ran wildly about; the birds sought their hiding places. The Pharisees tried to explain these signs as natural phenomena, but they succeeded badly, and soon they, too, were consumed with fear. The good thief, in deepest contrition, said to Jesus, "Remember me when you come into your kingdom." Jesus replied, "Amen. I say to you, this day you will be with me in paradise."

The Blessed Virgin Mary, Mary Cleophas, Mary Magdalene, and John the son of Zebedee were standing around Jesus' cross, between it and those of the thieves, and looking up at the cross. At that moment, Jesus cast an earnest and compassionate glance down upon the Blessed Virgin Mary and, turning his eyes toward John, said to her, "Woman, behold, this is your son!" To John he said, "Behold, this is your mother!"

Jesus, in unspeakable torture, suffered on the cross extreme abandonment and desolation of soul. Jesus endured, in infinite torment all that is suffered by a crushed, tortured creature, in the greatest abandonment, without consolation human or divine, when faith, hope, and love stand alone in the desert of tribulation, without prospect of return, and one is left there alone. By this suffering he gained for us merit to stand firm in our own last struggle when we too shall feel ourselves entirely abandoned. This is the context in which, toward the third hour, Jesus cried in a loud voice, *"Eli, Eli, lamma sabacthani!"* ("My God! My God! Why did you abandon me?"). From Judith von Halle, we have an alternate perspective. She experiences The Christ saying in a soft voice, *"Eloi, Eloi, l'ma shevachtanim"* meaning, "My God, my God, how you have raised me up!" Strangely, the Hebrew spelling for these two affirmations is identical, because in written Hebrew only the consonants are shown and different words are spelled the same way.[3]

Jesus was now completely exhausted. With his parched tongue he uttered the words "I am thirsty." At just after three o'clock in the afternoon, the hour of Jesus' demise had come. He spoke, "It is finished." Raising his head, he said, "Father, into your hands I commend my spirit." Then he bowed his head and the physical Jesus died. That cry rang through Heaven, Earth, and Hell. The earth quaked and the rock between the central cross and that of the criminal on the left was rent asunder. The heavens were still darkened. The radiant spirit of The Christ descended through the gaping hole in the rock. Thus began The Christ's mission to the souls in limbo and in hell.

A feeling of dread prevailed. At the time of the earthquake, in Jerusalem two central pillars, which upheld the veil of the Temple, were toppled, and the veil was rent into two pieces. Walls in the Temple fell; the dead arose from their graves, while mountains and buildings were overturned in many parts of the world.

Joseph had already heard of Jesus' death, and with Nicodemus had decided to bury Jesus' body in the new sepulcher hewn out of rock in his own garden, not very far from Calvary. Thus Joseph went to Pilate. He found Pilate very anxious and perplexed. Joseph begged openly and fearlessly that he might be allowed to take the body of Jesus, the King of the Jews, down from the cross, as he wanted to lay it in his own sepulcher. Pilate, perhaps wishing to palliate in some measure his cruelty, at once expedited an order for Joseph of Arimathea, by which he gave him the body of the King of the Jews with permission to take it down from the cross and bury it.

Meanwhile, on Calvary the executioners mounted up the cross, roughly felt Jesus' body, and declared that he was pretending to be dead. Although they felt that he was quite cold and stiff, yet they were not convinced that he was already dead. John, at the entreaty of the Blessed Virgin Mary, turned to the soldiers, to draw them off of Jesus' body. The

---

3   Von Halle 2007, pp. 69–71.

executioners next mounted the ladders to the crosses of the thieves. Two of them with their sharp clubs broke the bones of their arms above and below the elbows, while a third did the same above the knees and ankles. The left thief roared frightfully, consequently the executioners finished him by three blows of the club on the breast. The right thief moaned feebly, and expired under the torture. The executioners untwisted the cords, and allowed the bodies to fall heavily to the earth. Then tying ropes around them, they dragged them down the valley between the mount and the city wall, and buried them there.

The executioners appeared still to have some doubts as to the death of Jesus. His friends, after witnessing the terrible scene just described, were more anxious than ever for the executioners to withdraw. Cassius, the subaltern officer, was suddenly seized by a wonderful ardor. He drew his lance out to its full length, stuck the point upon it, turned his horses head, and drove him boldly up to the narrow space on top of the eminence upon which the cross was planted. He halted between Jesus' cross and that on the right side of the central cross. Grasping the lance with both hands, he drove it upward with violence into the right side of Jesus' body. When with all his force he drew the lance from the wide wound it had made in the right side of Jesus, a copious stream of blood and water rushed forth and flowed over his upraised face. He sprang quickly from his horse, fell upon his knees, struck his breast, and before all present proclaimed aloud his belief in Jesus.

Now began the transport to Mount Calvary of all that was necessary for the embalming. Besides the tools to be used in taking down Jesus' body from the cross, the servants of Nicodemus took with them two ladders. Each of these consisted of a single pole in which pieces of a thick plank were fitted so as to form steps. The poles were also provided with hooks, which could be hung higher or lower, as desired to steady the ladder or to hang on it articles relating to the work to be done. The servants left the city before their master.

Joseph of Arimethea and Nicodemus were in mourning attire: false sleeves, maniples, and wide girdles of black. They had drawn long, flow-ing, dark-grey mantles over their heads. These wide mantles covered all that they were carrying. Both directed their steps toward the Gate of Execution. As soon as the Centurion Abenadar arrived, they began, sadly and reverently, the taking down from the cross and preparation for burial of the body of the one they had so admired and loved. Nicodemus and Joseph placed the ladders behind the cross and mounted, carrying with them a very long strip of linen, to which three broad straps were fastened. They bound the body of Jesus under the arms and knees to the trunk of the cross, and the arms they fastened the same way at the wrists. Then by striking upon strong pegs fixed against the point of the nails at the back of the cross, they forced out the nails from Jesus' hands. The nails fell easily out of the wounds, for they had been enlarged by the weight of the body, which, supported now by means of the linen band, no longer rested upon them. Meanwhile Abenadar had, though with great effort, been driving out the enormous nail from the feet. As soon as the body was taken down, the men wrapped it in linen from the knees to the waist, and laid it on a sheet in the Blessed Virgin Mary's arms, which were stretched out to receive it.

When the preparations were complete, the men laid the body on a leathern litter, placed over it a brown cloth, and ran two poles along the side. Nicodemus and Joseph carried the front end on their shoulders; Abendar and John the son of Zebedee carried the back ends of the litter. Then followed the Blessed Virgin Mary and the holy women. Cassius and his soldiers closed the procession.

Two soldiers with torches of twisted branches walked on ahead, for light was needed in the grotto of the sepulcher. The procession moved on, for a distance of about seven minutes, singing psalms in a low, plaintive tone, through the valley to the Garden of the Tomb. The rock in which the sepulcher was cut lay at one end of the garden, entirely overgrown with verdure. The procession halted at the entrance to the garden. It was opened by removing some of the poles that fashioned the gate, which were afterwards used as levers for rolling away the stone from the entrance to the grotto. Before reaching the rock, they took the cover from the litter, raised the body, and placed it upon a narrow board that had previously been covered with a linen cloth. Nicodemus and Joseph took one end of the board and Abenar and John took the other. The grotto was perfectly new and had been cleaned out by Nicodemus' servants. It was very neat inside and the tomb was ornamented by a beautifully carved coping. The four men carried the body down into the tomb, set it down, strewed the stone couch with sweet spices, spread over it a linen cloth, and deposited the remains upon it. Then having with tears and embraces given expression of their love for Jesus, they left the tomb.

The Blessed Virgin Mary now went in, and she sat at the head of the tomb, which was about two feet from the ground. She was bending low over the corpse and weeping. When she left the tomb, Mary Magdalene hurried in with flowers and branches she had gathered from the garden and that she now scattered over the body. She wrung her hands and with tears and sighs embraced the feet of Jesus. When the men outside gave warning that it was time to close the doors, she went back outside where the women were waiting.

The men raised the cloth that was hanging over the side of the tomb, folded it around the body, and then drew the brown cover over the whole. Lastly they closed the bronze doors, which had a perpendicular bar intersected by a horizontal one. The great stone, intended for securing the doors was still lying outside the tomb. It was very large, enough for a man to lie at full length upon it, and it was very heavy. By means of the poles brought from the garden entrance, the men rolled it into place before the closed doors of the tomb.

It was now the hour at which the Sabbath began. Nicodemus and Joseph returned to the city by a little private gate that Joseph had been allowed to make in the city wall near the garden. They had previously informed the Blessed Virgin Mary, Mary Magdalene, John the son of Zebedee, and some of the women, who wanted to return to Mount Calvary to pray and to get some things they had left there, that this gate, as well as that to the Coenaculum, would be opened to them whenever they would knock.

Joseph of Arimathea left the Coenaculum at a late hour and, with some of the disciples and holy women, started for home. They were proceeding sadly and timidly along the streets of Sion when an armed band dashed suddenly from their place of concealment in the neighborhood of

Caiaphas's judgment hall and laid hands upon Joseph. His companions fled with cries of terror. They imprisoned the good Joseph in a tower of the city wall not far from the judgment hall. Caiaphas had committed the care of this seizure to pagan soldiers, who did not celebrate the Sabbath. The intention was to let Joseph die of starvation, and to keep his disappearance a secret.

On the night between Friday and Saturday, Caiaphas and some of the chief men among the Jews held a consultation about what ought to be done with regard to what had just taken place, and its effect upon the people. It was far into the night when they went to Pilate to tell him that as the seducer, while he was still alive, had said, "After three days, I will rise again," it would be right to command that the sepulcher be guarded until the third day; otherwise his disciples might come, steal him away, and say to the people, "He is risen from the dead," and the last error would be worse than the first. Pilate wanted to have nothing more to do with the affair, so he said to them, "You have a guard. Go do what needs to be done."

Thereupon, twelve men left the city before sunrise. They were accompanied by soldiers not wearing the Roman uniform; they were Temple soldiers. They took with them lanterns on long poles, in order to be able to distinguish things clearly in the dark, and also to have light in the dark sepulcher. On arrival, they rolled back the large stone, opened the bronze doors, and assured themselves that the body of Jesus was still present. Then they fastened a string across the doors of the tomb and another from that to the stone lying in front of them. After that, they sealed the two strings together with a seal in the form of a half-moon.

The twelve men returned afterward to the city, and the guards took up positions opposite the outer door to the sepulcher. Five or six of them took turns in watching, while some others went occasionally to the city for provisions.

Regarding friends of Jesus on the day after the crucifixion, about twenty men were in the Coenaculum celebrating the Sabbath and then taking a repast. Most of them remained quietly in the house, assembling at intervals for prayer and reading, and occasionally admitting a newcomer.

CHAPTER 21

THE RESURRECTION

APRIL 4 TO 16, 33 CE

O n the eve of the resurrection, an angel appeared to the Blessed Virgin Mary. The angel announced that The Christ was near, and told her to go out to the little gate belonging to Nicodemus. At these words, the heart of the Blessed Virgin Mary filled with joy. Without saying a word to the holy women, she wrapped herself in her mantle and hastened to the gate in the city wall through which she had come on her return from the Garden of the Tomb. It may have been almost nine o'clock when, in a narrow place near the gate, the Blessed Virgin Mary suddenly halted in her hurried walk. She gazed up, as if ravished in joyous longing, to the top of the wall. Floating down toward her, she saw The Christ. He uttered some words and appeared to embrace her. Then he vanished. Inexpressively consoled, she hurried back to the holy women, whom she found preparing ointment and spices on a table. She did not tell them what she had experienced, but she consoled and strengthened them in faith.

Joseph of Arimathea was praying in his prison cell. Suddenly the cell shone with light, and Joseph heard his name pronounced. The roof raised just where the cornice joined it to the wall, and a radiant figure let down a strip of linen. The figure commanded Joseph to climb.

Joseph grasped the linen with both hands and, supporting his feet on the projecting stones of the wall, he climbed to the opening, a distance of about twelve feet. As soon as he had passed through the opening, the roof immediately resumed its original position, and the angel disappeared. Unnoticed, Joseph ran a short distance along the city wall to the neighborhood of the Coenaculum, which was situated near the south wall of Sion. He climbed down and knocked at the door. The disciples were assembled with closed doors. They were sorrowful over Joseph's disappearance, for they credited the report that he had been thrown into a sewer. Joseph told them how an angel had helped him escape from his prison. They were greatly consoled by his account; they gave him food and thanked God.

At the sepulcher, all was calm and silent. About seven guards were in front and around the tomb, some sitting, others standing. It was night; the lanterns before the tomb shed a dazzling light. Jesus' body was wrapped in its winding sheet just as it had been laid on the stone couch. It was surrounded by a brilliant light; and, since the burial, two angels had in rapt adoration guarded the remains, one at the head, the other at the feet. However, these were not visible to the guards.

The Christ was seen, with spirits he had released from hell, floating through the rock and into the tomb. He showed them the marks of ill-treatment upon his martyred physical body. The linen bands and winding sheet seemed to have been removed, for the body could be seen complete with its wounds. It seemed as if The Christ, without restoring the body to life, was transported into the tomb and then both were transported out of the tomb. The two angels raised the tortured body, not in an upright position, but just as it lay in the tomb, and floated up with it to heaven. The rock trembled as they passed through it.

Four of the guards had gone to the city for provisions. The trembling of the rock caused the three remaining guards to fall to the ground unconscious. They ascribed the shock to an earthquake but knew nothing of its cause. At the time that the earth trembled, an angel dressed in warrior garb shot like lightening from heaven down to the tomb. The angel rolled the stone to one side, and then sat upon it.

On April 5, when the morning sky began to clear with a streak of white light, Mary Magdalene, Mary Cleophas, Joanna Chusa, and Salome, enveloped in their mantles, left their abode near the Coenaculum.[1] They

---

1   For the date of the Resurrection, see Powell, *Christian Hermetic Astrology*, p. 302.

carried the spices packed in linen cloths, and one of them had a lantern. They also brought fresh flower for strewing over the body and oils for pouring over it. The women walked anxiously to the little gate belonging to Nicodemus. They knew nothing of the miraculous events that had taken place. They did not even know of the guards at the sepulcher, for they had remained shut up in their house the whole of the previous day, which had been the Sabbath. They anxiously inquired of one another, "Who will roll away the stone in front of the doors?" Full of longing to show the last honors to the body in the tomb, they had entirely lost sight of the stone. At last the holy women concluded that they would set the flowers, spices, and oils in front of the stone and wait until some disciples came who would open it for them. Thus, they went on toward the garden.

Outside the tomb, the large stone was rolled to the right, so that the doors, which were merely lying to, could easily be opened. The linens in which the body had been enveloped were in the tomb in the following manner: the large winding sheet in which the body had been wrapped lay undisturbed, only empty and fallen together, containing nothing but the aromatic herbs; the long bandage that had been wound around it was still lying twisted and at full length just as if it had been drawn off, on the outer edge of the tomb; and the linen scarf with which the Blessed Virgin Mary had enveloped Jesus' head lay to the right of the tomb.

When the holy women, as they approached, noticed the lanterns of the guards and the soldiers lying around, they became frightened and went a short distance past the garden in the direction of Golgotha. Mary Magdalene however, forgetful of danger, hurried into the garden. Salome followed her at some distance and the other two waited outside. Mary Magdalene, seeing the guards, stepped back at first a few steps toward Salome, then both of them made their way into the sepulcher. They found the stone rolled away, but the doors to the tomb were closed. Mary Magdalene anxiously opened one of the doors, peered into the tomb, and found the linens lying apart and empty. Mary Magdalene was exceedingly troubled. She hurried out of the Garden of the Tomb, off through the gate belonging to Nicodemus, and back to the disciples. Salome, too, who only now entered the sepulcher, ran at once after Mary Magdalene. She encountered the women waiting outside the garden and told them what had happened. Though amazed and rejoiced at what they heard from Salome, they could not, at first, resolve to enter the garden. Eventually, with beating hearts the women did enter the sepulcher. When they drew near the tomb, they beheld the two angels of the tomb in priestly robes, white and shining. The women pressed close to one another in terror and, covering their faces with their hands, they trembled and bowed almost to the ground. One of the angels addressed them: "Fear not! Do not look for the crucified here. He is alive. He has risen. He is no longer among the dead." Then the angel pointed out the empty tomb, and ordered them to tell the disciples what they had seen and heard, and that The Christ would go before them into Galilee.

Meanwhile, Mary Magdalene reached the Coenaculum like one beside herself, and knocked violently at the door. Some of the disciples were still asleep on their couches about the walls, while several others had risen and were talking together. Peter and John opened the door. Mary Magdalene, without entering, told them, "They have taken the Lord from the tomb! We do not know where." Then she ran back in great haste to the Garden of the Tomb. As she was alone, she was afraid to enter the sepulcher at once; so she waited outside on the step at the entrance. She stooped down, trying to see through the low doors into the cave and even as far as the stone couch. She saw the two angels in white, priestly garments sitting at the head and foot of the tomb, and heard these words, "Woman, why are you weeping?" In her grief, she cried out, "They have taken my Lord away! I do not know where they have laid him." Saying this and seeing nothing but the linens, she turned weeping; her only thought was, "Jesus is not here! Where is Jesus?" She ran a few steps from the sepulcher and then returned like one half-distracted and searching for something.

About ten steps from the sepulcher and toward the east, where the garden rose in the direction of the city, Mary Magdalene spied, in the grey light of dawn, a figure clothed in a long white garment. Rushing toward it, she heard once more the words, "Woman, why are you weeping? Whom do you seek?" She thought it was the gardener. At the words, "Whom do you seek?" Mary Magdalene at once answered, "Sir, if you have taken him away, show me where you have laid him! I will take him away!" And she glanced around, as if to see whether he had not laid him someplace near. Then The Christ, in his well-known voice, said "Mary." Recognizing the voice, and forgetting the crucifixion, the death, and the burial now that he was alive, she turned quickly and, as once before, exclaimed, "Rabboni!" She fell on her knees before him and stretched out her hands toward his feet. But The Christ raised his hand to keep her off, saying, "Go to my brethren, and say to them, 'I ascend to my Father and to your Father, to my God and to your God.'" At these words The Christ vanished. After the disappearance of The Christ, Mary Magdalene rose up quickly and again, as if in a dream, ran to the tomb. She saw the two angels, she saw the empty linens, and hurried, *now certain of the resurrection*, back to her companions.

Scarcely had Mary Magdalene left the garden when John approached, followed by Peter. John stood outside the entrance of the cave and stooped down to look, through the outer doors of the sepulcher, at the half opened doors of the tomb, where he saw the linens lying. Then came Peter. He stepped down into the sepulcher and into the tomb, in the center of which he saw the winding sheet lying. It was rolled together from both sides toward the middle, and the spices were wrapped in it. The bandages were folded around it. The linen that had covered his face was lying to the right, next to the wall. It, too, was folded. John now followed Peter into the tomb, saw the same things, and believed in the resurrection. All that Jesus had said was now clear to them. Before, they had only an imperfect comprehension. Peter took the linens under his mantle, and both went back to the Coenaculum by way of the little gate belonging to Nicodemus.

Now for the first time, the guards rose up from where they were lying on the ground. They took their lances and also the lanterns that were hanging on poles at the entrance of the tomb, and hurried, in evident fear and trepidation, through the Gate of the Execution and into the city.

Meanwhile, Mary Magdalene had reached the holy women and told them she had seen The Christ. Then she, too, hurried on to the city through the neighboring Gate of the Execution. The other women went again to the garden, outside of which The Christ appeared to them in a white flowing garment that concealed even his hands. He said, "All hail!" They trembled and fell at his feet. While addressing some words to them, he waved his hand in a certain direction and then he vanished. The holy women then hastened through the Bethlehem Gate to Sion, so as to tell the disciples they had seen The Christ and what he had said to them. But the disciples would not at first credit either Mary Magdalene's report or that of the holy women. Until after the return of Peter and John, they had looked upon the whole affair as the effect of women's imagination.

Peter and John were amazed at what they had just seen. It rendered them silent and thoughtful. On their way back from the tomb they met James the Lesser and Thaddeus, who had set out for the tomb after them. They were very much agitated, for The Christ had appeared to them near the Coenaculum. Peter, as they went along, suddenly was startled and began trembling, as if he, too, had just gotten a glimpse of The Christ.

Four of the soldiers returned from the tomb and went directly to Pilate with a report of what had happened. The other guards went to a large court near the Temple in which a number of Pharisees were gathered. These latter consulted together and came to the conclusion that they would, with money and threats, force the guards to report that the disciples had stolen the body of Jesus. However, when the guards objected that their companions, who had informed Pilate of the whole affair, would contradict them, the Pharisees promised they would make it right with Pilate. Meanwhile the four guards who had been dismissed by Pilate arrived. They adhered strictly to the account they had given to the Governor. All seven guards defended themselves stoutly, and by no species of bribery could they be reduced to silence. The enemies of Jesus spread the report that his body had been stolen by the disciples. The Pharisees, Sadducees, and Herodians initiated this lie to be propagated everywhere. Their falsehood profited them little, for after the resurrection The Christ was seen by many.

In a portion of the Coenaculum, Nicodemus prepared a repast for ten of the eleven, the holy women, and the rest of the disciples. Thomas was not present at it; he kept himself apart from the other followers of Jesus. All that took place at this feast was in strict accordance with Jesus' directions. The meal was conducted with ceremony. The guests prayed standing and ate lying, while Peter and John taught. At the end of the meal, a flat, ribbed loaf was placed before Peter, which he divided into small pieces as marked by the ribs. These he distributed right and left on two plates. A large cup was then sent around, and out of it each one drank. Although Peter blessed the bread, it was not a sacrament, only an agape, a love feast. Peter said they should all desire to be one as the bread they were eating and the wine they were drinking. After that they sang psalms, standing.

Then Matthew was sent to Bethany, in order to reproduce, at a similar repast given at the house of the Apostle Lazarus, the instructions just heard and the ceremonies witnessed. There he taught a great many more of the disciples who were not so well instructed as the others were. They had the same kind of meal and went through similar ceremonies.

Luke had been among the disciples only a short time, but he had, before joining them, received the baptism of John the Baptizer. Luke was present at the love feast and at the instruction upon the Blessed Sacrament delivered by Matthew in the evening at the house of the Apostle Lazarus, in Bethany. After the instruction Luke went, troubled and doubting, to Jerusalem where he spent the night at John Mark's house. There he met several other disciples, among them Cleopas, a grandson of Mary Cleopas' paternal uncle. He had been at the instructions and the love feast given at the Coenaculum. The disciples were talking about the resurrection of The Christ and expressing their doubts. Luke and Cleopas, especially, were wavering in faith. The next morning, Monday, April 6, both resolved to go together to Emmaus.

These disciples were anxious and doubting, and they wanted to talk over all that they had heard. They were especially put out by Jesus being so ignominiously crucified. They could not understand how the redeemer and Messiah could have been so shamefully ill-treated. About the middle of their journey, The Christ drew near to them from a side path, but they did not know who it was. As soon as they saw him, they went more slowly, as if wanting the stranger to go on ahead. But The Christ likewise slackened his pace. He walked behind Luke and Cleopas for a while. Then drawing near, he asked them what they were discussing.

They stood still, looking sad. Then one of them, whose name was Cleopas, answered him, "Are you the only stranger in Jerusalem who does not know the things that have taken place there in these days?" He asked them, "What things?" They replied, "The things about Jesus of Nazareth, who was a prophet mighty in deed and word before God and all the people, and how our chief priests and leaders handed him over to be condemned to death and crucified him. But we had hoped that he was the one to redeem Israel. Yes, and besides all this, it is now the third day since these things took place. Moreover, some women of our group astounded us. They were at the tomb early this morning, and when they did not find his body there, they came back and told us that they had indeed seen a vision of angels who said that he was alive. Some of those who were with us went to the tomb and found it just as the women had said; but they did not see him." Then he said to them, "Oh, how foolish you are, and how slow of heart to believe all that the prophets have declared! Was it not necessary that the Messiah should suffer these things and then enter into his glory?"[2]

Then he interpreted for them the words of Moses and the prophets concerning the Messiah. When they came to the branch of the road that led to Emmaus, The Christ appeared as if he wanted to continue on the main road that led south to Bethlehem. But the two disciples encouraged him to go with them to Emmaus. They went to a public house and were offered a meal consisting of honeycomb, cake, and a Passover loaf. The latter was set before The Christ as being the guest. The Christ reclined at the table with the two disciples and ate with them of the cake and honey. Then taking the small loaf, The Christ broke off a piece, which he proceeded to divide into three small pieces. These he placed on the little plate and blessed them. Then he stood up, elevated the plate on high with both hands, raised his eyes, and prayed. The two disciples stood opposite him, both intensely moved, and, as it were, transported out of themselves. When The Christ separated the three pieces, they opened their mouths and stretched forward toward him. He reached his hand across the table and laid a particle in their mouths.

2   Luke 24:17–26 NRSV.

As The Christ raised his hand with the third particle to his own mouth, he disappeared. The two disciples stood a little while as if stupefied, and then cast themselves into each other's arms. This was an especially touching experience on account of The Christ's mild and loving manner, the calm joy of the two disciples even before they knew him, and their rapture as soon as they recognized him. After he disappeared, Cleopas and Luke hurried back to Jerusalem.

On the evening of April 6, many of the disciples and all of the eleven, excepting Thomas, assembled with Nicodemus and Joseph of Arimethea, in the Coenaculum, the doors being closed. Although the resurrected Christ had appeared to the Blessed Virgin Mary, Mary Magdalene, Peter, John, and James, the greater number of the eleven and also many of the other disciples would not fully believe in the resurrection. They still felt uneasy, as if his apparition was not a real and corporeal one. As if it were only a vision, similar to those that had been experienced by the prophets of old. All arranged themselves for prayer. Peter had just finished an instruction when Cleopas and Luke, hurrying back from Emmaus, knocked at the closed doors of the courtyard, and received admittance. The joyful news they related somewhat interrupted the prayer. However, scarcely was it again continued when all present started glancing in the same direction and became radiant with joyful emotion. The Christ had come in through the closed doors. They did not appear to be really conscious of his approach, until he passed through their circles and stood in their midst under the lamp. Then they became very much amazed and agitated. He showed them his hands and feet and, opening his garment, disclosed the wound in his side. He spoke to them and, seeing they were terrified, he asked for something to eat. On a side table stood a deep, oval dish covered with a little white cloth, which Peter took to The Christ. In the dish were a piece of fish and some honey. The Christ gave thanks, blessed the food, ate some himself, and then gave a portion of it to some but not all of those present. To the Blessed Virgin Mary and also other holy women, who were standing in the doorway of the outer hall, he likewise distributed some of the food.

Then The Christ started teaching and imparting strength. The circles around him were still triple, the ten of the original twelve forming the innermost. It appeared that this instruction was intended only for those in the inner circle. He never moved his lips. He was resplendent. Light streamed over those in attendance, from his hands, his feet, his side, and his mouth. As he breathed upon them, light flowed in upon them. It was interior speech, but without a whisper, without the softest word.

The Christ also spoke to the entire group about the mystery contained in the Ark of the Covenant. He said that this mystery was now replaced by his body and his blood, which he gave to them forever in the sacrament of the Holy Eucharist. He spoke of his own passion and of some wonderful things relating to David, of which they were ignorant and which he explained. Lastly, he told them to go in a couple of days to the region of Sichar, and there proclaim his resurrection. After that he vanished. The ten and the other disciples went around among one another, perfectly overjoyed. Then they assembled again under the lamp, to sing canticles of praise and thanksgiving.

On that same night, some of the eleven went to Bethany, while many of the disciples set out for Jerusalem. The older disciples remained in Bethany to teach the younger and weaker in the faith, which they did partly at the castle of the Apostle Lazarus and partly in the synagogue at Bethany. Nicodemus and Joseph of Arimathea were staying at the castle of the Apostle Lazarus. The rest of the eleven went with a troop of disciples, among them Luke, in the direction of Sichar. Peter said joyfully, as they were setting out, "We shall go to the sea and catch fish," by which he meant souls. They separated and went different ways, teaching at the inns and in the public places concerning the passion of Jesus and the resurrection of The Christ. This was in preparation for the conversion of Pentecost.

They met together in the inn outside Thanath-Silo. Thomas also, with two disciples, joined them as they were gathered at a meal prepared for them by Sylvan's father, who had care of the inn. Those of the eleven told Thomas of the appearance of the risen Christ in their midst. Nevertheless, Thomas raised his hands to silence them, and said that he would not believe it until he had touched the wounds himself. He did the same before the other disciples when they declared to him that they had seen The Christ.

Peter taught until late at night in the synagogue at Thanath-Silo. He spoke quite freely of how the Jews had dealt with Jesus. He related many things of Jesus' last predictions and teachings, of his unspeakable love, of his prayer on Mount Olivet, and of Judas' treachery and wretched end. Peter did not spare himself. He recounted his flight and denial with bitter tears. His hearers wept with him. Then with still more vehement expression of sorrow, he detailed how cruelly the Jews had treated Jesus, of his rising again on the third day, of his appearing first to the women, then to some of the others, and lastly to all in general. He called on all present that had seen The Christ to witness to his words. Some seventy hands were raised in response to his call. Thomas, however, remained silent and responded with no sign. He could not bring himself to believe. Peter then called upon the people to leave all things, to join the new community, and to follow The Christ. He invited the less certain to go to Jerusalem where the faithful would share all they had with them. All were very much impressed with Peter's words, and many were converted.

The ten cured numerous sick persons in Thanath-Silo. They went about these cures just as Jesus had done; that is, they breathed upon the sick and they imposed their hands while leaning over them. The other disciples performed no cures, but they served the ten by carrying, lifting, and leading the sick. The inhabitants of Thanath-Silo were very friendly. They wanted the ten to remain longer with them, but Peter said they must go back to Jerusalem.

In those days, the emissaries of the high priests went about visiting all the houses whose owners kept up communication with the disciples, discharging them from whatever public employment they might happen to hold, and arresting any followers of The Christ they found there. Nicodemus and Joseph of Arimathea, since the burial of Jesus, had nothing more to do with the high priests.

On Saturday, April 11, after the close of the Sabbath, the ten having laid aside their robes of ceremony, a great meal was spread in the outer hall of the Coenaculum. It was a love feast such as had taken place on the preceding Sunday. It was still early in the evening; the lamps were not yet lighted. Several of the eleven and the disciples were in the hall, and others were entering. They robed themselves again in long, white garments, and prepared for prayer as on the previous occasion. Peter, John, and James put on the vestments that distinguished them as priests. While these preparations were being made, Thomas entered the room in which the Last Supper had taken place. He passed through those who were already robed and put on his own long, white garment. As he went along, some of the ten accosted him. Some caught him by the sleeve, others gesticulating with the right hand as they spoke, as if emphatically protesting against him. But he behaved like one in a hurry to vest and as one who could not credit the account given him of the wonderful things that had happened in that place. While this was going on, a man entered the room; he appeared to be a servant. He wore an apron and had in one hand a small, lighted lamp and in the other a rod with hook in it. With the latter, he drew down the lamp suspended from the center of the ceiling, lit it, and again pushed it up. Then he left the room. Now the Blessed Virgin Mary, Mary Magdalene, and a third woman came into the house. When the Blessed Virgin Mary and Mary Magdalene entered the room, Peter and John came forward to greet them. The third woman remained in the antechamber. The entrance hall was opened into the room of the Last Supper and also into some of the side halls. The exterior doors leading into the courtyard, as well as those of the court itself, were shut. A great many disciples were in the side halls.

As soon as the Blessed Virgin Mary and Mary Magdalene entered, the doors were closed and all arranged themselves for prayer. The two holy women remained reverently standing on either side of the door. The eleven, kneeling before the Holy of Holies, prayed again as before; then standing under the lamp, they sang one psalm after another. After some time, there was a pause in the assembly, an intermission of prayer. Then they began to speak of going to the Sea of Galilee and of how they would disperse. Soon, however, they assumed an expression of rapt attention, called upon them by the approach of The Christ. At first he appeared in the courtyard. He was resplendent with light, clothed in a white garment with a white cincture. He directed his steps to the door of the outer hall, which opened of itself before him and closed behind him. The disciples in the outer hall saw the door opening of itself and fell back on both sides to make room. The Christ walked quickly through the hall into the room of the Last Supper and stepped between Peter and John who, like the others of the eleven, fell back on either side.

The Christ's first words were, "Peace be unto you!" Then he stepped under the lamp, and the eleven closed around him. Thomas, frightened at the sight of The Christ, timidly drew back. However, The Christ, grasping Thomas' right hand in his own right hand, took Thomas' forefinger and laid the tip of it on the wound of his left hand. Then taking Thomas' left hand in his own left, he placed the forefinger in the wound of his right hand. Lastly, taking again Thomas' right hand in his own right hand, The Christ put it, without uncovering his breast, under his garment and placed the fore and middle fingers in the wound of his right side. The Christ spoke some words as he did this. With the exclamation, "My Lord and my God!" Thomas sank down like one unconscious, The Christ still holding his hand. The nearest of the eleven supported Thomas and The Christ raised him up by the hand.

The Christ did not disappear immediately after Thomas' declaration of faith. He still continued to speak to the eleven, and asked for something to eat. A little oval dish was brought to him, again from the partitioned recess in which the table stood. It was not the same as that presented to him on the previous occasion. There was something in the dish that looked like a fish, of which he ate; then he blessed and distributed what was left to those around him, beginning with Thomas.

After that The Christ told them why he stood in the midst of them, although they had abandoned him, and why he did not place himself nearer to those who had remained faithful to him. He told them also that he had commissioned Peter to confirm his brethren, and explained why he had given him that charge. Then turning to the entire gathering he told them, although Peter had so recently denied him, why he wished to give them Peter for a leader. He said, "He must be the shepherd of the flock." And he enlarged on Peter's zeal.

John brought out from the Holy of Holies the large, colored, embroidered mantle that James had received from the Blessed Virgin Mary and on which, in those last days, the holy women had worked at Bethany. Besides that, he also brought a hollow, slender staff, high and bent at the top like a shepherd's crook.

Peter knelt down before The Christ, who gave him to eat a round morsel, like a little cake. It was not clear where The Christ got the morsel, but it shone with light. Peter received with it some special power; strength and vigor poured into Peter's being when The Christ breathed upon him. This action of The Christ was not a simple, ordinary breathing. It was a power, something substantial that Peter received. The Christ put his mouth to Peter's mouth, then to both his ears, and poured that strength into each of the three. It was not the Holy Spirit, but something that the Holy Spirit was to quicken and vivify in Peter at Pentecost. Then The Christ placed upon him the mantle that John was holding on his arm and put the staff in Peter's hand. While performing this action, The Christ said that the mantle would preserve in him all the strength and virtue that he had just imparted to him, and that he should wear it whenever he had to make use of the power with which he had been endued.

Peter addressed the assembly in his new dignity. He had become, as it were, a new being, a man full of vigor and energy. His hearers were greatly moved; they listened with tears. He consoled them and alluded to many things that Jesus had told them before, which were now being fulfilled. He told them that Jesus, during his eighteen-hour passion, had born insult and outrage from the whole world. While Peter was speaking, The Christ vanished. No alarm, no exclamations of surprise broke in upon the attention with which Peter's words were received. He appeared to be endowed with an entirely new strength. The discourse ended, they sang a psalm of thanksgiving.

Before going to Galilee, on Wednesday, April 16, the eleven went over the way of the cross to Mount Calgary, and on to Bethany, from which they took with them some disciples. They went by different routes, remote from cities, and in several companies to the Sea of Galilee. Peter went with John, James the Greater, Thaddeus, Nathanael, John Mark, and Silas, seven in all, to Tiberius, leaving Samaria to the west. They went to a fishery outside Tiberius that Peter had held on lease, but that was now owned by another man. They took a repast with this man, and Peter said he had not fished here in three years.

They went aboard two ships, one somewhat larger and better than the other. They gave Peter the choice of the former, into which he mounted with Thaddeus, Nathanael, and one of the fisherman's servants. In the second ship were John, James, John Mark, and Silas. Peter would not suffer another to row. He wanted to do it himself. Although so distinguished by The Christ, he was exceedingly humble and modest, especially before Nathanael, who was polished and educated

They sailed about the whole night with torches, casting the nets here and there between the two ships, but always drawing them up empty. At intervals they prayed and sang psalms. When day was beginning to dawn, the ships approached the eastern shore of the sea, on the opposite side of the Jordan River. The seven were worn out and wanted to cast anchor. They had set aside their outer garments while fishing. When about resuming their clothing, in preparation for taking a little rest, they saw a figure standing behind the reeds on the shore. He cried out, "Children, have you any meat?" They said, "No!" Then the figure told them to cast the net on the west side of Peter's ship. They did, and John had to sail around the other side of the ship. Now the net was heavily filled. John recognized The Christ, and called to Peter across the silent deep, "It is the Lord!" At these words, Peter instantly girded his coat about him, leapt into the water and waded through the reeds to where The Christ was standing.

In back of a little mound on the shore, there was a hollow where there was a fire pit. No one saw The Christ kindling a fire, catching a fish, or getting one any other way. Fire, fish, and everything necessary appeared at once as soon as it entered The Christ's mind that a fish should here be prepared for eating.

Peter was already standing by The Christ when John came up. Those on the ships began to cry to them to help draw in the net. The Christ told Peter to go bring in the fish. They drew the net to land, and Peter emptied it on the shore. There were on the ships several men in the employ of the fisherman from Tiberius, and they took charge of the ships and the fish, while the seven went with The Christ to the hollow where he invited them to eat. The seven were much surprised to see the fire and a fish, not of their own catching, and the bread and honey cakes. The seven reclined by the fire while The Christ played the host. He handed to each on a little roll a portion of fish from the pan. The amount of fish in the pan did not diminish as the portions were distributed. He gave them also of the honey cakes and then reclined with them by the fire and ate. All this took place very quietly and solemnly.

After the meal, The Christ and the seven rose from the fire. They walked up and down the shore, and at last stood still while The Christ gravely addressed Peter, "Simon, son of John, do you love me more than these?" Peter timidly answered, "Yes, Lord, you know that I love you!" The Christ said, "Feed my lambs!" At that moment, there appeared a vision of the early church and its chief pastor. The vision included Peter teaching and guiding the first Christians, as well as his baptizing and cleansing the first Christians who appeared like so many lambs.

After a pause, The Christ again said to Peter, "Simon, son of John, do you love me?" Peter very timidly and humbly, for he was thinking of his denial, answered again, "Yes, Lord, you know that I love you!" Then The Christ addressed him solemnly, "Feed my sheep!" Once more there was a vision of the rising church and its persecutions. The vision included Peter as the chief bishop gathering together the numerous scattered Christians, protecting them, providing them with a shepherd, and governing them.

After another pause and still walking, The Christ said once more, "Simon, son of John, do you love me?" Peter grew troubled at the thought that The Christ asked him so often as if he doubted his love. It reminded Peter of his denial, repeated three times, and he answered, "Lord, you know all things, you know that I love you!" At this point, John was thinking, "Oh, what love must The Christ have, and what love ought a shepherd have, since three times he questioned Peter, to whom he consigns his flock, concerning his love!" Again The Christ said, "Feed my sheep!" Then he added, "Amen, amen, I say to you, when you were younger, you did gird yourself and walked wherever you wished. But when you shall be old, you shall stretch forth your hands, and another shall gird you, and lead you where you would prefer not to go. Follow me!" Then there was a third vision of the spreading church. It showed Peter in Rome bound and crucified, also the martyrdom of the saints.

On Thursday, April 16, Peter, accompanied by the eleven, some other disciples, and many who had heard him preach on the previous day, went westward from Tiberius to an elevated region that had on the north an extraordinary fertile valley. Five pathways planted with hedges and trees ran up the mountain, whose summit afforded ample space for about a hundred persons to walk about it freely. From it the view extended far around the country and over the Sea of Galilee. It was a beautiful prospect. The eleven, the holy women, and many other disciples all knew they were supposed to meet there. Peter placed five of the eleven on the five different pathways that led up the mountain, and they taught the people, because they could not all hear Peter on account of the crowd. He himself stood on the teacher's pillar in the center and published details of the passion, the resurrection, the appearances of The Christ, and the obligations of following him.

The Christ approached by the same route that Peter had come. He went up the mountain. The holy women, who were standing on that particular pathway, prostrated themselves before him, and he spoke to them as he passed by. The Christ, resplendent with light, stepped through the crowd and went to the pillar on which Peter was standing. Peter resigned his place and took up a position opposite The Christ, who now addressed the multitude. He spoke of abandoning one's relatives, of following him, and of the persecutions that they would have to endure. About two hundred of his hearers withdrew when they heard him talking of such things. After all these were gone away, The Christ said that he had spoken to them mildly in order not to scandalize the weak. Then he uttered some very grave words upon the sufferings and persecutions of those that would follow him on earth, and he alluded to their eternal reward. Then The Christ vanished. His disappearance was like a light suddenly extinguished in their midst. Many fell prostate on their faces. Peter again taught and prayed. This was The Christ's principal appearance in Galilee, where he gave proof of his resurrection from the dead.

CHAPTER 22

THE ASCENSION

MAY 14, 33 CE

The Christ communicated with the eleven quite freely in those days immediately preceding the ascension. He ate and prayed with them, walked with them in many directions, and repeated all that he had previously told them. He appeared also to Simon of Cyrene as he was working in the garden between Bethpage and Jerusalem. The Christ, resplendent in light, approached him as if floating in the air. Simon fell on his knees and kissed the ground at the feet of The Christ, who signed him with his hand to keep silence and then he vanished. When The Christ was walking with the eleven in Jerusalem, some of the Jews perceived the resurrected Christ, and were terrified. They ran to hide themselves, or to shut themselves up in their houses. Even the eleven and the disciples accompanied him with a certain degree of timidity, for there was in him something too spiritual for them. The Christ appeared also in other places, Bethlehem and Nazareth for instance, to those with whom he and the Blessed Virgin Mary formerly had relations. He scattered blessings everywhere, and they that saw him believed and joined with the eleven and the disciples in Jerusalem.

On May 12, The Christ with five of the eleven was approaching Bethany from the east. The Blessed Virgin Mary, with other holy women, was also coming from Jerusalem. Many of the faithful were gathered at Lazarus' castle. They knew that The Christ was soon to leave them; they wanted to see him once more and to bid him goodbye. The Christ took a singularly touching leave of the Apostle Lazarus. He gave him a shining morsel, blessed him, and extended to him his hand. The Apostle Lazarus, who generally remained hidden in his own residence, did not accompany The Christ when they left for Jerusalem with the eleven and the other disciples.

They took the Palm Sunday route, though with many turnings into sideways. They went in four companies, allowing considerable distance to intervene between them. The eleven went with The Christ; the holy women followed last. The Christ was shining with light, a conspicuous figure in their midst. All were anxious and some were depressed. Others were talking to one another: "He has often vanished from us." They did not want to think that he would really leave them. Only Peter and John appeared calmer, as if they understood The Christ better. He did often speak to them interiorly and explained many things. He also disappeared and then suddenly reappeared in the midst of the disciples, as if he desired to prepare them for his final departure.

Nicodemus and Joseph had prepared a meal, which was served in the Coenaculum. The table for The Christ and the eleven was set in the entrance hall. On it stood little mugs and a large dish ornamented with delicate foliage, in which lay a fish along with some small rolls. The tables for the disciples were laid out in the covered walkway to the courtyard. On these tables were fruits and three-cornered dishes containing honeycombs. Flat boned knives were placed around. Near every dish lay three slices of bread, for there was one dish for every three of the guests.

The sun had set and it was beginning to grow dark before The Christ and his procession drew near. Nicodemus, Joseph, and the Blessed Virgin Mary received The Christ at the gate. He went with Mary into her little abode, while the eleven proceeded to the entrance hall. When the remaining disciples and the holy women arrived somewhat later, The Christ joined the eleven in the entrance hall. The table was only set on one side. The eleven reclined on cross seats, but The Christ stood. The lamp over the table was lighted. Nicodemus and Joseph served. The Christ blessed the fish, the bread, and the herbs and passed them around with words of earnest instruction. At the end of the meal, The Christ blessed the cup, drank from it, and passed it around.

When this love feast was over, all assembled outside the hall under the trees. The Christ addressed to them an extended instruction, and ended by giving them a blessing. To the Blessed Virgin Mary, who was standing in front of the holy women, he extended his hand. All were very much affected, and Mary Magdalene, who ardently longed to embrace the feet of The Christ, restrained her desire, for his demeanor was so grave that it inspired a holy fear. When he left them, they wept very much. It was not, however, an exterior weeping; it was like the weeping of the soul. The assembly broke up before midnight.

On the morning of May 14, morning prayers were solemnly recited in the Coenaculum as usual under the lamp. The Christ was present and once more imparted to Peter jurisdiction over the others, again laid upon him the previously mentioned mantle, and repeated what he had said on the mountain by the Sea of Galilee. He also gave some instruction on baptism and the blessing of water.

As the day dawned, The Christ left the Coenaculum with the eleven. The Blessed Virgin Mary followed them closely; the disciples, at some little distance, brought up the rear. They passed through the streets of Jerusalem where all was quiet, the inhabitants still buried in sleep. At each moment The Christ became more earnest, more rapid in speech and action. He went with them over all the paths he had taken during his passion in order to inspire them by his teachings and admonitions with a lively appreciation of the fulfillment of the promise. Just before the gate that led out to Mount Calvary, they stepped aside from the road to a delightful spot shaded by trees. The Christ paused to teach and comfort the little flock. Meanwhile, the day dawned brightly; their hearts grew lighter, and they even began to think that The Christ would still remain with them.

New crowds of believers arrived. The Christ again took the road that led to Mount Calvary and the garden of the Tomb. But he did not follow it up to those points; he turned off and went around the city to the Mount of Olives. The Christ paused awhile with the increasing crowd in a cool spot with beautiful long grass. The multitude that surrounded him here was so great that it could no longer be counted. The Christ spoke to them a long time, like one who is about to close a discourse and come to a conclusion. His hearers divined that the hour of parting was near, and yet they had no idea that the intervening time was to be so short. The Christ went only to Gethsemane and from the Garden of Olives up to the summit of the mount. The Christ at each instant shone more brightly and his motions became more rapid. The disciples hastened after him but it was impossible to catch up with him. When he reached the top of the mountain, he was as resplendent as a beam of sunlight. The pressing crowd stood in a wide circle as if blending with the light from above. The Christ laid his left hand on his breast and, raising the right hand, turned slowly around, blessing the whole world. The crowd stood motionless.

And now the rays of light from above united with the glory emanating from The Christ, and he began to disappear, dissolving in the light from above, vanishing as he rose. It appeared as if one sun was lost in another, as if one flame entered another, as if a spark floated into a flame. It was as if one was gazing into the full midday splendor of the sun. At first, one could no longer see his head, then his whole person was engulfed, and lastly his feet disappeared in celestial glory.

After some moments, when the splendor began to diminish, the whole assembly in deep silence—their souls swaying by varying emotions—gazed fixedly up at the brightness, which remained visible for some time. The brightness remained for a while longer and then disappeared like daylight retiring before the darkness of night.

CHAPTER 23

PENTECOST

MAY 24, 33 CE

The holy day of Pentecost occurred on May 24. On the eve of the feast, the whole interior of the Coenaculum was ornamented with green bushes in whose branches were placed vases of flowers. Garlands of green were looped from side to side. The screens that cut off the side halls and vestibule were removed; only the gate of the outer court was closed. In his episcopal robe, Peter stood at a table, spread over in red and white, under the lamp in front of the covered Holy of Holies. Opposite him, in the doorway leading to the entrance hall, the Blessed Virgin Mary stood, her face veiled, and behind her in the entrance hall stood the holy women. The twelve (recall that Matthias had been selected to replace Judas Iscariot) stood in two rows facing Peter along either side of the hall. From the side halls, the disciples ranged behind the twelve and took part in the prayers and the hymns. When Peter broke and distributed the bread that he had previously blessed, first to the Blessed Virgin Mary, then to the twelve and to the disciples who stepped forward to receive it, they kissed his hand. Besides the holy women, there were in the Coenaculum one hundred and twenty followers of Jesus Christ.

After midnight there arose a wonderful movement in all nature. It communicated itself to those present as they stood in deep reflection, their arms crossed on their breast, near the pillars of the supper room and in the side halls, silently praying. Stillness pervaded the house, and silence reigned throughout the whole enclosure.

Toward morning, above the Mount of Olives, a glittering white cloud of light came down from heaven and drew near the house. In the distance it appeared as a round ball carried along on a soft breeze. But coming nearer, it looked larger and floated over the city like a luminous mass of fog until it stood over Sion and the Coenaculum. It seemed to contract and to shine with constantly increasing brightness. At last, with a rushing roaring noise as of wind, it sank like a thunder cloud floating low in the atmosphere.

The luminous cloud descended over the house and with increasing sound, the light became brighter. Then there shot from the rushing cloud streams of light down upon the house and its surroundings. The assembled faithful were enthralled. Each involuntarily threw back the head and raised their eyes on high. Into the mouth of every one there flowed a stream of light like a burning tongue of fire. The flames descended on each person in different colors and in different degrees of intensity. A new life full of confidence and courage had been infused into all. Meanwhile, the light vanished.

They gathered around the Blessed Virgin Mary who was the only one perfectly calm, the only one that retained a quiet, holy self-possession. The twelve, who can now legitimately be called Apostles, embraced one another and, urged by joyous confidence, exclaimed, "What were we? What are we now?" Their joy found vent in thanksgiving. They arranged themselves for prayer, gave thanks, and praised God with great emotion.

Later, Peter imposed hands on five of the new apostles who were to help teach and baptize at the nearby pool of Bethsaida. Baptism at this site had been arranged by The Christ himself for this day's feast, and the disciples had in consequence made all kinds of preparations at the pool as well as in the old synagogue that they had taken over for their own use. The walls of the synagogue were hung with tapestry, and from the building down to the pool a covered tent-way was erected.

The apostles and disciples went in solemn procession, two by two, from the Coenaculum to the pool. The five apostles upon whom Peter had imposed hands separated, each one taking one of the five entrances to the pool, and they addressed the people with great enthusiasm. When the apostles spoke, the multitude was amazed, for everyone listened to what sounded to them as their own language. It was owing to this astonishment that Peter lifted up his voice and said,

"Men of Judea and all who live in Jerusalem, let this be known to you, and listen to what I say. Indeed these are not drunk, as you suppose, for it is only nine o'clock in the morning. No, this is what was spoken through the prophet Joel:

'In the last days it will be, God declares, that I will pour out my Spirit upon all flesh, and your sons and your daughters shall prophesy, and your young men shall see visions, and your old men shall dream dreams. Even upon my slaves, both men and women, in those days, I will pour out my Spirit; and they shall prophesy. And I will show portents in the heaven above and signs on the earth below, blood, and fire, and smoky mist. The sun shall be turned to darkness and, the moon to blood, before the coming of the Lord's great and glorious day. Then everyone who calls on the name of the Lord shall be saved.' ...

"You that are Israelites, listen to what I have to say: Jesus of Nazareth, a man attested to you by God with deeds of power, wonders, and signs that God did through him among you, as you yourselves know—this man, handed over to you according to the definite plan and foreknowledge of God, you crucified and killed by the hands of those outside the law. But God raised him up, having freed him from death because it was impossible for him to be held by his power.

"For David said concerning him, 'I saw the Lord always before me; for he is at my right hand, so that I will not be shaken; therefore my heart was glad, and my tongue rejoiced; moreover my flesh will live in hope. For you do not abandon my soul to Hades, or let your Holy One experience corruption. You have made known to me the ways of life; you will make me full of gladness with your presence.' ...

"Fellow Israelites, I may say to you confidently of our ancestor David that he both died and was buried, and his tomb is with us to this day. Since he was a prophet, he knew that God had sworn with an oath to him that he would put one of his descendants on his throne. Foreseeing this, David spoke of the resurrection of the Messiah, saying, 'He was not abandoned to Hades, nor did his flesh experience corruption.'

"This Jesus God raised up, and of that all of us are witnesses. Being therefore exalted at the right hand of God, and having received from the Father the promise of the Holy Spirit, he has poured out this that you both see and hear. For David did not ascend into the heavens, but he himself says, 'The Lord said to my Lord, "Sit at my right hand, until I make your enemies your footstool."'

"Therefore let the entire house of Israel know with certainty that God has made him both Lord and Messiah, this Jesus whom you crucified."[1]

Now, when they heard this, they were cut to the heart and said to Peter and to the other apostles, "Brothers, what should we do?" Peter said to them, "Repent, and be baptized every one of you in the name of Jesus Christ so that your sins may be forgiven; and you will receive the gift of the Holy Spirit. For the promise is for you, for your children, and for all who are far away, everyone whom the Lord our God calls to him." And he testified with many other arguments and exhorted them, saying, "Save yourselves from this corrupt generation."

As many presented themselves for baptism, Peter assisted by John and James solemnly blessed the water. Peter sprinkled the holy water they had brought in a leather bottle from the Coenaculum in fine streams far over the pool. The preparations and the baptism itself occupied the whole day. The people added to the community on that day amounted to three thousand.

---

1   Acts 2:14–21, 25–40 NRSV.

Appendix: The Bare-Bones Story

DATE	EVENT	COMMENT
Sept. 7, 21 BCE	Birth of Solomon Mary	
Dec. 18 BCE	Solomon Mary took vow to become a temple virgin	
July 17, 17 BCE	Birth of Nathan Mary	
Mar. 5, 6 BCE	Birth of Solomon Jesus	Mary was 14½ years old
Apr. 17, 6 BCE	Presentation of Solomon Jesus to the temple	
Dec. 26, 6 BCE	Adoration of the Magi as described in Matthew	This took place ½ month after the birth
Feb. 29, 5 BCE	Flight into Egypt	
Sept. 15, 5 BCE	Slaughter of Innocents	Occurred when Solomon Jesus would have been 1½ years old
Mar. 30, 2 BCE	Visit of Nathan to her cousin Elizabeth	
June 3, 2 BCE	Birth of John the Baptizer	
Dec. 6, 2 BCE	Birth of Nathan Jesus / Adoration of the Shepherds as described in Luke	Occurred 4 years and 9 months after the birth of Solomon Jesus
Jan. 1 BCE	Presentation of Nathan Jesus to the temple	
Jan 28, 1 BCE	Death of Herod the Great	
Sept. 2 BCE	Return of the Solomon Holy Family from Egypt	Return to Nazareth rather than to Bethlehem
Before Passover of 12 CE	Death of Solomon Joseph	
Apr. 3, 12 CE	Transfer of Zarathustra individuality from Solomon Jesus to Nathan Jesus	The new name Jesus of Nazareth is used to recognize his change of status
June 4, 12 CE	Death of Solomon Jesus	Solomon Jesus lived only 17 years
Aug. 4, 12 CE	Death of Nathan Mary	Nathan Mary lived only 28 years; Date for this event not available but occurred not long after death of Nathan Mary; Merger of two families: Nathan Joseph, Nathan Jesus, Solomon Mary, and her six children born after Solomon Jesus (James, Joseph, Simon, Judas, and two sisters)

DATE	EVENT	COMMENT
Before Passover of 29 CE	Death of the Nathan Joseph	
Sept. 23, 29 CE	Departure of Zarathustra individuality; Baptism of Jesus of Nazareth by John the Baptizer; Incarnation of Christ Being; now called Christ Jesus; transfer of Nathan Mary individuality to Solomon Mary, now called Blessed Virgin Mary	
Apr. 8, 30 CE	Conversation with Nicodemus Beheading of John the Baptizer	
Apr. 3, 31 CE	The Transfiguration	
July 26, 32 CE	Raising of Lazarus from the dead	Now called Lazarus–John
Mar. 19, 33 CE	Triumphant Entry into Jerusalem	
Apr. 3, 33 CE	Crucifixion of Christ Jesus	
Apr. 5, 33 CE	The Resurrection	Now called The Christ
Apr. 6, 33 CE	Appearance to the two disciples: Emmaus	
Apr. 15, 33 CE	Appearance to the seven: Sea of Galilee	
May 14, 33 CE	The Ascension	
May 24, 33 CE	Pentecost Disciples became Apostles	The Blessed Virgin Mary becomes Mary–Sophia
Aug. 15, 44 CE	Death of Mary–Sophia	In Ephesus at age 65

Adapted from Tidball 2005; see pp. 17–79

BIBLIOGRAPHY

de Voragine, Jacobus (1993). *The Golden Legend: Readings on the Saints*, 2 vols. (trans. W. G. Ryan), Princeton, NJ: Princeton University.

Emmerich, Anne Catherine (1986). *The Life of Our Lord and Savior Jesus Christ Combined with The Bitter Passion and the Life Of Mary* (trans. anonymous; ed. Rev. C. E. Schmöger), Fresno, CA: Academy Library Guild, 1954b; reprint, *The Life of Jesus Christ and Biblical Revelations: From the Visions of the Venerable Anne Catherine Emmerich as recorded in the journals Clemens Brentano*, 4 vols., Rockford, IL: TAN.

Fahsel, Helmut Kaplan (1942). *Der Wandel Jesu in der Velt, nach den visionen der Anna Katherina Emmerich*, Olten, Switzerland: Basel and Rickenback.

Funk, Robert W., Roy W. Hoover, and The Jesus Seminar (1993). *The Five Gospels: The Search for the Authentic Words of Jesus*, New York: HarperCollins.

The New Oxford Annotated Bible: New Revised Standard Version (1991). Ed. B. M. Metzger and R. E. Murphy. New York: Oxford University.

Pagels, Elaine (2003). *Beyond Belief: The Secret Gospel of Thomas*, New York: Random House.

Powell, Robert (1988). *Christian Hermetic Astrology: The Star of the Magi and the Life of Christ*, Hudson, NY: Anthroposophic Press.

———(1996). *Chronicle of the Living Christ The Life and Ministry of Jesus Christ: Foundations of Cosmic Christianity*, Hudson, NY: Anthroposophic Press.

Steiner, Rudolph (1986). *Gospel of St. Mark* (trans. C. Maizner; ed. S. C. Easton), Hudson, NY: Anthroposophic Press.

———(1995). *The Fifth Gospel: From the Akashic Record* (trans. A.R. Meuss, London: Rudolf Steiner Press.

———(2001). *According to Luke: The Gospel of Compassion and Love Revealed* (trans. C. E. Creeger), Great Barrington, MA: Anthroposophic Press.

Tidball, Charles S. (2005). *Jesus, Lazarus, and the Messiah: Unveiling Three Christian Mysteries*, Great Barrington, MA: SteinerBooks.

Tomberg, Valentin (1992). *Lazarus, Come Forth! Meditations of a Christian Esotericist on the Mysteries of the Raising of Lazarus, the Ten Commandments, the Three Kingdoms & the Breath of Life* (trans. R. Powell and J. Morgante, Great Barrington, MA: Lindisfarne Books.

von Halle, Judith (2007). *And if He Has Not Been Raised...: The Stations of Christ's Path to Spirit Man* (trans. B. Stevens), London: Temple Lodge.

CHARLES S. TIDBALL was born in 1928 in Geneva, Switzerland. At age seven his family moved to the United States of America, where later he earned a B.A. in Chemistry from Wesleyan University, an M.S. degree in Pharmacology from the University of Rochester, a Ph.D. degree in Physiology from the University of Wisconsin, Madison, and an MD from the University of Chicago. Following two years of postgraduate clinical training, he joined the faculty of the School of Medicine of The George Washington University in Washington, DC, in 1959, where he subsequently became Professor and Chair of the Department of Physiology. In 1967, he received the Washington Academy of Science Award for Scientific Achievement in the Biological Sciences. In addition to the duties of managing the Department, he maintained an active research program while directing the education of medical students, graduate students, and the further training of postdoctoral fellows.

In 1973, Professor Tidball founded the Office of Computer Assisted Education at the Medical Center, and additionally pioneered the online training of medical library personnel in computerized citation retrieval. For more than ten years he participated in the Association for the Development of Computer-based Instructional Systems both as incorporator and officer of the Health Education Network, Inc., sponsored by the National Library of Medicine. While on sabbatical leave from 1978 to 1979, he was consultant to the Deputy Director of the Clinical Center of the National Institutes of Health where he developed a multimedia training program to assist physicians in learning computerized patient management. Starting in 1980, he developed, for the Department of Education at GWU, an Educational Computing Technology Program, which he directed, while on leave from the School of Medicine from 1982 to 1984. Dr. Tidball then returned to the

217

Medical Center as Professor of Computer Medicine and staff physician for the medical center Multitest Facility. He had supervisory responsibility for administering a medical computing proficiency requirement for all medical students at GWU and was instrumental in developing patient management software for the GWU Department of Neurological Surgery.

Since 1987, Dr. Tidball has continued his service to the Washington National Cathedral as Volunteer Manager of the Cathedral Information Systems Program which is developing a computer database of the works of art that has been crafted into the building along with a companion database containing biographical information on those who have been responsible for bringing about the Cathedral's structure and its programs. In 1992, The George Washington University designated him Professor Emeritus of Computer Medicine and of Neurological Surgery. Recently, Professor Tidball has been engaged in collaborative research with his wife, Professor M. Elizabeth Tidball. In 1994 they were both appointed Distinguished Research Scholars at Hood College where they are codirectors of the Tidball Center for the Study of Educational Environments. He is a coauthor, with his wife and two other colleagues, of *Taking Women Seriously: Lessons and Legacies for Educating the Majority* (American Council on Education/ Oryx Press, 1999). In 1994, Wilson College, Chambersburg, Pennsylvania, awarded him the Doctor of Humane Letters degree, and in 1999 Hood College honored him with a Doctor of Science degree.

Dr. Tidball has had a lifelong interest in Anthroposophy and in 1948 and 1970 visited the Goetheanum in Dornach, Switzerland. Since retiring, he has been able to devote himself to the study of Dr. Rudolf Steiner's writings. He has been an active member of the Rudolf Steiner Study Group of the Anthroposophical Society Greater Washington Branch for two decades. Encountering Dr. Powell's *Chronicle of the Living Christ* encouraged him to expand his interests to include the contributions of revelations in furthering an understanding of biblical texts. Dr. Tidball's previous book is *Jesus, Lazarus, and the Messiah: Unveiling Three Christian Mysteries* (SteinerBooks, 2005), portions of which were delivered as illustrated lectures in Baltimore, Maryland (2001), and in Washington, DC (2002 and 2004).

CPSIA information can be obtained at www.ICGtesting.com
Printed in the USA
BVOW062346130512

289979BV00001B/3/P